9/11 and the Future of
Transportation Security

9/11 and the Future of Transportation Security

R. William Johnstone

James Dunton, Imprint Adviser

Praeger Security International
Westport, Connecticut • London

Library of Congress Cataloging-in-Publication Data

Johnstone, R. William, 1953–
    9/11 and the future of transportation security / R. William Johnstone.
        p. cm.
    Includes bibliographical references and index.
    ISBN 0-275-99075-3 (alk. paper)
    1. Transportation—Security measures—United States.   2. Aeronautics,
Commercial—Security measures—United States.   3. Airports—Security measures—United
States.   4. Transportation—Effect of terrorism on—United States.   5. September 11
Terrorist Attacks, 2001.   I. National Commission on Terrorist Attacks upon the United
States.   II. Title.
    HE194.5.U6J64   2006
    363.325′9363120973–dc22   2006004354

British Library Cataloguing in Publication Data is available

Library of Congress Catalog Card Number: 2006004354
ISBN: 0–275–99075–3

First published in 2006

Praeger Security International, 88 Post Road West, Westport, CT 06881
An imprint of Greenwood Publishing Group, Inc.
www.praeger.com

Printed in the United States of America

The paper used in this book complies with the
Permanent Paper Standard issued by the National
Information Standards Organization (Z39.48–1984).

10 9 8 7 6 5 4 3 2 1

Contents

Preface

Our failure took place over many years and Administrations. There is no single individual who is responsible for this failure. Yet individuals and institutions are not absolved of responsibility. Any person in a senior position within our government during this time bears some element of responsibility for the government's actions. It is not our purpose to assign blame. As we said at the outset, we look back so that we can look forward. Our goal is to prevent future attacks.

> — Hon. Thomas Kean, Chairman and Hon. Lee Hamilton, Vice Chairman, National Commission on Terrorist Attacks Upon the United States "Release of 9/11 Commission Report," Public Statement, July 22, 2004

This book had its origins in work done by the National Commission on Terrorist Attacks Upon the United States (hereafter referred to as the 9/11 Commission) staff working group on aviation and transportation security. This team, of which I was a member, focused on three major topics: (1) uncovering the details of the 9/11 hijackings themselves, and investigating the civil aviation security system that failed on that occasion; (2) examining how transportation security has evolved from 9/11 to the present; and (3) making recommendations to lessen the chances for future successful terrorist attacks on the U.S. transportation system.

Some of our work was made public in the 9/11 Commission's second and seventh public hearings (May 2003 and January 2004, respectively) and, in particular, in Staff Statements Three (about the pre-9/11 aviation security system) and Four (about the four hijackings) we delivered at that latter event. The Commission's widely read final report, published in July 2004, provided additional results from our findings about pre-9/11 aviation security "layers" and the chronological details of the hijackings, as did the subsequently released *Staff Report: Monograph on Four Flights and*

Aviation Security.[1] Finally, in addition to the relatively limited number of aviation and transportation security-related recommendations contained in the Commission's final report, our staff working group's ninety-one transportation security recommendations were transmitted to the Congress in September of 2004. (See Appendix A for a complete list of these recommendations, as well as the transmittal letter to Congress.)

However, given that aviation and transportation security was but one of a number of areas that the 9/11 Commission was mandated by law to investigate (we were one of eight staff working groups), that the Commission was under a tight statutorily imposed reporting deadline, and that the interests of time and space militated against completeness in publicizing all of the information discovered by the Commission and its staff, much of the work that I and my teammates did—work that was financed by American taxpayers, created through the efforts of the families of the 9/11 victims, and rightfully the property of the American public, in my view—did not make it to the public record.

More specifically, while our findings with respect to what happened and when it happened, on the four hijacked flights, and what aviation security defenses were defeated by the hijackers and how they were defeated have been generally well covered in what has already been made public, in my opinion not enough has been put on the record that attempts to explain *why* the system failed. Similarly, although our recommendations themselves have received some circulation and even some action by the Congress, their basis, most important including consideration of the current state of transportation security, has not.

This book, then, is an attempt to build on and supplement the work of the 9/11 Commission by explaining the aviation security system failure on 9/11, and using this as a means for both evaluating post-9/11 transportation security efforts and proposing remedies for continuing shortcomings. It is based on information provided to the 9/11 Commission, augmented by reports and other material that has come to light since the issuance of the Commission's final report in July 2004.

Part One seeks to answer the question of why the aviation security system failed on 9/11, based on an analysis of that system's history and institutions. Part Two looks at what has been done in aviation and transportation security since 9/11, including the 9/11 Commission's recommendations and the Congressional response thereto. Finally, Part Three outlines a suggested approach for improving current transportation security efforts, beginning by positing fundamental policy questions that must be answered if we are to optimize transportation security efforts, and concluding with a presentation of underlying principles for action and recommendations.

The conclusions and opinions expressed in this book are entirely those of the author. Specifically, neither the 9/11 Commissioners nor the other

Commission staff members bear any responsibility for them. However, many individuals contributed importantly to the facts and interpretations contained herein. These included past and current government officials of the Department of Homeland Security (DHS) and its Transportation Security Administration (TSA) division, the Federal Aviation Administration (FAA), and the Federal Bureau of Investigation (FBI), as well as outside transportation security experts and industry stakeholders.

The Government Accountability Office (GAO)[2] supplied valuable assistance throughout the work of the Commission, including detailing Dr. Gerald Dillingham to work on the Commission's aviation and transportation security staff where he concentrated on analyzing the current state of transportation security.

I owe an especial debt of gratitude to John Raidt, who was the only other staff member beside myself to work on all stages of the aviation and transportation security investigation. Mr. Raidt is responsible for a major portion of our work that has been made public to date, as well as for many of the insights contained in this book.

1   Introduction

9/11 Systems Failure

> Despite the current security requirements at the nation's checkpoints, poten-
> tial vulnerabilities exist. . . . The Commission is concerned over the minimal
> security controls for the shipping of cargo by aircraft and the absence of con-
> trols for mail; the lack of controls over checked baggage; limited employment
> checks for airport employees; limited control over those gaining access to an
> aircraft, such as caterers and cleaning crews; and the limited effectiveness of
> screening passengers and their carry-on articles.[1]

The Commission in this case was the President's Commission on Aviation
Security and Terrorism created by President George Herbert Walker Bush
in response to the 1988 terrorist bombing of Pan Am Flight 103. Many of
these same deficiencies were noted by the 9/11 Commission over a decade
later and, even more disturbingly, persist to this day.

Before September 11, 2001, transportation security within the United
States was limited in extent and purpose. Total federal spending for all
transportation security was less than $200 million a year, with most of
that devoted to passenger aviation. Transit police and subway surveillance cameras sought to deter or detect criminal activity. Customs agents
at our ports looked for smugglers. In aviation, the only sector that
had received significant security policy attention and resources from
the federal government, the emphasis was overwhelmingly directed
overseas.

During 2001, the U.S. intelligence system was "blinking red" and "counterterrorism officials were receiving frequent but fragmentary reports
about threats. Indeed, there appeared to be possible threats almost ev-
erywhere the United States had interests—including at home."[2]

Many have explained the success of the 9/11 attacks as primarily the result of flawed intelligence, but the available evidence indicates the principal failure was that of the aviation security system. The entire history of that system, as well as the testimony received by the 9/11 Commission, demonstrated that its defenses could only respond effectively with the kind of specific and "actionable" intelligence that all agree is always in short supply.[3]

In the absence of such intelligence, or disasters like the downing of Pan Am 103, aviation security operated as a "junior partner" to safety and economic efficiency within the airlines, the airports, and the federal government. The former head of the Federal Aviation Administration, the federal agency charged with the responsibility of both promoting and regulating civil aviation, told the 9/11 Commission, "On September 10 we were not a nation at war. On September 10, we were a nation bedeviled by delays, concerned about congestion, and impatient to keep moving."[4]

Writing in 1999, aviation security expert Brian Jenkins detailed a number of factors that served as "obstacles" to implementation of aviation security measures, and that "may be inevitable in a democratic process," including "lack of consensus on the threat, the highly competitive airline industry's resistance to spending money or increasing charges to passengers, effective lobbying at the White House and in Congress, efforts to achieve a balanced federal budget, a slow, often cumbersome rule-making process, and fleeting focus as other issues commanded immediate attention."[5] Although there remains a greater awareness of the threat in the post-9/11 world, the other items and their analogs in the other transportation modes have continued to impact security through 9/11 and beyond.

The result was a situation under which

> plotters who were determined, highly motivated individuals, who escaped notice on no-fly lists, who studied publicly available vulnerabilities of the aviation security system, who used items with a metal content less than a handgun and most likely permissible, and who knew to exploit training received by aircraft personnel to be non-confrontational were likely to be successful in hijacking a domestic U.S. aircraft.[6]

When it came,

> the 9/11 attack was an event of surpassing disproportion. . . . While by no means as threatening as Japan's act of war [at Pearl Harbor], the 9/11 attack was in some ways more devastating. It was carried out by a tiny group of people, not enough to man a full platoon. Measured on a governmental scale, the resources behind it were trivial. The group itself was dispatched by an organization based in one of the poorest, most remote countries on earth.[7]

The shock of 9/11 represented a crisis as the Chinese understand the term, danger with opportunity. The danger appeared clear enough in the days and weeks following the terrorist act, but so did the opportunity in the unprecedented national policy attention and resources devoted to what has come to be called homeland security.

Transportation Security Today

The federal government responded to 9/11 with a flurry of Congressional and Executive Branch initiatives, including:

- The Aviation and Transportation Security Act of 2001 (ATSA),[8] which created the Transportation Security Administration (TSA) to be responsible for the security of all modes of transportation and established deadlines for the implementation of a number of specific aviation security measures.
- The Maritime Transportation Security Act of 2002 (MTSA),[9] which set security guidelines for ports and ships.
- The Homeland Security Act of 2002 (HSA),[10] which established a new Department of Homeland Security (DHS) by combining twenty-two separate federal agencies, including TSA, the Coast Guard, the Customs Service, and the Federal Emergency Management Agency (FEMA).
- The 2002 legislation creating the 9/11 Commission,[11] which was to "examine and report upon the facts and causes relating to the terrorist attacks of September 11, 2001 . . . and investigate and report to the President and Congress on its findings, conclusions and recommendations for corrective measures that can be taken to prevent acts of terrorism."
- A series of Homeland Security Presidential Directives (HSPDs),[12] including the December 2003 HSPD-7, which called for DHS to "produce a comprehensive integrated National Plan for Critical Infrastructure and Key Resources Protection."
- The Intelligence Reform and Terrorism Prevention Act of 2004,[13] which turned many of the 9/11 Commission's recommendations, including those relating to transportation security, into statutory mandates.

The increased federal policy attention was accompanied by a substantial rise in federal funding for transportation security, which rose from less than $150 million in Fiscal Year (FY) 2001 (almost all of which went for aviation security) to more than $7.7 billion in FY2005 (with 70 percent devoted to aviation).[14]

   To be sure, there have been improvements in many areas of transportation security over the past four years. Passenger aircraft are much less vulnerable to another 9/11-style of attack. More air and sea cargo is being scrutinized in some fashion. More attention has been given to vulnerability assessments of America's transportation infrastructure and to security training for law enforcement and transportation workers. Above all, there is greater awareness of the terrorist threat.

But four years after 9/11, after a series of federal laws, executive directives, and reorganizations, after more than $25 billion in new federal security investments, major questions remain about the effectiveness of all elements of the new system.

The Heritage Foundation and the Center for Strategic and International Studies (CSIS) reported that DHS "is weighed down with bureaucratic layers, is rife with turf warfare, and lacks a structure for strategic thinking and policymaking."[15] The 9/11 Commission found that "The current efforts do not yet reflect a forward-looking strategic plan systematically analyzing assets, risks, costs, and benefits."[16] A January 2005 GAO report indicated that this is still the case.[17] And a December 2005 survey of past and current homeland security officials and independent experts reported that DHS continues to suffer from "haphazard design, bureaucratic warfare, and unfulfilled promises."[18]

Nor have assessments of TSA performance produced more positive reports. Governmental organization expert Paul Light wrote in April 2005 that TSA "still fails too often at detecting guns, knives and improvised explosive devices, and it's years behind in developing 'smart' technologies that could help screeners do their work."[19] The successor to the 9/11 Commission, the 9/11 Public Discourse Project, reported that, as of December 2005, DHS and TSA progress to date in implementing the Commission's transportation security recommendations ranged from "C" (for checkpoint screening for explosives) to "F" (for airline passenger prescreening).[20]

Aviation Security

Among the layers of aviation security, TSA's *intelligence* division is more relevant to its agency leadership and decision-making process than its predecessor within the FAA, but, though it is twice as large as its predecessor, it remains significantly under-staffed,[21] and its agents are now spread much thinner with responsibilities for all transportation modes, not just aviation.[22]

Progress has been reported in *airport perimeter security* through a reduction in airport access points, an increase in surveillance of individuals and vehicles entering airports, and some improvement in airport employee background checks. However, little has changed in the old system's divided responsibilities for access control, with the federal government, airport authorities, and to a lesser extent the airlines, all having a role.[23]

The number of names currently on the *no fly list* used to prevent known or suspected terrorists from boarding commercial aircraft, and the *automatic selectee list* that subjects them to additional security scrutiny,[24] is much greater than the very small number in effect on 9/11.[25] However, administrative problems[26] and the intelligence community's concern about sharing sometimes highly classified names with the private airlines that still implement the no fly and automatic selectee programs, have dramatically limited the usefulness of the government's consolidated terrorist watch list, with many identified terrorists still not appearing on either aviation security list.[27]

The *prescreening* system in use today is largely the same as the one that selected ten of the hijackers on 9/11,[28] with the added consequence of subjecting the selectee to a search of their person and carry-on bags. Testing of the follow-on program, called *Secure Flight*, has progressed very slowly.[29] Privacy groups remain concerned about the potential impact of the program, describing it as "an unprecedented government role, designating citizens as suspect," and criticizing TSA for being "incredibly resistant" to providing the public with necessary information.[30]

Problems have persisted in *checkpoint screening of passengers* and *checked bag screening*—by far the recipient of the most post-9/11 policy attention and funding. The current federalized checkpoint screening workforce is more numerous, better paid, more experienced, and the recipient of better training than its pre-9/11, private contractor counterpart.[31] But a series of reports by the DHS Inspector General (DHS IG) have documented continuing poor performance.[32]

By the latter part of 2003 all checked bags were being screened for explosives in some fashion, compared to just 5 percent before 9/11,[33] and by the end of 2005 the DHS IG was reporting that TSA had "largely" succeeded in implementing the ATSA mandate that all of this screening be done by explosive detection equipment.[34] However, concerns continue to be expressed about the capabilities of existing explosives detection equipment,[35] especially about the placement of many of these machines in airport lobbies, rather than "in-line" with baggage conveyor systems.[36]

The *onboard security* layers underwent the most immediate transformation after 9/11 with all U.S. airlines and international airlines flying to the United States having installed reinforced cockpit doors,[37] the *Common Strategy* training program for flight crews (which as of 9/11 had called for accommodation with hijackers) having been revised to take into account the 9/11 tactics,[38] and the number of Federal Air Marshals (FAMs) having been increased dramatically, with its agents now assigned to domestic as well as international flights.[39]

Deficiencies have been noted in each of the onboard security measures, however. The effectiveness of the hardened cockpit doors has been questioned because of reported failures by crew to secure the door throughout a flight.[40] The quality of the new security training has also been doubted, with flight attendant representatives indicating "we still have not been trained to appropriately handle a security crisis or terrorist attack onboard our airplanes."[41] The rapid expansion of the FAM program has produced operational and management problems, including an abbreviated training curriculum, and budget constraints have "not permitted the Service to reach its target staffing levels."[42]

General aviation security has not been substantially upgraded, with neither pilots, passengers, baggage, nor cargo subjected to security screening. Threat and vulnerability assessments have yet to be undertaken for most general aviation airports.[43] A December 2004 Congressional report criticized TSA for failing to understand the risks from small private planes, provide useful threat information to general aviation airports, and enforce security compliance by charter airlines and flight schools.[44]

Similar shortcomings continue to exist in *air cargo* security. Reportedly only 5 percent of all air cargo is currently screened, and the GAO has reported that aircraft carrying cargo continue to be highly vulnerable to terrorist sabotage.[45] TSA has proposed a set of regulations for air cargo security but, typical for rule making, the process is moving very slowly. Even if finalized, the new rules would provide few details on how the freight industry, which is expected to implement the security program, is to fulfill this unfunded mandate.[46]

Maritime Security

The potential vulnerability of the U.S. maritime sector was noted before 9/11 (for example, by the 2000 federal Interagency Committee on Crime and Security in U.S. Seaports), but little was done to address those vulnerabilities. After 9/11, the situation changed somewhat, though the resources and policy focus have been far less than in the aviation sector.

The Coast Guard has been entrusted with the primary responsibility for *port security*. MTSA mandated that all U.S. ports, facilities, and vessels develop and submit for Coast Guard approval comprehensive security and incident response plans, based on the Coast Guard's vulnerability assessments and security recommendations.[47] Though there have been problems with the vulnerability assessments, DHS has indicated that "over 99 percent" of the port and facility security plans have been received,[48] totaling 9,000 domestic vessel security plans and 3,200 domestic facility plans by the end of 2004.[49]

Though the content of the port and vessel security plans varies, among the reported security enhancements made to date are: increased identification checks on crewmembers and visitors, additional canine bomb detection teams, increased passenger and baggage screening, enhanced perimeter fencing with surveillance cameras, greater restrictions on access to secure areas of ports, deployment of X-ray machines on all large cruise ships, additional security training for workers, and increased security patrols.[50]

In April 2003 testimony to the 9/11 Commission, the GAO indicated that, "an effective port security environment may be many years away,"[51] and later that year it reported continuing concerns about the quality of the port security assessments, the limited number of ports covered by the vessel identification system, and the approval process for foreign vessel security plans.[52]

A 2005 maritime security report observed:

> A compressed and disjointed timeline for implementing the act has definitely affected what the MTSA has actually accomplished. . . . It remains to be seen whether or not the thousands of facility security plans, scores of area plans and an overarching national plan collectively have achieved unity of purpose and coherent operational procedures for preventing attacks on the maritime transportation system. . . . Overall, too many facility plans are little more than lists of activities that individually and collectively fall far short of the goals set by MTSA.[53]

The DHS IG, GAO, and its own Commandant have all reported on the difficulties the Coast Guard has encountered in trying to fulfill its new homeland security responsibilities together with its traditional rescue, drug interdiction, and other missions under current funding levels.[54]

The Customs and Border Protection (CBP) division of DHS has responsibility for *container security*. Its Container Security Initiative (CSI) identifies and prescreens *high-risk* containers bound for the United States from the largest ports outside the country. The Customs-Trade Partnership Against Terrorism (C-TPAT) creates government–industry partnerships that offer expedited customs processing for shipping companies that reduce their security vulnerabilities.[55]

By the end of 2004, CSI operated in thirty-four overseas ports, and C–TPAT had more than 4,000 certified partners,[56] but recent GAO reports found significant inadequacies in staffing for both CSI and C–TPAT, and noted shortcomings in their performance measurement and strategic planning as well.[57] The bottom line is that, with all of the efforts made since 9/11, just 6 percent of all containers currently entering the United States receive any physical inspection,[58] and less than half are subjected to risk assessment prescreening.[59]

A November 2004 analysis of the nation's seaborne cargo supply chain found that the maritime sector was "still vulnerable" and that current programs to improve security are "rife with weaknesses." Among the flaws cited by the report were the voluntary nature of the programs and the absence of federal funding for security measures, both of which limited adoption of the recommended measures, and reliance on companies' own security reporting and a one-time government inspection in certifying freight as low-risk.[60]

Land Transportation Security

Though terrorists have repeatedly demonstrated both an interest in and the capability of attacking the land transportation modes, exemplified most recently by the bombings of Madrid commuter trains in 2004 and London subways in 2005, "the least emphasis has been placed on this area because it was perceived as least pressing, and also because it is hardest to protect."[61]

With a total proposed FY2006 budget of just $32 million, and employing only 100 inspectors for land transportation security,[62] TSA and DHS continue to play a minimal part in such security, and various Department of Transportation agencies (including the Federal Railroad Administration, the Federal Transit Administration, the Federal Highway Administration, and the Federal Motor Carrier Safety Administration) retain substantial security roles. These, too, are operating with very limited resources, with less than $60 million in total included in the FY2006 budget request.[63]

DHS has used grants as its principal method for promoting land transportation security, though, in part because of uncertain federal leadership, less than half of the $300 million provided by the Department to rail, transit, bus, and trucking operators had actually been expended as of August 2005.[64]

These limited federal investments, directed primarily at rail and transit systems, have yielded a number of security measures including vulnerability assessments, increased law enforcement presence, enhanced surveillance, expanded security training of land transportation workers, and limited deployment of explosives detection capability (such as canine teams). However, with an almost complete absence of performance data on the effectiveness of these measures, it is difficult to discern what impact they have had.

Summing up the current state of land transportation security efforts, an assessment by the Dartmouth Institute for Security Technology Studies reported that, "A non-prohibitive, cost efficient security strategy for surface transportation has yet to be developed," and "efforts to secure surface transportation systems have only minimally reduced the risk of terrorist attacks."[65] The DHS IG reported in December 2004 that TSA "is moving slowly to improve security in the surface transportation modes,"[66] and reaffirmed that finding at the end of 2005.[67] Writing shortly after he left the job of DHS Inspector General, Clark Kent Ervin was even more direct in noting, "too little attention has been paid and too few resources devoted to modes of transportation other than aviation."[68]

Where Do We Go From Here?

In spite of the massive increase in attention and resources devoted to transportation—especially aviation—security in the wake of the 9/11 catastrophe, and of some improvements in areas such as checked bag screening, onboard aircraft security procedures, and a start to better air and maritime cargo security, many of the 9/11 systemic weaknesses continue.

- Reactivity and incident-driven decision making still predominate in transportation security.
- The clash of security with other societal imperatives, including consumer convenience, citizen rights, and taxpayer and shareholder satisfaction continues to strongly influence the performance of the transportation security system.
- The system of shared responsibilities and dispersed accountability that marked the 9/11 aviation security system remains in force today for all transportation security efforts.
- The layered approach to transportation security, under which the failure of a single component does not lead to a systemwide failure, that was the goal of both the pre- and post-9/11 aviation security systems[69] continues to be honored more in the breach than the observance.
- As was true on 9/11, security is still not being engineered into and integrated with basic transportation operations.
- Transportation security is not being handled as a national security issue.

Despite its proposed increase in funding for aviation and maritime security, the FY2006 budget is reminiscent, in a number of respects, of the pre-9/11 mindset. Thus, "In protecting America, the Federal Government must defeat terrorism before it reaches our shores," indicating the focus is "over there." Or, "Private owners remain responsible for security" of most critical infrastructure.[70] And, finally, even in the case of aviation, the one area of transportation where the federal government has accepted primary responsibility, the budget reaffirms the pre-9/11 philosophy that system users rather than the general treasury should shoulder most of the burden for financing security measures, specifically by more than doubling the typical fee on aviation passengers.[71] (Both houses of Congress rejected the fee increase during their consideration of the FY2006 DHS Appropriations bill.)[72]

In the pre-9/11 world, efforts to significantly enhance security were likely to fail, with neither the White House, nor the Congress, nor the American public prepared to accept the financial costs and inconveniences that would have been entailed. However, 9/11 was a watershed event, and in its aftermath there was a sea change in attitudes toward the terrorist threat and the priority attached to homeland security. The national leadership responded with a multibillion-dollar increase in federal expenditures, and a raft of legislative initiatives. It has clearly become possible to do much more to bolster transportation security than was ever the case prior to 2001. If significant systemic problems persist in aviation and transportation security, as the available evidence indicates, the post-9/11 failure is, then, one of policy and national policy makers.

Key Questions, Hard Choices

To succeed in avoiding the mistakes of the past and preparing to meet an unknown future, any plan for improving transportation security must face up to and provide appropriate answers for three fundamental policy questions. Without better guidance than has been provided to date as to their authorities, roles, and funding sources, neither DHS, nor TSA, nor the other federal and nonfederal components of transportation security will be able to succeed, regardless of the best efforts of their workforces.

First, *how is security to be prioritized and balanced with other societal imperatives, including fiscal responsibility, economic efficiency, and civil liberties?*

Before 9/11, many other values were allowed to outweigh security considerations with respect to aviation security. Whereas in the immediate aftermath of the terrorist attacks, it was perhaps true that the country and its leaders were willing to subordinate other competing priorities to homeland security needs, with the passage of time and in the absence of further incidents, these other claims have predictably, and necessarily, reasserted themselves. Thus, TSA has had to back away from the more ambitious Computer Assisted Passenger Prescreening System II (CAPPS II) program for targeting aviation security resources because of its inability to successfully address public and Congressional concerns about the program's impact on civil liberties. For fiscal reasons, Congress has limited TSA spending on and deployment of checkpoint screeners, and the deployment of in-line explosives detection equipment has slowed.

The available evidence indicates there is a continuing, unmet need to debate fully the costs and benefits of proposed security measures and, through our democratic institutions, to determine the proper balance among security for the society, individual rights, personal convenience, and financial cost. There are no easy answers here and to pretend otherwise, or even worse, to ignore such a need, was an invitation for disaster on 9/11, and continues to be so.

Second, *how is transportation security to be organized: Who is to be responsible for what?*

One facet of the 9/11 aviation security failure was the lack of accountability afforded by the system of divided responsibilities. Unfortunately, for the most part, little has been accomplished post-9/11 to clarify the situation. In particular, other than for passenger aviation, the security roles and responsibilities of federal, state, local, and private entities over the whole range of transportation modes have gone largely undefined.

Transportation security today is full of examples where large questions remain unanswered about the federal role, including in airport access, general aviation, port security, and the entire realm of land transportation. In addition, important decisions have yet to be made as to how certain transportation security functions are to be handled within the federal government, many of them centering on the future of TSA.

Third, *how are security measures to be funded: Who will pay?*

From the pre-9/11 aviation security system where documented screening performance shortcomings went unfixed and mandated explosives detection systems went undeployed in large part because of the unresolved question of how those measures were to be financed, all the way through to the November 2004 legislation implementing the 9/11 Commission recommendations, which deleted the Commission's requirement that the national transportation security plan provide a means for adequately funding its security measures,[73] this hard question has not so much been poorly answered as *ignored* by federal policy makers. Even today, the primary federal security efforts for air cargo, ports, and mass transit are little more than unfunded mandates.[74] In the absence of clear cost-allocation decisions by the federal government, attempts to increase security investments in such areas as airport access control, airline flight crew security training, general aviation, port security, rail transportation, mass transit, highways, bridges, tunnels, and pipelines will continue to be deferred and/or denied.

Principles for Action

Unless these foregoing fundamental questions are effectively addressed, transportation security efforts are doomed to flounder. But, though they are a necessary prerequisite for better security, they alone are not sufficient guides to policy makers. For that, it is useful to look at the lessons learned from the previous and current systems and the policy recommendations made by the many commissions and other organizations that have examined aviation and transportation security in recent years.

Such a review suggests a number of cornerstone principles for transportation security that appear to be lacking, in varying degrees, in current efforts. To maximize its effectiveness, the United States should build a transportation security system that

- Treats the issue as a matter of national security, with commensurate resources and policy focus, rather than as a "second tier" activity as suggested by current funding levels and bureaucratic clout.

- Prioritizes budgets and policy measures, within and across program lines, based on relative risks rather than on responding to the latest incident, bureaucratic inertia, or pork barrel politics.
- Builds a comprehensive and sustainable "baseline" of standard security across all transportation modes and intermodal connections rather than a series of largely unconnected systems based on ad hoc, reactive decision making.
- Improves both the quality and flow of relevant security information to state, local, and private stakeholders and the general public rather than relying on an approach that continually calls for "heightened alert" to a high, but nonspecific threat while offering largely unfounded reassurances about current vulnerabilities.
- Provides response and recovery efforts with sufficient authority, resources, and leadership to deal effectively with disasters rather than the kind of "too little, too late" response exemplified in the case of Hurricane Katrina.
- Clearly assigns transportation security roles to federal and nonfederal agencies and holds those assigned fully accountable for security performance rather than continuing the old and current systems of often ill-defined "shared responsibilities" where no agency is held to account.

Priorities

Securing the nation's transportation systems is very, very difficult. Would-be defenders are confronted with the daunting assignment of protecting a vast, nationwide array of airports, ports, tracks, roads, tunnels, bridges, stations, cargo, passengers, and workers. They must do so in a manner that minimizes disruption to commerce, inconvenience to riders, and costs to customers, shippers, and taxpayers. They must continually defeat a terrorist enemy that can choose the time, place, and method of attack, utilizing publicly available information on security vulnerabilities. And they must cope with the fact that the nature of this particular threat means that protections must be maintained even though incidents may be few and far between.

In response to all of these challenges, the federal government has, to date, done considerably more with respect to transportation security than was the case before 9/11. Even so, many independent analyses have concluded that these efforts fall far short of the need. Most glaring, more than four years after 9/11, the federal government has yet to come to grips with basic questions about priorities, roles, and funding. Unless and until it does so, significant and sustained progress is not likely to be made.

Part One: The 9/11/01 Systems Failure of Civil
Aviation Security

2 The Pre-9/11 Aviation Security System

As a staff member of the 9/11 Commission, I have been impressed and heartened by the widespread attention and general receptivity given the Commission's final report. Based on what they learned from the 9/11 tragedy, on a unanimous, bipartisan basis the Commissioners proposed a wide-ranging set of recommendations for improving homeland security, which were largely incorporated into legislation enacted in the closing days of the 108th Congress.

Whereas much of the media attention and public debate has, perhaps understandably, focused on the Commission's documentation of the intelligence failures that contributed to the 9/11 catastrophe and the accompanying recommendations designed to remedy those defects, the final report is equally importantly a story of the failure of the nation's law enforcement, border and immigration control, and transportation security systems that were supposed to protect the American people.

Indeed, with respect to the specific 9/11 attacks, in my view, the facts indicate clearly that this latter failure, of aviation security, was paramount; whereas the shortcomings in intelligence collection, analysis, and dissemination were secondary. The entire history of the civil aviation security system, as well as all of the testimony received by the 9/11 Commission, demonstrated that that system's defenses could only respond effectively with the kind of specific and "actionable" intelligence that all agree is always in short supply.[1]

Prior to 9/11, the FAA had, in fact, received a number of intelligence reports, including from its own intelligence division, which highlighted the threat posed by Usama bin Laden to U.S. civil aviation. For example, of 105 daily intelligence summaries provided to the FAA's leadership by the agency's intelligence office between April 1, 2001, and September 10,

2001, fifty-two mentioned bin Laden or al Qaeda by name, and five of these cited the possibility of airplane hijacking. Two of the fifty-two addressed suicide operations, though not in connection with aviation. However, none of this information pointed specifically to an al Qaeda intent to hijack commercial planes within the United States and use them as weapons with which to attack targets on the ground.[2]

In brief, without precise details as to names, flights and dates, it is unlikely that improved intelligence would have produced timely responses by the aviation security system that would have or could have prevented the hijackings.

Furthermore, as will be outlined in the following, the civil aviation system received numerous indications *on 9/11 from the hijackers themselves* that something was amiss, and yet even this individual, site, and date-specific intelligence was not translated into effective defense.

The central question, then, is why, on Tuesday, September 11, 2001, when the U.S. aviation system was supposed to be operating at only one notch below its highest level of security alert, each of three teams of lightly armed terrorists were able to accomplish their mission of hijacking a U.S. airliner and using it as a weapon against high-value symbols of American economic and military power, while a fourth came within twenty minutes of doing so.

The short answer is because they chose to. With the weapons and tactics they employed, they very likely would have succeeded on any previous day in the history of a U.S. civil aviation security system that had never been designed or operated to counter such attacks. To understand why this was so requires consideration of the evolution of that system and its key attributes.

Evolution of the Civil Aviation Security System to 1995

Until the late 1960s and early 1970s, when a rapidly increasing number of U.S. airliners were hijacked to Cuba, the federal government as well as the airlines and airports gave aviation security matters little attention. In response to the hijacking epidemic, a security system was created that included X-ray machines, magnetometers, and training programs for screening personnel, to prevent would-be hijackers from carrying weapons onboard, and federal air marshals to thwart in-progress hijackings. These measures, combined with other changing circumstances, helped lead to a dramatic reduction in the incidence of hijackings, especially within the United States.[3]

However, even as the hijacking threat ebbed, a new danger to civil aviation emerged in the form of aircraft sabotage via explosives. In the decade of the 1980s, twenty-five planes were attacked by explosives, resulting in

1,207 casualties as compared to 650 deaths caused by explosions in the 1970s and 286 such deaths in the 1960s.[4] Most notably, on December 21, 1988, a terrorist bomb, concealed in a checked bag unaccompanied by the Libyan agent who planted it, exploded in the cargo hold of Pan Am Flight 103 over Lockerbie, Scotland, killing 270 people.[5]

In response, the Bush Administration announced a series of initiatives to strengthen anti-explosives procedures at aviation facilities considered high risk, located mostly overseas. The procedures called for mandatory X-ray screening of all baggage and a 100 percent passenger/bag match requirement. Four months after the downing of Pan Am 103, the Department of Transportation announced plans to spend more than $100 million to purchase equipment specifically designed to detect explosives, unlike the X-ray machines in use at the time.[6]

On August 4, 1989, President George Bush signed Executive Order 12686 creating the *President's Commission on Aviation Security and Terrorism.* The panel (sometimes referred to as the Pan Am/Lockerbie Commission), comprised primarily of members of Congress, examined the Pan Am 103 disaster and on May 15, 1990, issued a comprehensive report, including sixty-four recommendations to improve aviation security. The Commission concluded that, "the U.S. civil aviation security system is seriously flawed and has failed to provide the proper level of protection for the traveling public."[7]

In November of 1990, Congress passed the Aviation Security Improvement Act (Public Law 104–604) to implement a number of the Commission's key recommendations. These included the creation of several new aviation security and intelligence positions at the FAA; mandatory agency reports on aviation threats and system vulnerability; and new FAA authorities to impose security measures at airports, including flight cancellation. The legislation also implemented a key Commission recommendation with regard to performance problems with the explosives detection units sought by the Department of Transportation, requiring that these systems not be deployed until the Department could certify their reliability or otherwise assure they contributed to security.[8]

The Bojinka Plot (1995)

In the period after the implementation of the new aviation security system prescribed by the Presidential Commission and enacted by Congress, the evidence seemed to suggest that threats to domestic civil aviation had been dealt with effectively, and the remaining risk was primarily overseas. For example, between 1992 and 1996, there were a total of eighty-nine hijacking incidents, none of which occurred in the United States or involved a U.S. air carrier. During that same period, two bombings and two attempted bombings of civilian aircraft occurred, once again all overseas and all involving non-U.S. air carriers. However, one of these (the December 1994 bombing of a Philippines Airlines aircraft) later proved to be a test-run of a plot devised by Ramzi Yousef to place explosive devices on twelve U.S.-registered aircraft flying routes in the Western Pacific.[9]

An accidental fire in a Manila apartment in the early morning hours of January 7, 1995, led to a discovery by Filipino police of what appeared to be a "bomb factory," plus a number of documents. At first, suspicion turned to a possible bomb threat against the Pope who was to visit the city two weeks later, but when U.S. officials were called in, an FAA security representative recognized a series of numbers on one of the documents as flight codes, which helped lead to the realization that the plot had been to bomb twelve 747s, owned by United, Delta, and Northwest, on flights originating in Manila, Tokyo, Singapore, Bangkok, Taipei, and Seoul. A laptop computer in the apartment, which contained much of the plot details, was subsequently traced to Ramzi Yousef, architect of the 1993 World Trade Center bombing.

Another FAA official was able to figure out the bomb assembly to have been used in the plot, and then "for three weeks, aviation authorities in the United States and Asia-Pacific hectored and cajoled airline officials, demanding that they push their people to unprecedented levels of vigilance and intrusiveness, and industry officials, who could seldom remember the authorities being so agitated, responded." Yousef was arrested on February 7, 1995, in Islamabad, and after several months had passed without incident, the heightened security measures were eased.[10]

After the discovery of the plot (called Bojinka by its planners)[11] and the linkage of several of the plotters to Usama bin Laden, FAA intelligence was increasingly concerned about bin Laden's interest in civil aviation as a target.[12]

The federal government's response to the Pan Am 103 tragedy and the Bojinka plot beefed up somewhat the FAA's security organization and authorities and gave impetus to the deployment of more advanced explosive detection technology. Nevertheless, the general structure of the U.S. civil aviation security system in which the FAA set and enforced standards, while the aviation industry implemented them, remained intact.

TWA 800, the Baseline Working Group, and the Gore Commission (1996–1997)

On the night of July 17, 1996, TWA Flight 800, which had departed from New York's JFK International Airport bound for Paris, France, crashed into the Atlantic Ocean near East Moriches, New York, killing all 230 individuals on board. Though terrorism was initially suspected, the National Transportation Safety Board (NTSB) later determined that the probable cause was an explosion of a fuel tank most likely caused by a short-circuit.[13]

Notwithstanding the NTSB's findings, it was clear even before the downing of TWA 800 that the United States was facing a new, more dangerous, threat environment as illustrated by the 1993 bombing of the World Trade Center in New York by radical Islamic fundamentalists.

Aviation authorities were cognizant of this new threat. Former FAA Administrator Jane Garvey told the 9/11 Commission that, "It was not immediately clear what the threat might be with respect to domestic civil aviation but evaluation of the intelligence . . . drove the FAA Office of Intelligence to the conclusion that some terrorist groups were preoccupied with the idea of attacking civil aviation and that, in fact, the domestic threat to civil aviation had . . . increased."[14]

In July of 1996, FAA's Aviation Security Advisory Committee created a Baseline Working Group (BWG), comprised of federal officials, representatives of the aviation industry, and public interest groups. The BWG's charge was to "review the threat assessment of foreign terrorism within the United States, consider the warning and interdiction capabilities of intelligence and law enforcement, examine the vulnerabilities of the domestic civil aviation system (in particular checked baggage and checkpoint screening), and consider the consequences of a successful attack." The goal of the group, which was created "in part because of disruptions in airline and airport operations caused by contingency plan-based security measure adjustments," was "to strengthen the domestic aviation security 'baseline' to a level commensurate with the new threat environment."[15]

In December 1996 the BWG issued its *Domestic Security Baseline Final Report*, which called for "effectiveness," rather than cost or expediency to be the primary determining factor in establishing a baseline for security. This new system was to be built in to the standard security programs for airlines and airports, thus making it both more enforceable from the FAA's standpoint and more predictable from the aviation industry's vantage, as compared to security measures based on temporary Security Directives or Information Circulars.[16]

The BWG proposed "airlines will apply a FAA-approved passive profile to all passengers enplaning at U.S. airports to identify selectees, whose persons and property (checked baggage and carry-on bags/items) will be subjected to security scrutiny." Furthermore, it called for an expanded role for the FBI with respect to aviation security via a full-time FBI presence at all of the largest (Category X) airports, a joint FAA/FBI effort to secure legislation to provide direct FAA access to the FBI's criminal record database (National Crime Information Center [NCIC]), and joint FAA/FBI exploration of the possibility of expanding FBI background checks "to include a search of all available intelligence files for possible 'terrorist' connections."[17]

The BWG also recommended an end to "unfunded federal mandates" on the various components of the civil aviation security system by providing "a Congressional appropriation from the General Fund" to meet "the full cost of implementing and maintaining an improved domestic security baseline." Finally, it called for a series of measures to rapidly improve the security system, via the timely deployment of available technologies (including liquid explosives scanning devices and trace portals for the larger airports), and "institutional and procedural changes" in the system (including expansion of the Federal Security Manager program, designation by air carriers and airport operators of a security head "who should be a senior management official," and streamlining the rule-making process for security). The group estimated the ten-year cost of implementing its recommendations to be $9.9 billion.[18]

The Office of Management and Budget (OMB) strongly objected to the BWG majority on the issues of the source and amount of funding to be provided:

> [These recommendations]... are inconsistent with the current practice of FAA programs, contradicting long-standing government-wide budget policy, and reflect an unrealistic outlook regarding the availability of discretionary funds. First, aviation system users currently pay for on-going aviation security costs. These are considered to be costs incurred by the private aviation industry for doing business in modern society.... Continuing efforts to balance the budget will significantly limit the amount of General Fund monies available to support this, or other potentially worthy expenditures.... Finally, a dedicated funding system for operating costs, if not paid by the users, provides little incentive for cost discipline in the provisions of these services and will result in waste and increased cost to the public.[19]

Ironically, though the BWG had been conceived of as a way to break the usual cycle of aviation security measures being driven solely in response to disasters and emergencies, the group held its first meeting on the same day that TWA 800 exploded, and its analyses and recommendations served primarily as a basis for the work of the Presidential Commission that was established one month later.

In response to mounting concerns about the terrorist threat to aviation, as manifested by the Bojinka plot and precipitated by the explosion of TWA Flight 800, on August 22, 1996, President Bill Clinton created the *White House Commission on Aviation Safety and Security*, chaired by Vice President Gore and commonly referred to as the Gore Commission.[20]

The final report of the Gore Commission described the evolving threat to civil aviation in this time period as follows:

The Federal Bureau of Investigation, the Central Intelligence Agency, and other intelligence agencies have been warning that the threat of terrorism has been changing in two important ways. First, it is no longer just an overseas threat from foreign terrorists.... The second change is that in addition to well-known, established terrorist groups, it is becoming more common to find terrorists working alone or in ad-hoc groups, some of which are not afraid to die in carrying out their designs.[21]

The Gore Commission's most significant security recommendations, issued in February 1997, were directed at dealing with the bomb threat. These included:

1. Immediate deployment of explosives detection technology to the airports for baggage screening.
2. Partial implementation of full bag–passenger match on domestic flights. (This measure, which had previously been applied overseas, was explicitly linked to the need to determine the presence of explosives in checked baggage. Under it, a checked bag was not to be loaded onto an aircraft until it could be matched to a boarded passenger.)
3. Additional deployment of canine explosives-sniffing teams. (There were eighty-seven such teams deployed in 1996, not all of which met the same performance standards.)
4. Establishment of automated profiling to identify passengers "who merit additional attention." (The Commission specifically endorsed the automated profiling system then "under development by the FAA and Northwest Airlines," which subsequently became known as the Computer Assisted Passenger Prescreening System, or CAPPS.)
5. Federal certification of screening companies and minimum training requirements for screeners.
6. Elevation of aviation security to a national security issue, which should entail "substantial" federal funding, defined to be approximately $100 million a year for capital improvements to achieve the Commission's objectives.[22]

In the period between 1996 and the end of 2000, the FAA moved administratively to implement, or to begin implementation of, each of these major items and many of the remaining Gore Commission security recommendations.[23] However, the lack of more specific requirements and deadlines made it difficult to gauge actual implementation.

For example, rule making on screener company certification, which had been called for by the Gore Commission, was still not completed as of September 10, 2001 (in spite of the statutory requirements outlined in the following).[24]

Commission member Victoria Cummock, whose husband had been lost on Pan Am 103, dissented from the final report:

> Sadly, the overall emphasis of the recommendations reflects a clear commitment to the *enhancement of aviation* at the expense of the Commission's mandate of enhancing aviation *safety and security.* . . . In summary, our final report contains no specific call to action, no commitments to address aviation safety and security system-wide by mandating the deployment of current technology, with actionable timetables and budgets.[25]

In January 2004 testimony to the National Commission on Terrorist Attacks Upon the United States, Cathal "Irish" Flynn, who was head of FAA security from 1993 through 2000, indicated that the failure of the Gore Commission to follow the BWG in stressing the importance of intelligence and law enforcement, emphasizing the threat from foreign terrorists, and recommending a multibillion-dollar federal investment in aviation security, was "disappointing."[26]

The Congress generally responded affirmatively to the Gore Commission's and the Clinton Administration's calls for increased funding and tightened regulations for aviation security. Passage of the Federal Aviation Reauthorization Act of 1996 followed in the immediate aftermath of the preliminary Gore Commission security recommendations, but preceded the issuance of the Commission's final report. Among the Act's key elements were provisions to:

- Direct FAA to certify screening companies and improve training and testing of security screeners.
- Require criminal history background checks for baggage and passenger screeners.
- Encourage FAA to facilitate the interim deployment of available explosive detection equipment.
- Encourage FAA, the Department of Transportation, the intelligence community, and law enforcement agencies to assist air carriers in developing passenger profiling programs.
- Direct FAA and the FBI to conduct joint threat and vulnerability assessments at least once every three years at airports determined to be high risk.
- Require airports and air carriers to conduct periodic security system vulnerability assessments, and the FAA to periodically audit such assessments as well as to conduct periodic and unannounced inspections of airport and air carrier security systems.[27]

Four years later, Congress adopted the Airport Security Improvement Act of 2000. Its major features included:

- Specifying that criminal background checks be done for airport security applicants.

- Directing FAA to issue the final rule on the certification of screening companies by May 31, 2001.
- Establishing new minimum standards for the training of security screeners.
- Requiring FAA to work with airport operators and air carriers to improve airport access controls by January 31, 2001.
- Directing FAA to require augmenting the Computer Assisted Passenger Prescreening System by randomly selecting additional checked bags for screening and directing the FAA to maximize the use of explosive detection equipment in this process.[28]

3 Attributes of the Security System

Institutions of Civil Aviation Security

By 1974, the main structure of the civil aviation security system that was in place on September 11, 2001, had been established. It provided for a set of shared and "complementary" responsibilities, divided among the FAA, the airlines and airport authorities, and the Congress.

The FAA was responsible for setting minimum-security requirements governing airports (as defined in 14 CFR Part 108) and air carriers (14 CFR 107) with the power to enforce the standards through inspections, fines, and revocation of operational certificates.[1]

Air carriers were responsible for screening passengers, baggage, and cargo; protecting aircraft from unauthorized access; and training personnel in emergency procedures and tactics. The details of how they were to conduct those functions were spelled out in the Air Carrier Standard Security Program, issued by the FAA.[2]

The airports were responsible for providing law enforcement and facility security, including the control of access to Air Operations Areas (AOA).[3] The details of how they were to conduct those functions were spelled out in the FAA-approved Airport Standard Security Program.[4]

Congress was responsible for making aviation security law (imbedded primarily in Title 49 of the United States Code) and for performing oversight of the implementation of those laws. It was also responsible for funding and financing the federal components of the aviation security system.

In his book, *After: How America Confronted the September 12 Era*, Stephen Brill wrote about some of the consequences of the system:

For years, the airlines—an industry whose product is regulated from Washington like almost no other—and the FAA have had a mutual support relationship. Their personnel regularly switched sides, going from the agency to one of the airlines' large Washington lobbying offices and back again. . . . [T]hey thought of themselves more as partners than adversaries, which had its positive side in the sense that overbearing regulators could easily strangle an industry like this. So, the airlines rarely complained publicly about the FAA, and the FAA didn't hassle the airlines about issues like security.[5]

Although recognizing that "the terrorist threat is changing and growing," the Gore Commission generally ratified the existing system of shared and complementary responsibilities in civil aviation security and concluded that "because of its extensive interactions with airlines and airports, the FAA is the appropriate agency" to implement and oversee aviation security. It sought to make improvements by creating "a new partnership" between government and industry "that will marshal resources more effectively, and focus all parties on achieving the ultimate goal: enhancing the security of air travel for Americans."[6]

In this same time period, Congress appeared to take some tentative steps to reevaluate and revise the organization of the civil aviation security system, but it too essentially accepted the basic, long-standing elements of that system. Though the Federal Aviation Reauthorization Act of 1996 formally removed the so-called dual mandate by explicitly making safety and security the FAA's highest priority, the Joint Explanatory Statement of the Congressional conference committee that drafted the final bill stated:

The managers do not intend for enactment of this provision to require any changes in the FAA's current organization or functions. Instead, the provision is intended to address any public perceptions that might exist that the promotion of air commerce by the FAA could create a conflict with its safety regulatory mandate.[7]

The system of dispersed responsibilities for civil aviation security created multiple opportunities for delaying the regulatory process and avoiding accountability.[8] The 1990 President's Commission on Aviation Security and Terrorism had referred to the situation as "a division of security responsibilities that leaves no entity accountable."[9]

In the aftermath of 9/11, in words eerily reminiscent of the finding from eleven years before, some experts perceived shared responsibility among the FAA, air carriers, and airports as fragmentation in which "everyone was involved in aviation security, but no one was singularly responsible."[10]

Reactive System

In 1990 the Presidential Commission on Aviation Security and Terrorism, which itself had been established only after the Pan Am 103 disaster, reported to the nation that the FAA was "a reactive agency—preoccupied with responses to events to the exclusion of adequate contingency planning in anticipation of future threats."[11] This attribute, "that we are continually fighting the last war and allowing the perpetrators of violence to educate us about the vulnerabilities of the system,"[12] continued to hold true right through the events of 9/11. Furthermore, the culture of reactivity was present not just at the FAA but also throughout the entire civil aviation security system, including the air carriers, the airports, and the Congress.[13]

Thus, the primary features of the pre-9/11 security system could be summarized as:

- Antihijacking measures (including checkpoint screening,[14] profiling,[15] and air marshals), which were created in the early 1970s in response to the Cuba hijackings; and
- Antisabotage measures (including X-ray screening and positive passenger bag match at high-risk airports), which were undertaken in response to the 1988 bombing of Pan Am 103,[16] and additional such measures (explosive detection equipment, canine teams, and CAPPS), which were begun after the explosion of TWA 800 in 1996.[17]

Furthermore, reactivity was built into the very operation of the system—driven by either cumbersome and time-consuming rule making (which history had shown could be hastened only in the wake of a disaster) or Security Directives (which were implemented mainly in response to an actual event or very specific threat information).[18]

The major exception to this history of reactive policy making was the 1996 Baseline Working Group established by the FAA to strengthen the overall civil aviation security program outside of the crisis mode. However, when TWA 800 exploded on the day of the BWG's first meeting, most of the impetus for action passed to the subsequent Gore Commission, thereby repeating the familiar reactive pattern.[19]

It should be noted that even after a major event, the reaction could be short-lived. A noted aviation security author observed more broadly that "democratic states often find their enthusiasm for further, possibly expensive, preventative actions, quickly dissipates after the initial surprise of a terrorist attack. Thus it is only after a real disaster or a sustained series of attacks that democracies take real action."[20] This was demonstrated for the U.S. civil aviation system in the aftermath of TWA 800 when funding for the deployment of explosives detection equipment was greatly diminished after it was determined that the plane was most likely downed by a mechanical problem rather than a terrorist bomb.

Decision Making

The civil aviation system decision-making process was bifurcated, with serious flaws within each part:

- Rule making, for permanent changes in the security program.
- Security Directives (SDs) through which the FAA could mandate "temporary" security measures for airlines and airports.[21]

The rule-making process, which consisted of numerous and repetitive steps,[22] was subjected to a type of cost–benefit analysis[23] under which security measures in particular had a difficult time gaining support even within the originating agency (FAA), let alone at the departmental or Office of Management and Budget level. Under such circumstances, FAA security officials came to regard the process as the "bane" of security. One FAA official told the 9/11 Commission that the agency had to prioritize potential new regulations, and it was rare for a security rule to crack the list of its top ten priorities.[24]

In addition to concerns about the timeliness and accountability of FAA rule making, the partial deregulation of U.S. civil aviation in the 1970s had significant consequences within that process, as described in a 2001 textbook on aviation safety and security:

> Over the past two decades, vigorous industry economic competition has made rulemaking a distinctly adversarial process. Carriers, labor groups, aircraft manufacturers and general aviation supporters carefully scrutinize every proposed safety regulation and question its efficacy and impact on costs. Often such activities, in concert with administrative policies and bureaucratic labyrinths, have effectively blocked safety regulations for years.[25]

Contributing to the difficulties in the rule-making process was the position of U.S. air carriers, which, unlike the situation in many other countries where civil aviation is run directly or indirectly by national governments, are privately owned, for-profit enterprises. Whenever the FAA considered security enhancements, the airlines would "push back on anything that cost them money or their passengers time."[26]

The long-time Inspector General of the Department of Transportation, Kenneth Mead, testified to the 9/11 Commission that there were great pressures within the civil aviation security system on behalf of the air carriers to control security costs and to "limit the impact of security requirement on aviation operations, so that the industry could concentrate on its primary mission of moving passengers and aircraft.... [T]hose counterpressures in turn manifested themselves as significant weaknesses in security."[27]

Many of the problems with rule making were clearly illustrated by the FAA's efforts to revise Federal Aviation Regulation, Part 108, through which the FAA set the security framework for the airlines. That particular rule making began in August of 1997, but the final rule was not promulgated until almost four years later, on July 17, 2001, with an effective date of November 14, 2001.

Based on an assessment that estimated the potential threat to *domestic* civil aviation to be "equivalent to some portion" of the Bojinka plot ("12 . . . explosions . . . that involve the loss of an entire aircraft and incur a large number of fatalities"), the rule sought to make improvements in a number of areas including FAA inspection authority and compliance enforcement, training requirements for certain security personnel, and the issuance of Security Directives (SDs). As was often the case, over the course of the rule-making process, certain FAA proposals were dropped in response to comments received from the interested public.

- The FAA had proposed to prohibit persons "from carrying a deadly or dangerous weapon, explosive, or incendiary" but this was dropped in the final rule because, "the FAA has determined that airport operators . . . are able to handle such occurrences through their local laws that control the presence of weapons and other deadly items on airport property. . . . While the FAA will not take action at this time, it will continue to assess the need for any future comprehensive security enhancements regarding weapons and other destructive substances that may be detrimental to the flying public."[28]

- The FAA had initially included an accountability compliance element for air carriers, including penalties. In response to the original proposal, comments were received as follows: "The UPS [United Parcel Service], the Denver Airport and ATA [Air Transport Association] agree that individuals should be held accountable, but strongly object to delegating enforcement authority to the air carrier." In the final rule, the compliance program was deleted, while the comment period on the proposal was reopened, and the FAA indicated "the omission of security compliance programs from the final rule does not stop an aircraft operator from voluntarily adopting a compliance program at any time."[29]

- Last, the FAA had proposed that air carriers be required to "detect and prevent" the carrying of explosives or dangerous weapons onto an aircraft or into a secure area. Comments received included: "Alaska Airlines, FedEx, UPS, United Express, CAA, RAA [Regional Airline Association] and ATA state that the air carrier cannot 'detect' introduction of deadly or dangerous items 100% of the time; they believe that 'deter' should be substituted for 'detect.' In the final rule, the FAA has decided to accept the commenters' suggestion so the language . . . remains 'prevent or deter.' Both phrases adequately reflect the overall intent that aircraft operators must use the measures in their security programs to keep deadly or dangerous weapons, explosives or incendiaries off the aircraft and out of the sterile area."[30]

Although the FAA perhaps saw little distinction in this last change, the airlines viewed things somewhat differently. In testimony to the 9/11 Commission, the head of the airlines' Air Transport Association indicated that, "This [pre-9/11 aviation security] system was specifically designed, according to statute actually, as a 'prevent or deter' system and was not a more intrusive 'prevent and detect' system."[31]

The difficulties with rule making led the FAA to turn increasingly to SDs, which allowed the agency to implement urgent security measures immediately.[32] In addition to being temporary and not as amenable to enforcement actions as the regulatory process, SD decision making was based almost entirely on threat assessment. Even this was problematic, especially with respect to the gathering of intelligence about threats to domestic civil aviation and the awareness of such information by the FAA and other civil aviation security decision makers. Furthermore, FAA officials involved in assessing the threat were reluctant to quantify their analysis because of the inherent uncertainties in intelligence data.[33]

With the growing use of SDs, while threat assessments dominated the civil aviation security system's decision-making process, they were not connected in any significant way to vulnerability assessments, which were handled by different divisions in the FAA[34] that, in turn, had little involvement in informing either the tasking or analysis of the threat evaluations. Beyond that, while the FAA and others (such as GAO[35] and the Department of Transportation Inspector General[36]) routinely conducted vulnerability assessments on at least some of the aviation security system's layers, there is little evidence of such evaluations having a major impact on the system (as witnessed by the system's limited response to the long-documented problems with checkpoint screening).

Finally, there was no discernable attempt at the FAA, or elsewhere within the civil aviation security system, to factor consequence assessment into the equation. Thus, whereas there may have been claims about the use of risk management in civil aviation security decision making, the record does not bear out such a contention.[37]

This perhaps helps explain why the FAA decision-making system could discount its own consideration of potential suicide hijacking in the United States,[38] which would have simply been scored as *very low* in the threat analyses. Had vulnerability and consequence evaluations been factored in, the results should have been different. For example, a domestic Bojinka-type threat, which was the very one cited in the cost–benefit analysis accompanying the July 2001 FAA rule making to revise the basic airline and airport security programs,[39] would have scored *very high* in consequence assessment, and if one used the FAA's own test results for vulnerability to such a scenario, that ranking would have had to be *high* as well.

Dual Mandate

The institutional outlook and attitudes of the FAA and the other elements of the U.S. civil aviation system with respect to security were heavily influenced by the fact that the agency, and its predecessors, were tasked from the beginning with what has come to be called the "dual mandate" of both regulating and promoting civil aviation. From the Aeronautic Branch of the Department of Commerce created by the Air Commerce Act of 1926 with responsibility for "fostering air commerce, issuing and enforcing air traffic rules, licensing pilots, certificating aircraft, establishing airways, and operating and maintaining aids to air navigation,"[40] to its ultimate successor, the FAA, the U.S. Government's lead civil aviation agency was confronted with what aviation security author Andrew Thomas called "two competing and divergent goals. How can it nurture both market forces and public safety at the same time? A formidable, if not almost impossible, task, to be sure."[41] This divided focus had significant implications for the FAA's ability to carry out its security mission.

The Federal Aviation Act of 1958, which created the FAA, described the FAA's security role as "to establish security provisions which will encourage and permit the maximum use of the navigable airspace by civil aircraft consistent with the national security."[42] Former Department of Transportation Inspector General Mary Schiavo wrote in her 1997 book, *Flying Blind, Flying Safe*:

> The FAA's dual mission did not leap out at anyone in 1958 — or in most of the years following—as a glaring paradox. In those days, aviation was heavily regulated. The government controlled prices, routes, even the purchase of airplanes. The aviation industry thrived under the care and nurturing of the government. The government and the military were intrinsic to the development of aviation; the same people guided and assisted aviation on both sides. The aviation industry urged Congress to pass the very legislation that created the FAA. The FAA's mandate was essentially a national industrial policy designed to foster commercial aviation.[43]

As was customary in the civil aviation system, the impetus for a change in the dual mandate came in *reaction* to a disaster. In this case, it was the May 1996 explosion of a ValuJet DC-9 over the Everglades. When the National Transportation Safety Board (NTSB) investigation revealed safety lapses by the FAA, the air carrier, and one of the carrier's contractors to have been responsible for the crash, Transportation Secretary Pena announced on July 18, 1996 "that he would urge Congress to make safety FAA's single primary concern."[44]

In introducing legislation to implement the change advocated by Secretary Pena, Senator Olympia Snowe (R-ME) stated, "We cannot expect the FAA to regain the trust of the public while it maintains the mission to both ensure their safety while continuing to promote the growth of the carriers. The current mission of the FAA places it in the untenable position of being both the enforcer and the best friend of the airlines – no one can perform both roles and do them well."[45]

Though, as previously noted, concerns about the *appearance* of a conflict between FAA's promotional and regulatory roles led Congress to formally eliminate the promotional mandate in 1996,[46] the FAA's legal authorities that were still in effect on September 11, 2001, included all of the following:

- Under Section 40101 of 49 USC 449, the FAA was to consider a number of factors in carrying out its safety and security responsibilities, including "encouraging and developing civil aeronautics."
- Section 40104 provided that "The administrator of the Federal Aviation Administration shall encourage the development of civil aeronautics and safety of air commerce in and outside the United States."
- Section 44903 required that, in carrying out its authority to protect passengers "against an act of criminal violence or aircraft piracy," the FAA was to consider whether any proposed regulation was consistent with "protecting passengers; and the public interest in promoting air transportation and intrastate air transportation." Furthermore, "to the maximum extent practicable," the FAA was to "require a uniform procedure for searching and detaining passengers and property to ensure their safety; and courteous and efficient treatment" by the air carrier and any governmental personnel involved in the process.[47]

Safety Versus Security

A final attribute of the pre-9/11 aviation system in the United States was the different approaches it took toward safety and security. Aviation safety, which refers to countermeasures related to accidents, is based on quantifiable assessments of accident probabilities derived from a wealth of data built up over many years within civil aviation itself. Aviation security, which encompasses protective efforts against hostile or malicious acts, involves the vagaries of human behavior and intentions and "is much more difficult to measure because it depends on our estimate of the threat of a hostile act."[48] And such a threat estimate would typically come from "outside" the world of civil aviation (i.e., the intelligence community).

The National Research Council (NRC) contrasted aviation safety, where "one agency (the FAA) has a dominant role in ensuring safety through multiple, coordinated means," with aviation security, where "tactics and techniques emerged piecemeal, in reaction to a series of individual security failures." The NRC concluded, "Given the outstanding performance of the aviation safety system, it is notable that aviation security . . . was not handled in a similarly holistic fashion."[49]

Indeed, though safety was built in to the basic operation of the civil aviation system from the outset (with the 1926 Air Commerce Act "passed at the urging of the aviation industry, whose leaders believed the airplane could not reach its full commercial potential without federal action to improve and maintain safety standards"[50]), security was generally regarded as "disruptive" to the regular operation of civil aviation.[51]

In an August 16, 2001, speech at an Air Line Pilots Association Safety Forum, Carol Hallett, then President of the airline industry's trade association, remarked that by the 1930s, "safety truly became an integral part of aviation. It was woven into every aspect of our industry—from design to operations, from maintenance to marketing. Safety became a discipline and a cornerstone of our operations."[52] In contrast, security — other than internal security directed at such criminal acts as fraud or theft—was a relatively recent, and "external," addition to airline concerns.

Assessments of Aviation Security System Performance

The civil aviation security leadership viewed the pre-9/11 system as "adequate for the conditions of low threat that prevailed,"[53] and "responsive to the assessed threat based on information from intelligence and law enforcement agencies."[54] Perhaps most important, the effectiveness of the antihijacking measures adopted over the years seemed to be demonstrated by a dramatic decline in the number of domestic hijackings after 1983. As illustrated by Fig. 3.1, although foreign hijackings had continued, no airline hijacking had occurred within the United States since 1991.

More specifically with respect to terrorism, the consensus view of pre-9/11 civil aviation security was expressed by terrorism and aviation security expert Brian Jenkins, who wrote in 1999:

> Commercial aviation has long been a favorite target of terrorists, who have viewed airliners as nationally-labeled containers of hostages in the case of hijackings, or victims in the case of sabotage. This set off a deadly contest between terrorists and security which has continued for the past 30 years with security gradually gaining. In the early 1970s, more than 30 percent of international terrorist attacks were targeted against commercial aviation; it is less than 10 percent today.[55]

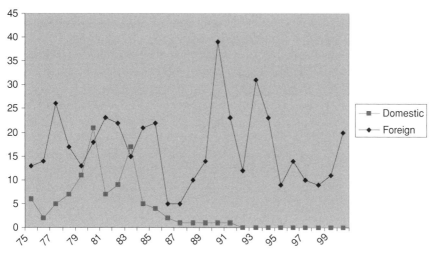

Figure 3.1. Hijackings of U.S.-Registered versus Foreign-Registered Air Carriers 1975–2000. (*Source:* Federal Aviation Administration, *Criminal Acts Against Aviation 2000* (Washington, DC: 2001), pp. 75–76.)

However, in the same article, Jenkins noted that the terrorist threat was "dynamic" and that the threat inside the United States was "real."[56]

Whatever the evaluations of the system's overall effectiveness, abundant and publicly available information pointed to "significant, long-standing vulnerabilities in aviation security." Most prominent were "failure to detect threats when screening passengers and their carry-on bags prior to their boarding aircraft and the absence of any requirement to screen checked baggage on domestic flights; [and] inadequate controls for limiting access to secure areas at airports."[57]

Among many other similar reports it had issued beginning in the latter half of the 1980s, GAO reported to Congress in June of 2000 that, caused primarily by the rapid turnover (itself a product of the prevalent low wages, limited benefits, and tedious nature of the work) and inadequate training of screeners, 20 percent of the simulated weapons used in FAA testing in 1987 escaped detection at airport checkpoints and that subsequent FAA test data had shown *declining* performance throughout the 1990s. Moreover, the more realistic the testing the worse were the results.[58]

Starting in 1997, the Department of Transportation's Inspector General (DOT IG) had documented substantial "underutilization" of the explosives detection machines deployed at airports to screen checked baggage, primarily because the airlines were reluctant to inconvenience their passengers. In 1998 and 1999, agents of the DOT IG's office were able to gain unauthorized access to secure areas in 68 percent of the tests they conducted at eight major U.S. airports, mainly because airport security personnel failed to follow prescribed procedures. Finally, in 2000 the DOT IG issued a report that found the FAA's background investigation requirements for airport personnel were ineffective because of limitations in the content and timing of these requirements.[59]

Apart from all of these published reports that documented aviation security flaws, the FAA leadership had data from its own "Red Teams," which conducted undercover testing of airport security employing simulated terrorist tactics. A former Red Team member testified to the 9/11 Commission that in testing between 1996 and 2001, the FAA Red Team found major flaws in checked baggage screening, access control, and checkpoint screening.[60]

As Dr. Gerald Dillingham of the GAO testified at an April 2000 Senate hearing, "Taken together these problems show the chain of security protecting our aviation system has not one but several weak links." He went on to add, "It must be remembered that the responsibility for these problems does not rest with the FAA alone. The aviation industry is responsible for undertaking the security measures at airports and many of the problems identified—such as rapid screener turnover—more appropriately rest with it."[61]

4 The 9/11 Hijackings

The World of September 11, 2001

In the period leading up to 9/11, aviation security efforts were directed at implementing a three-year-old mandate to deploy explosives detection machines at all of the largest airports and completing a nearly four-year rule making to mandate certification of checkpoint screening companies, increase screener training, and impose stricter background checks on screeners and airport employees. But security was not the primary focus of the civil aviation system and its components.

In addition to continuing attention to safety issues, throughout 2001 the top leadership of the FAA was focused on congestion and delays within the system, with the Administrator recalling that, "we were a nation bedeviled by delays, concerned about congestion, impatient to keep moving."[1]

In response to constituent demands, Congress directed its legislative and oversight attention to reducing flight delays, requiring the airlines to provide passengers with better information, and improving the handling of baggage.[2]

The American public—the customers of the aviation industry and the constituents of members of Congress—offered a relatively benign view of the threat with respect to commercial aviation safety and security in the period leading up to 9/11. In an ABC poll taken just after the 1999 EgyptAir crash off the East Coast of the United States, 58 percent of the respondents indicated their belief that flying was safer than driving, and in a Fox News/Opinion Dynamics survey conducted during the same period, fully 78 percent cited poor maintenance as "a greater threat to airline safety" than terrorism.[3]

Although there was an acknowledgment of a continuing, and evolving, potential terrorist threat to civil aviation, those who looked at civil aviation security prior to September 11, 2001, could observe that there had not been a hijacking or bombing of a U.S. air carrier since 1991, and that aviation security measures had apparently been "gaining" ground against the terrorists.[4]

With such perceptions—and realities—and with a security system that was largely paid for and carried out by an industry that was still struggling economically,[5] it is perhaps somewhat easier to understand some of the constraints operating on the aviation security system on September 11, 2001. But, as observed previously, even with a pre-9/11 mindset, the system's flaws were well known.

As DOT Inspector General Kenneth Mead testified to the 9/11 Commission:

> I think that the system we had in place before September 11th had in fact undergone incremental improvements over the years . . . and I believe in fact provided a deterrent value for certain types of threat. Overall, though, the model on which the system was based did not work very well, and there were significant weaknesses in the protections it provided, even for the types of threats the system was designed to prevent.[6]

Given that the threat assessments that drove aviation security decision making were very problematic, especially with respect to domestic aviation; that top-level FAA and other civil aviation security decision makers were largely unaware of such threat information as did exist; and that the security measures then in place were virtually inapplicable to the weapons and tactics that were to be employed, the U.S. civil aviation security system and its individual members were utterly unprepared for the terrorist hijackings that occurred on 9/11.

On September 11, 2001, the prescreening of civil aviation passengers in the United States was solely designed to prevent individuals from placing explosives in their checked baggage.[7] The screening checkpoints were geared to preventing the carrying of handguns or large knives on board a plane. Any items with a lesser metal content, say box cutters or short-bladed knives, would likely not have been detected, barring an effective physical search by a security screening workforce whose performance difficulties had been publicly documented by the GAO and others for more than a decade.[8]

In the event such a weapon were discovered, security checkpoint rules in effect at that time would have caused the box cutters to be placed in checked baggage, whereas short-bladed knives would have been permitted to be carried into the passenger cabin.[9] Once onboard, a would-be hijacker would have been confronted with flight crew tactics that were designed to avoid attempts to overpower the hijackers and that did not address the possibility of suicidal intent.[10]

All of these design features were, at least to some degree, knowable to interested parties via a review of the public record and/or carefully planned "test-runs." Would-be hijackers of domestic U.S. airliners who were determined and highly motivated, and therefore largely immune to whatever "deterrent" value was possessed by the civil aviation security system, who escaped notice in FAA Security Directives (which essentially supplied the pre-9/11 "no fly" lists for the air carriers),[11] who used as weapons items with a metal content less than that of a handgun, and who did not conform to the traditional, nonsuicide hijacking paradigm were likely to succeed.

Why Did the System Fail?

Having considered the civil aviation security system's history and major features, we can now return to the central question posed at the outset: Why did that system fail on 9/11? One possible answer would be the skills of these particular terrorists, and indeed their plan was nearly flawless in taking advantage of the shortcomings in the antihijacking countermeasures then in place. However, their execution was far from perfect.

Repeatedly, the hijackers' actions on 9/11 came to the attention of U.S. government and airline authorities in ways that could have—and perhaps should have—exposed their plot. Leaving aside the clues they had previously left as they made their way through the U.S. immigration system and the fact that two were on the State Department's terrorist watch list (which the FAA had not been made aware of), seven of the nineteen were identified by the FAA's CAPPS as potential threats to civil aviation based on their ticketing information, and an eighth (the ringleader, Atta) was selected for extra security attention through CAPPS' random selection feature. At least two others raised such suspicion by their behavior when they checked in at the airport that they, too, were made selectees for additional security scrutiny, and two more had difficulty in responding to the routine security questions they were asked at the ticket counter. Thus, before the hijackers even reached the airport security checkpoints on 9/11, twelve of the nineteen had, in one way or another, alerted the civil aviation security system that they might be potential threats.[12]

Of the seven who were observed, via closed circuit cameras, progressing through checkpoints at the Portland, Maine and Washington Dulles airports, three set off alarms on the magnetometers, and two of these set off a second magnetometer.[13]

Even after the takeovers occurred, the hijackers continued to make potentially crucial mistakes. On the very first hijacked aircraft, Flight 11, the hijackers inadvertently transmitted messages intended for the passengers to the air traffic control system instead, potentially exposing their plot to conduct multiple hijackings within the first ten minutes of its beginning by indicating that "we have some planes."[14] On the last of the hijackings, Flight 93, the terrorists apparently departed from their operational plan by delaying their takeover by fifteen minutes compared to the other flights, and they allowed passengers to communicate with friends and relatives on the ground thereby learning of the earlier hijackings, both of which perhaps contributed to their failure to accomplish their mission.[15]

The breakdowns in operational discipline by the hijackers afforded the civil aviation security system one final opportunity to stop at least the last of the hijackings, an opportunity that it once again failed.

By 9:00 a.m. on the morning of September 11, 2001, American Airlines was aware that Flight 11 had been hijacked, that an aircraft of some type had hit the World Trade Center (WTC), and that contact had been lost with Flight 77.[16] United knew that a hijacked American aircraft had hit the WTC and that Flight 175 had been hijacked.[17] By 9:05 a.m. American became aware that Flight 77 had been hijacked. Clearly, had the airlines more effectively pooled the information they each possessed by this point, both would have been far better informed on the nature of what was transpiring. However, it is not clear what meaningful difference such awareness would have made, at least with respect to three of the hijacked flights: Flight 11 (at 8:47 a.m.) and Flight 175 (at 9:03 a.m.) had both crashed by this time period, and Flight 77 had been taken over by the hijackers (by 8:54 a.m.).[18]

Awareness within the Air Traffic Control (ATC) system was similarly muddled in the first forty-five minutes of the 9/11 hijackings. Herndon Command Center was advised by the Boston ATC Center of the hijacking of American 11 at 8:28 a.m.[19] and by 8:52 a.m. was advising United Airlines that the 8:47 a.m. crash into the WTC had been a hijacked American Airlines jet.[20] However, though the New York ATC Center was aware of the Flight 175 hijacking by 8:55 a.m., there is no evidence that this crucial piece of information reached Herndon until after Flight 175 had crashed.[21]

Perhaps most to the point, by 9:07 a.m. the Boston Air Traffic Control Center instructed its controllers to notify all aircraft within the Center's airspace of the two crashes in New York City and advise them to heighten cockpit security. The Boston Center then immediately requested that Herndon issue a similar alert nationwide ("to get messages to airborne aircraft to increase security for the cockpit"), but there is no evidence that this was ever done.[22]

In the absence of any FAA guidance, United did not take decisive action to warn its airborne aircraft to take defensive action until 9:19 a.m., when on his own initiative a United dispatcher began transmitting the message to "Beware any cockpit intrusion" to his sixteen transcontinental flights. This was twenty-seven minutes after United was aware of the crash of an American airliner into the WTC, nineteen minutes after it knew of the hijacking of Flight 175, and nine minutes after the airline knew of the second crash into the WTC (though not that this was Flight 175). It was also twelve minutes after Boston Air Traffic Control Center asked the Herndon Command Center to contact aircraft about increasing cockpit security.[23]

Furthermore, because the United dispatcher in question was still responsible for his other flights, his warning message was not transmitted to Flight 93 until 9:23 a.m., and therefore was not received in the cockpit until 9:24 a.m., and responded to by the Flight 93 pilot at 9:26 a.m., just two minutes before the presumed takeover of the aircraft.[24]

In this crucial interval between 9:00 a.m. and 9:24 a.m. when the dispatcher's message finally was transmitted to Flight 93, a large number of conflicting, and for the most part what later turned out to be inaccurate, reports about other flights were being received by the FAA and the airlines. In addition, the airlines lacked vital information from air traffic control about communications and flight data it had received from Flights 11, 175, and 77, whereas the FAA similarly lacked important information about calls to the airlines from flight attendants on the hijacked flights.[25]

Given what was known within the various parts of the civil aviation system by shortly after 9:00 a.m. on the morning of September 11, 2001, it seems clear that the FAA and/or the airlines should have transmitted cockpit warnings to all airborne aircraft well before 9:19 a.m. Although it will never be possible to know for certain, had this occurred, and more specifically had the warning been transmitted to Flight 93 several minutes earlier than 9:24 a.m., the subsequent cockpit takeover of Flight 93 may well have been averted.

A second potential answer as to why the aviation security system failed on 9/11 would be the security shortcomings of particular components of the system. However, the 9/11 Commission found no evidence that specific airports or airlines were targeted by the terrorists because, based on all of the performance results it examined, nothing stood out about any of them on the only level that really mattered: the security layer of checkpoint screening. Though there were indications that there was more local reporting of security problems at Logan Airport and that, within the world of civil aviation security, United Airlines had a better reputation for security consciousness than did American, there was nothing to suggest that such issues entered into the terrorists' targeting of well-fueled East-to-West transcontinental flights. They simply booked the flights that took off (or were at least scheduled to take off) near simultaneously.[26]

If they considered contract checkpoint screening performance at any length, the hijackers would have been able to discern what the 9/11 Commission learned, and what the Congress, FAA officials, the airports, and airlines were all aware of well before 9/11: that this layer represented a "lowest common denominator" where, as one former FAA security official who was responsible for performing liaison with several airlines over his career noted to the Commission, a now-defunct airline with a one-man security office had about as good a performance result as the airline with the largest security staffing and greatest attention to security concerns.[27]

But beyond that, what if a superior screening workforce had somehow, in contravention of everything we have learned about the history of civil aviation security, been brought about prior to a hijacking disaster? The small knives that seem to have been the weapons of choice were expressly *permitted* to be brought on the planes, so even if found by an alert screener, what would have been the difference?[28] Mace and pepper spray were not permitted, but were exceedingly hard to find, even with the very best of screening efforts.[29] Thus, it seems hard to maintain that better checkpoint screening would have made any significant difference on 9/11, given the *system* then in place.

So why were U.S. antihijacking defenses so insufficient that even marginal execution was adequate to defeat them?

The late 1990s were, or at the time at least seemed to be, good times for air travel in the United States. The strong competitive forces set in motion by the deregulation of civil aviation in the late 1970s had provided American consumers with more choices and lower prices; increased ridership and a strong economy provided the aviation industry with record-high economic performance. The FAA was overseeing ongoing improvements in what was already considered to be an outstanding safety program, while preparing to build an air traffic system for the twenty-first century that could cope with the anticipated ever-growing demand for more flights and at more convenient times.

Perhaps most important for the 9/11 story itself, the FAA, the Congress, the aviation industry, and the general public all took note of the absence of major security incidents. The last domestic hijacking occurred in 1991, the 1995 Bojinka plot to blow up twelve U.S. airliners overseas had been thwarted, and the 1996 crash of TWA 800 was ultimately attributed to an accidental explosion of a fuel tank.

But these apparent successes of the 1990s contained within them the seeds of the systemic failure of 9/11. The increasingly crowded airports and skies led to escalating pressures on the capacity of the airlines and the air traffic control system, which in turn drew the priority attention of the traveling public, the Congress, the FAA, and the Administration. Economic reverses in 2000 and early 2001 (including the "dot.com" crash and higher fuel prices) dramatically worsened the financial position of the aviation industry, intensifying its efforts to contain costs.[30]

These twin pressures of higher demand, in the form of longer lines, and cost restraint played out at the airport security checkpoints operated for the air carriers by private screening companies. Constant pressure to reduce the waiting time in lines, along with chronically low pay and difficult work conditions produced staggeringly high turnover rates and poor performance, as documented by a number of sources, inside and outside of the FAA.[31]

The absence of evidence of domestic security incidents was readily seen as the evidence of absence of such a threat by a civil aviation security system that for the most part had been created and continued to evolve primarily in the wake of disasters. Furthermore, based on at least a decade of experience, the system's "mindset" was that the threat was almost exclusively overseas. When added to the fact that the agency (CIA) responsible for gathering and disseminating information on the foreign threat was better-equipped in mission and outlook to do so than was its counterpart on the domestic side (the FBI), this took the form of a self-fulfilling prophecy in that we saw the greater threat where we looked for it, "over there."[32]

Furthermore, the civil aviation security system had been from the outset one of "shared responsibilities" between the FAA, the airlines, and the airports, which in turn created, whether intentional or not, multiple opportunities for "plausible deniability" as to who was responsible, for example for determining precisely what items should be kept out of aircraft cabins, or who should notify flight crews of potential security emergencies.

Finally, the failure of imagination throughout America's counterterrorism efforts, documented by the 9/11 Commission's final report, was abundantly present in the field of civil aviation security. Perhaps nowhere is this more apparent than in the one-hour period between the first transmission from Flight 11 after it had been hijacked (at 8:19 a.m. Eastern time) and the time when Flight 93 became the fourth hijacking (at 9:28 a.m.) when aviation authorities lurched from one mistaken preconception to another (domestic hijackings would not happen anymore, then multiple simultaneous hijackings were unheard of, and finally no enemy was planning for suicide hijackings), only too late coming to grips with what was actually transpiring.[33]

Does all of this mean that the 9/11 failure of the civil aviation security system was inevitable, and that, in a sense, everyone was to blame? I believe the answer is no, on both counts.

A key attribute of any system of governance must be accountability, that both those in charge and those who carry out their orders are held to account for their actions.

In the first place, as previously mentioned, the 9/11 hijackers made many mistakes along the way and there were a number of individuals— ranging from ticket counter personnel, to checkpoint screeners, to air traffic controllers, to FAA security officials, and many others—who were in a position where they could have hampered, mitigated, or even prevented one or more of the hijackings. To be sure, in most cases, to have done so would have required the individual to perform well beyond what his or her job description and training had prepared him or her to do. That is exactly what flight attendants on all four flights did, when they transcended their training to directly relay vital information to the ground, or what the passengers on Flight 93 (and perhaps on the other flights) did when they themselves rewrote the nation's strategy for dealing with hijackers onboard aircraft.

But it is to leadership we must turn to find those who were entrusted with the responsibility for protecting their citizens, their constituents, and their customers. To be sure, there are extenuating circumstances that must be taken into account in arriving at a fair evaluation of leadership performance related to 9/11, including the ever-present competing priorities of safety, customer service, economics, and keeping government expenditures down. Furthermore, the American people themselves, who had been little prepared for the growing terrorist threat inside the United States, largely set these priorities.

Under such circumstances, what could reasonably be expected from leadership in improving the flawed aviation security system? For example, would a different administrator or head of security at the FAA have been able to muster the necessary support from elected officials in both the executive and legislative branches of government and from the powerful industry, state and local stakeholders who largely would be the ones to implement increased security, in the face of different priorities from the public, and absent either an actual disaster or compelling and highly specific intelligence information about an imminent threat?

In the period leading up to 9/11, the top leadership at the FAA had chosen to largely delegate the responsibility for security to the agency's security division, which lacked the resources or the clout to initiate major improvements in the system.

Although some attempts to place accountability for the lack of preparedness for 9/11 begin and end with the FAA, it must be emphasized that FAA itself was but a part of the larger aviation security system (in some ways, perhaps not even the most influential part), and that none of the leadership of the other components distinguished themselves with respect to security.

Congress, which provided the money and was responsible for oversight of the system, collectively and, with few exceptions, individually did not steer the FAA toward strengthening security, in its hearings or in its spending decisions.

The Office of Management and Budget, on behalf of all recent administrations from both parties, consistently hampered attempts to direct more policy attention and resources toward civil aviation security.

And, again with very few exceptions, the leadership of the airlines, which long ago accepted the necessity for assisting government efforts to improve safety for their customers, and which, on 9/11, had ultimate responsibility for the single most important antihijacking defense (checkpoint screening), consistently and persistently fought virtually all efforts to increase security measures, absent a disaster or very specific and "credible" threat intelligence. As mentioned previously, such intelligence was, is, and always will be in small supply.

(While holding others to account, the author of this piece must point out that I served for many years as a Congressional staffer, and must candidly admit that I can claim no credit for being prescient enough to see the need for a major increase in aviation security prior to 9/11; thus I, too, must share in the responsibility.)

To transcend the many limitations built in to the pre-9/11 system would indeed have required a massive effort, with considerable expenditure of political, as well as financial, capital. However, if the national leadership had stayed the course on the largely unprecedented security recommendations of the FAA-chartered Baseline Working Group as presented at the end of 1996, which entailed a substantial increase in both federal spending and federal responsibility for aviation security, and which included greater emphasis on such items as expanded security training, comprehensive screening of individuals identified as potential threats, and increased FBI attention to civil aviation, the system in place by 9/11/01 may very well have made a difference in whether the terrorists would have tried or succeeded in attacking a more hardened target.

Beyond its failure to improve civil aviation defenses to counter the growing terrorist threat, the system's leadership failed over many years to convey realistic "risk assessments" to the media or the public. The country had been vulnerable to the kind of plot carried out on 9/11 for many years, and yet when it happened, it produced shock and a shutdown of a key part of our economy. Thus, the system's response to the attacks exacerbated the psychological and economic consequences in just the ways that the terrorist leadership would have hoped, with the public (and news media) moving from an underappreciation of the terrorist threat to a wildly exaggerated overestimate of what was, in essence, the same threat that had existed for some time.

Part Two: Transportation Security Today

5   Response to 9/11

Is History Repeating Itself?

Before 9/11 aviation security proceeded in fits and starts, with major changes generally occurring only in the immediate aftermath of and in direct reply to a major incident. As time passed after the event, the institutional forces of inertia, both within and outside of government, were strong enough to prevent significant modifications to the system.

Up to the present time, the U.S. response to the 9/11 hijackings has followed this historical pattern. The terrorist attacks were succeeded in short order by the aviation security system's adoption of a host of measures (hardened cockpit doors, new onboard security procedures, more air marshals) designed to counter the newly recognized suicide hijacking threat. What followed that initial action was outlined in a 2002 report by the National Research Council, and though some of the particulars are different, the general description fits the responses to both Pan Am 103 and TWA 800.

> In seeking to regain public confidence in aviation security after September 11, federal policy-makers did not have a coherent system in place that could be readily fixed, prompting Congress to take dramatic and hurried measures, from the federalizing of airport screeners to ambitious deadlines for the deployment of costly and potentially unready explosive detectors.[1]

The issue of the federalized screener workforce is a case in point with respect to the reassertion of nonsecurity priorities as the precipitating crisis recedes in memory. By mid-2002, TSA was under fire in Congress for hiring too many screeners and for spending at a higher rate than what had been appropriated.[2] Such concerns culminated in October 2003 legislation that capped the screener level at 45,000,[3] and despite concerns raised in a February 2004 GAO report that insufficient staffing levels were leading to underutilization of deployed detection equipment and of screener training programs,[4] TSA implemented the Congressionally mandated staffing level.[5] And all of this has occurred, as far as can be discerned, without any comprehensive assessment of how many screeners are, in fact, needed to discharge their currently assigned duties.[6]

Last, the 9/11 response followed the Pan Am and TWA disasters in another key respect: the empanelment of an outside commission to ascertain the causes and to suggest remedial action to prevent a reoccurrence. Although it is true that the most recent commission took note of and sought to avoid "fighting the last war,"[7] it is worth recalling that such was also the intent of the 1989–1990 Pan Am/Lockerbie Commission, but its legacy was largely to help redirect the aviation security system away from hijacking ("For all practical purposes, the focus of the security procedures for domestic flights is to deter hijackings. . . . Aided substantially by the closing of Cuba as a safe harbor for hijackers, the emphasis has been successful."[8]) and toward what was seen as the greater threat of in-air bombings.

Transportation Security After 9/11

In late 2001 and 2002, three major pieces of legislation were enacted in response to the 9/11 attacks. The Aviation and Transportation Security Act (ATSA), which was signed into law on November 19, 2001, established a new Transportation Security Administration (TSA) within the Department of Transportation and gave it responsibility for the security of all modes of transportation, including the security functions of the FAA. Furthermore, ATSA mandated a series of aviation security measures, many of which had specific implementation deadlines. It also required TSA to "receive, assess, and distribute intelligence, . . . assess threats . . . [and] develop policies, strategies and plans" for securing the various transportation modes.[9]

In November of 2002, both the Maritime Transportation Security Act (MTSA) and the Homeland Security Act (HSA) were signed into law. The former established general maritime security requirements, mandated vulnerability assessments for all vessels and facilities on or near U.S. waters, and authorized increases in maritime security personnel, technologies, and infrastructure.[10] The HSA created the Department of Homeland Security and transferred TSA, the Coast Guard (which was given the lead role in maritime security), and twenty other federal agencies into the new department. Among many other provisions, the Act required DHS to develop a strategic plan.[11]

Subsequently, on December 17, 2003, President Bush issued Homeland Security Presidential Directive-7 (HSPD-7), which "establishes a national policy for federal departments and agencies to identify and prioritize United States critical infrastructure and key resources and to protect them from terrorist attacks." It required DHS to "produce a comprehensive integrated National Plan for Critical Infrastructure and Key Resources Protection to outline national goals, objectives, milestones, and key initiatives within 1 year from the issuance of this directive." The strategy was to identify and prioritize critical infrastructure and key resources; indicate how vulnerabilities of these assets are to be reduced; outline how DHS is to coordinate and share threat and vulnerability information with other federal, state, local, foreign, and international agencies, as well as the private sector; and specify how DHS is to coordinate and integrate its activities with other federal emergency management and preparedness activities.[12]

In implementing HSPD-7, DHS is developing thirteen Sector Specific Plans (SSP), with TSA assigned as the lead agency for the Transportation SSP. The transportation plan is supposed to include the following elements: "(1) identify participants in the sector, their roles and relationships, and their means of communication; (2) identify assets in the sector; (3) assess vulnerabilities and prioritize assets in the sector; (4) identify protective programs; (5) measure performance; and (6) prioritize research and development." Additionally, TSA intends that the plan include specific annexes for each transportation mode to "provide security planning guidance to modal security plan writers and industry stakeholders."[13] Last, the plan is to "form the basis for allocating resources in a risk-based and cost-effective way, as recommended by the 9/11 Commission."[14]

9/11 Commission Recommendations and Congressional Response

Another Congressional action of November 2002 was the passage of legislation creating a National Commission on Terrorist Attacks Upon the United States (the 9/11 Commission) that was to "examine and report upon the facts and causes relating to the terrorist attacks of September 11, 2001; . . . make a full and complete accounting of the circumstances surrounding the attacks, and the extent of the United States' preparedness for, and immediate response to, the attacks; and investigate and report to the President and Congress on its findings, conclusions and recommendations for corrective measures that can be taken to prevent acts of terrorism."[15]

After reviewing over 2.5 million documents, interviewing more than 1,200 individuals, and holding nineteen days of public hearings, the 9/11 Commission issued its Final Report in July of 2004.[16] That document summed up the major challenges facing the U.S. transportation security system:

> Hard choices must be made in allocating limited resources. The U.S. government should identify and evaluate the transportation assets that need to be protected, set risk-based priorities for defending them, select the most practical and cost-effective ways of doing so, and then develop a plan, budget and funding to implement the effort.[17]

The Commission went on to make a number of specific proposals that would significantly, and in the relatively short term, enhance transportation security.

1. The nation's transportation security plan should clearly define the security roles and missions of the different governmental and private authorities that operate the country's transportation system and provide an adequate means for funding the implementation of the plan. Furthermore, the Congress should set a date-certain for the completion of the plan.
2. Security plans for all transportation modes should incorporate the principle of multiple, independently effective layers of protection.
3. The Transportation Security Administration (TSA) should take immediate steps to keep known terrorists from using the U.S. transportation network by taking complete control of the implementation of "no fly" and screening "selectee" lists.
4. Congress and TSA should give priority attention to improving the detection of explosives on airline passengers.
5. TSA should require that all security selectees be screened for explosives.
6. TSA should conduct a detailed human factors study to better understand and address problems in screener performance.
7. To enhance security and improve efficiency, explosives detection equipment should be moved from airport lobbies and placed where they can accomplish their vital mission "in line" as checked luggage is moved from the check-in counter to the aircraft. Cost-sharing between government and the industry should be used, based on the relative "security" versus "efficiency" benefits to be derived.
8. Every passenger aircraft that is used to carry cargo should be equipped with a hardened container to carry the cargo.
9. TSA needs to intensify its efforts to identify, track and screen potentially dangerous cargo in both the aviation and maritime sectors.[18]

Both houses of Congress addressed these recommendations as part of the legislation designed to implement the full range of the Commission's proposals, including reform of the intelligence community. The Senate bill

(S. 2845) largely tracked the Commission's transportation security suggestions, whereas the House measure (HR 10) incorporated some, but not all, of them. An agreement was reached by the conference committee convened to reconcile the differences between the two measures, but because of opposition from some House Republicans, Speaker of the House Hastert (R-IL) did not bring the agreement up for a final vote prior to the November 2004 general election. However, after further discussion and clarification of certain provisions (primarily concerning the flow of tactical military intelligence to military units), in December of 2004 the House and Senate took up and passed the conference measure, thus clearing it to be signed into law by the President, as the Intelligence Reform and Terrorism Prevention Act of 2004 (Public Law 108-458).[19]

Table 5.1 summarizes Congressional action on the 9/11 Commission's transportation security recommendations.

In addition to the measures designed to implement the recommendations of the 9/11 Commission, the new law contained a number of additional provisions concerning transportation security. Some of these were similar to the suggestions submitted to the Congress in September 2004 by the aviation and transportation security staff of the 9/11 Commission[20] to supplement the Commission's recommendations and to help inform Congressional action on the transportation portions of the implementing legislation:[21] (See Appendix A for a full list of the staff recommendations, as well as the transmittal letter to Congress.)

- The addition of damage mitigation and recovery measures to the transportation security strategy's content requirements (Sec. 4001).
- The addition of a threat matrix to the aviation security plan (Sec. 4001).
- Provision for the use of biometrics to confirm the identity of those seeking to gain access to secure areas of airports and of law enforcement officers seeking to board aircraft (Sec. 4011).
- A requirement that employees being given unescorted access to secure areas of airports be screened against terrorist watch lists (Sec. 4012).
- A requirement for the development of advanced airport checkpoint screening devices (Sec. 4014).
- Support for operational anonymity of federal air marshals (Sec. 4016).
- Provision for in-flight counterterrorism training for federal law enforcement officers (Sec. 4016).
- A requirement for the development of standards for determining the appropriate security staffing levels for airports (Sec. 4023).
- A requirement that cruise ship passengers be prescreened against terrorist watch lists (Sec. 4071).

Table 5.1. 9/11 Commission Transportation Security Recommendations

9/11 Recommendation	Senate Bill (S. 2845)	House Bill (HR 10)	Conference Agreement
Security Plan should define roles and missions for all modes, provide adequate funding, and be subject to specific Congressional deadline. (pp. 391–392)	Incorporates Commission recommendations. (§1032)	Partially incorporates Commission recommendations, but confines plan to aviation, and does not address funding issue. (§2172)	Similar to Senate bill, but weakens mission assignment language (changing from the Plan "assigns" to "sets forth the agreed upon" roles and missions) and deletes funding language. (§4001)
TSA should take over implementation of "no fly" and "automatic selectee" programs. (pp. 392–393)	Incorporates Commission recommendation. (§1033)	Largely incorporates Commission recommendation, goes beyond Commission in specifying appeals process for passengers included on lists, but somewhat weakens deadline by not setting deadline for completion of testing. (§2173)	Same as House bill. (§4012)
TSA and Congress must give priority to detection of explosives on passengers. (p. 393)	Incorporates Commission recommendation. (§1034)	Incorporates and goes beyond Commission recommendation by including nonmetallic weapons. (§2174)	Incorporates and goes beyond Commission recommendation by including nonmetallic, chemical, biological, and radiological weapons. (§4013)
"Selectees" should be screened for explosives. (p. 393)	Incorporates Commission recommendation. (§1034)	No provision.	Same as Senate bill. (§4013)
TSA should do "human factors" screening study. (p. 393)	Incorporates Commission recommendation. (§1034)	Incorporates Commission recommendation. (§2178)	Incorporates Commission recommendation. (§4015)
"In-line" baggage screening for explosives should be employed, with appropriate cost-sharing between government and industry. (p. 393)	Incorporates Commission recommendation. (§ 1034)	Largely incorporates Commission recommendation, but omits cost-sharing provision. (§2188)	Same as Senate bill. (§4019)
Hardened containers for cargo on passenger flights. (p. 393)	Converts requirement into a pilot test program. (§1034)	Converts requirement into a pilot test program. (§2175)	Converts requirement into a pilot test program. (§4051)
TSA should intensify aviation and maritime cargo security efforts. (p. 393)	Incorporates Commission recommendation for air cargo. (§1034)	Incorporates Commission recommendation for air cargo. (§2176)	Incorporates and goes beyond Commission recommendation for air cargo by establishing a detailed program for security enhancement. §§4052–4054)

Note: Page citations in first column refer to National Commission on Terrorist Attacks Upon the United States, *The 9/11 Commission Report: Final Report of the National Commission on Terrorist Attacks Upon the United States,* authorized ed. (New York: W.W. Norton, 2004). Section citations in remaining columns refer, respectively, to the legislation passed by the Senate (S. 2845), and the House (HR 10), and the final version that was signed into law (Conference Agreement).

Last, the new law contained a number of transportation security provisions that were not in the recommendations of either the 9/11 Commission or its aviation and transportation security staff, including: (a) calling for international agreements to allow maximum deployment of Federal Air Marshals (Sec. 4017); (b) establishing a program for training foreign air marshals (Sec. 4018); (c) calling for the monitoring of checked baggage screening areas in order to deter theft (Sec. 4020); (d) mandating studies of wireless communication methods to aid flight crewmembers communicate about security threats (Sec. 4021) and of secondary flight barriers to further secure cockpits (Sec. 4028); (e) requiring improved, more tamperproof pilot's licenses (Sec. 4022); (f) adding butane lighters to the list of items prohibited from being carried onto aircraft (Sec. 4025); (g) outlining a program to address the threat of Man-Portable Air Defense Systems (MANPADS) (Sec. 4026); and (h) imposing deadlines for a number of the provisions of the Maritime Transportation Security Act of 2002, including the National Maritime Transportation Security Plan, vessel and facility vulnerability assessments, and Transportation Security Card regulations (Sec. 4072).

The quick legislative action on the 9/11 Commission's recommendations, including the key aviation and transportation security proposals, is noteworthy. However, after recalling the evolution of the aviation security system and its history of sometimes vigorous response to incidents followed by gradual ebbing of attention, and observing the failure of many previous Commissions to ultimately achieve their security enhancement goals despite initial success, it is vital that good intentions get translated into sound policy over the long haul.

The successor to the 9/11 Commission, the 9/11 Public Discourse Project, issued a "Report on the Status of the 9/11 Commission Recommendations" on September 14, 2005. (See Appendix B.) For transportation security, the report found the progress to date to be either "Unsatisfactory" (for the National Strategy for Transportation Security and airline passenger prescreening) or "minimal" (for checkpoint screening for explosives and checked bag and cargo screening).[22] In its Final Report three months later, the group assigned letter grades for the federal government's implementation of the recommendations. In the area of transportation security, the marks were as follows.

- National Strategy for Transportation Security C-
- Airline passenger prescreening F
- Airline passenger explosive screening C
- Checked bag and cargo screening D[23]

6   The New Organization of Transportation Security

DHS and TSA

The FAA, whose responsibilities were limited to the civil aviation mode, faced a daunting challenge in securing more than 19,000 airports throughout the United States (of which 563 were "certificated" by the agency and 458 were required to have a formal security program[1]), and more than 25,000 daily flights by U.S. airlines that served 1.8 million passengers.[2] Furthermore, although FAA directed security operations through rules and directives, actual implementation of most security measures was left up to the airlines and the airports.

Today, TSA has, at least in theory, inherited not only the same range of civil aviation security responsibilities possessed by the FAA (the main difference being the new federalized checkpoint screening workforce added to TSA), but also the obligations for an array of other transportation modes, each with its own set of challenges and vulnerabilities:

- *Mass transit*, which involves 6,000 local operators (public and private) serving 14 million Americans each weekday.[3]
- *Rail*, which includes more than 300,000 miles of freight rail lines, and more than 10,000 miles of commuter and urban rail system lines.
- *Surface modes*, which include 4 million miles of interconnected roadways, 600,000 bridges, and 45,000 miles of interstate highways.[4]
- *Pipelines*, which span some 2.2 million miles and transport potentially dangerous materials, including oil and natural gas.[5]

The Coast Guard, which like TSA, is now a part of the Department of Homeland Security, has primary responsibility to protect "the U.S. maritime domain and the U.S. marine transportation system and deny their use and exploitation by terrorists as a means of attack on U.S. territory."[6] It should be noted that 95 percent of all U.S. overseas trade passes through the nation's 361 seaports.[7]

DHS' Customs and Border Protection (CBP) division is primarily responsible for the security of *cargo containers*, of which several million are transported yearly to the United States through public and private seaports with more than 3,700 cargo and passenger terminals.[8]

Further complicating the situation is the fact that the various modal agencies within the Department of Transportation have retained varying levels of security responsibilities, ranging from considerable (in the cases of FTA and FRA) to limited (FAA, which retains responsibility for hazardous materials brought onto aircraft, security of its own facilities, and management of the national airspace).

With the breadth and diversity of these transportation targets, the high volume of traffic they handle, the limited federal ownership or control over most of them, the openness and accessibility of the American transportation and commerce system, and their "entwinement in society and the global economy,"[9] DHS and its constituent parts indeed face a far more severe security challenge than did FAA prior to 9/11.

Both DHS and its TSA component have been confronted from the outset with additional managerial and coordination challenges. DHS opened for business on March 1, 2003, as an amalgamation of twenty-two separate federal agencies, with different institutional histories and cultures and some (especially FEMA, the Coast Guard, Immigration and Naturalization Service [INS], and Customs) bringing with them significant nonsecurity missions.

TSA was faced not only with rapid shifts in its organizational status, moving from a small component within the FAA, to separate agency status within DOT, to being a part of the new DHS all within the space of fifteen months. TSA also had to cope with a formidable array of legislated deadlines, primarily from the Aviation and Transportation Security Act of 2001.

Thus, there is some reason why DHS has focused much of its attention on "building a new information-technology infrastructure to support and unify its 22 components" rather than in establishing clear linkages with other federal and nonfederal components.[10] TSA has thus far concentrated its time and budgetary resources on meeting the statutory deadlines (mainly in the area of commercial aviation passenger and baggage screening) but has executed detailed memoranda of understanding (MOU) to coordinate efforts only with the FAA among all of the DOT modal agencies with which it shares at least some security functions.[11]

Taking the challenging circumstances into account, it is nonetheless sobering to read the largely negative assessments of DHS and TSA progress to date. In its end of the year performance reports for both 2004 and 2005, the DHS Office of Inspector General indicated that "While DHS has made progress, it still has much to do to establish a cohesive, efficient, and effective organization," and "structural and resource problems continue to inhibit progress" in consolidating the various components of the Department, including TSA.[12]

A major analysis conducted jointly by the Heritage Foundation and CSIS summarized its findings about the effectiveness of the new department with respect to management, roles and missions, authorities, and resources:

> Putting it bluntly, the current organization of DHS must be reformed because it hampers the Secretary of Homeland Security's ability to lead our nation's homeland security efforts. The organization is weighed down with bureaucratic layers, is rife with turf warfare, and lacks a structure for strategic thinking and policymaking. Additionally, since its creation, whether one looks at the department's capacity to organize and mobilize a response to catastrophic terrorist attack or at the international dimension of DHS programs, the department has been slow to overcome the obstacles to becoming an effective 21st century national security instrument.[13]

A February 2005 *Washington Post* survey of past and present administration officials and independent experts found that

> As the leadership changes for the first time, the Department of Homeland Security remains hampered by personality conflicts, bureaucratic bottlenecks and an atmosphere of demoralization, undermining its ability to protect the nation against terrorist attack. . . . It remains a second-tier agency in the clout it commands within President Bush's Cabinet. . . . Pockets of dysfunction are scattered throughout the 180,000-employee department. Several current and former officials said the department remains underfinanced and understaffed, and suffers from weak leadership.[14]

An updated survey at the end of the year indicated that DHS continued to be marred by "haphazard design, bureaucratic warfare, and unfulfilled promises."[15]

Nor have assessments of TSA performance produced more positive reports. Governmental organization expert Paul Light wrote of TSA in April 2005:

> The three-year old agency has been ridiculed for everything from pat-downs of women and U.S. Senators, to a "no-fly" passenger list that has produced story after story of mistaken identity, to a recent $16 million purchase of new uniforms with sturdier epaulets. More importantly, it still fails too often at detecting guns, knives and improvised explosive devices, and it's years behind in developing "smart" technologies that could help screeners do their work.[16]

In a 2005 poll of federal workers, which was designed to identify the "Best Places to Work in the Federal Government," based on such workplace environment factors as organizational leadership, teamwork, the connection between employee skills and agency mission, and organizational cultural values, the Department of Homeland Security ranked twenty-ninth out of thirty departments and independent agencies, and FEMA, Customs and Border Protection, and TSA tied for last (with a number of other agencies) among all federal departmental subcomponents. Of the DHS entities involved in transportation security, only the Coast Guard scored relatively well at twenty-fourth place out of the 220 subdepartmental units examined.[17]

DHS and TSA Planning

The strategic planning process mandated by both the Homeland Security Act and HSPD-7 is supposed to clarify the roles and responsibilities not only of DHS and TSA but also of the other relevant federal and nonfederal entities involved in transportation security. Yet, the 9/11 Commission found that

> The current efforts do not yet reflect a forward-looking strategic plan systematically analyzing assets, risks, costs, and benefits. Lacking such a plan, we are not convinced that our transportation security resources are being allocated to the greatest risks in a cost-effective way. . . . Despite Congressional deadlines, TSA has developed neither an integrated strategic plan for the transportation sector nor specific plans for the various modes—air, sea, and ground.[18]

Under HSPD-7, the National Critical Infrastructure Protection Plan and its Transportation Sector Specific Plan component were to have been completed by December 17, 2004. After missing this deadline, DHS issued an "Interim National Infrastructure Protection Plan" in February of 2005. However, this document was little more than a "plan to plan," with a self-description as "the starting point for developing the national cross-sector plan for critical infrastructure protection."[19]

A draft final plan was issued in November 2005. In a briefing to the staff of the House Committee on Homeland Security, DHS representatives indicated that the plan simply "established the risk management framework" and was issued in order to facilitate more engagement between the department and its governmental and non-governmental partners involved in infrastructure protection.[20]

The 9/11 Public Discourse Project gave the plan a "D" in its report card on implementation of the 9/11 Commission recommendations, commenting:

> No risk and vulnerability assessments [are] actually made; no national priorities established; no recommendations made on allocation of scarce resources.

All key decisions are at least a year away. It is time that we stop talking about setting priorities, and actually set some.[21]

Former DHS Inspector General Clark Kent Ervin has reported "According to members of Congress who have seen the list [of critical infrastructure] compiled so far, there is no apparent rationale for some entries other than parochialism and pork."[22]

There were some indications that the completion of the infrastructure plans was being subordinated to the effort to produce the transportation security strategy called for by the 9/11 Commission and mandated by the November 2004 legislation implementing the Commission's recommendations. The security strategy, which was supposed to have been delivered by April 1, 2005, was finally provided to Congress in September 2005, though in classified form under which "its details cannot be discussed in a public forum."[23]

The publicly released Overview of the transportation security strategy states that the plan "identifies *asset categories* at greatest risk for each mode (e.g., Aviation: major and mid-sized commercial airport facilities; Transit, Commuter and Long-Distance Passenger Rail: passenger trains). Corresponding risk based priorities to mitigate the risk and defend the *asset categories* were then established." (*Emphasis added.*) The Overview also reports that the strategy "addresses the roles and responsibilities of those involved with securing the transportation system," but the discussion that follows is little more than a restatement of previous DHS pronouncements on the subject (such as "The state, local and tribal governments, and the private sector own/operate the vast majority of the transportation infrastructure and are primarily responsible for security measures to secure the individual pieces of the transportation system").[24] If these comments are at all representative of the strategy's content, it is difficult to discern any significant improvement over the situation noted by the 9/11 Commission.

In giving the National Strategy for Transportation Security a "C-" in its "Final Report on 9/11 Commission Recommendations," the 9/11 Public Discourse Project stated, "While the strategy reportedly outlines broad objectives, this first version lacks the necessary detail to make it an effective management tool."[25]

The GAO has called for the use of risk management principles ("a systematic process to analyze threats, vulnerabilities, and the criticality of assets to better support linking resources with prioritized effort for results") in the design of strategic plans for federal homeland security efforts.[26] The 9/11 Commission echoed this call.[27]

Assessing the current state of risk management in transportation security policy making is complicated by several factors. First of all, the full application of risk management techniques, especially consequence assessment, is "a new area of expertise"[28] and is currently at a "conceptual" stage[29] at DHS. The authors of a report on the Navy's risk management effort cited the specific challenges of how to quantify threats, vulnerabilities, and consequences in a meaningful way for decision makers, and what level of precision to require. Thus, it should be expected that, as with any major institutional change, the shift to a risk-based approach will require much time and effort to perfect. But the pursuit of perfection should not be allowed to stymie all progress. As the Navy planners observed, the real-world goal "is to perform the *minimum* level of analysis that is at least *barely adequate* for decision-making." (Emphasis in original.)[30]

In its 2004 "Homeland Security Strategic Plan," DHS addressed its approach to risk management in several places. However, although the concept as defined by GAO and the 9/11 Commission was largely present in the "Implementation" discussion ("As part of managing risks, we assess continuously what can go wrong; evaluate the potential consequences if an event happens; determine the likelihood of an event succeeding; prioritize the risks; and implement strategies to deal with those risks. We will direct our resources toward those priority threats and vulnerabilities based on potential consequences and likelihood of success."[31]), the more specific discussions of vulnerability and consequence assessments (Objectives 1.2[32] and 1.3[33]) were primarily confined to "critical infrastructure and key assets." This may be derived in part from DHS's inheritance of the mission and resources of the National Infrastructure Protection Center, which was previously housed within the FBI.[34]

A second complicating factor is the large (and growing) number of entities, spread across several agencies of the federal government, which are involved in each portion of the risk management process for homeland security.

As illustrated in Table 6.1, many different federal agencies are involved in compiling transportation security-related risk information. Note the diversity of *threat assessment* entities (as well as the *two* joint efforts to consolidate such information across agency lines) against the relative lack of *vulnerability* and *consequence assessments*, especially with respect to integrated evaluations. This is in keeping with statements from Admiral James Loy, formerly head of TSA and later Deputy Secretary of DHS, that TSA's and DHS's risk management approach is "threat-based."[35]

However, one analyst observed that

> So far, threat information [within DHS] has been in short supply, especially for state and local officials. As a result, the nation has not really accomplished *threat* assessment. Instead, it has focused on *vulnerability* assessment. Because any democracy's vulnerabilities are legion, the consequence of highlighting them has been mostly to frighten citizens and local authorities.[36]

Former DHS Inspector General Ervin has written, "As it stands now, the Department of Homeland Security is on the margins of the nation's

Table 6.1. Federal Agency Responsibilities for Transportation Security Risk Assessment

Entity/Agency	Relevant Responsibilities
I. THREAT ASSESSMENTS	
Directorate of Intelligence (DI)/CIA	Provide timely and objective assessments of intelligence to senior policy makers.
Counter-terrorist Center (CTC)/CIA	Produce in-depth analyses of terrorist groups, methods, and plans.
Analysis branch of Counter-terrorism Division/FBI	Provide strategic assessments and reports to policy makers.
Terrorist Threat Integration Center (TTIC)/CIA (FBI, DHS)	Integrate and disseminate terrorist threat-related information and analysis via daily President's Terrorism Threat Report (PTTR) and Terrorism Threat Matrix (TTM), which is unanalyzed compendium of threat reports.
Terrorist Screening Center (TSC)/FBI (CIA, DHS)	Maintain single, consolidated watch list of terrorist suspects to be shared with federal, state, local, and private entities in accordance with applicable law.
Information Analysis and Infrastructure Protection Directorate (IAIP)/DHS	Assess nature and scope of terrorist threats to homeland security.
Transportation Security Intelligence (TSI)/TSA-DHS	Analyze and disseminate information on threats to transportation security.
Federal Transit Administration (FTA)/DOT	Assess threats to mass transit systems.
II. VULNERABILITY ASSESSMENTS	
Information Analysis and Infrastructure Protection Directorate (IAIP)/DHS	Map threat information against vulnerabilities of critical infrastructure; develop remediation and action plans to reduce risk and mitigate vulnerabilities of critical infrastructure and key assets; and develop standards for vulnerability assessments and best practices.
Internal Affairs Program Review (IAPR)/TSA-DHS	Perform performance tests on TSA security components (primarily aviation security to date).
U.S. Coast Guard (USCG)/DHS	Assess vulnerabilities of ports, vessels, and facilities.
Federal Transit Administration (FTA)/DOT	Assess vulnerabilities of mass transit systems.
Federal Highway Administration (FHWA)/DOT	Assess vulnerabilities of critical highway infrastructure.
Federal Railroad Administration (FRA)/DOT	Assess vulnerabilities of national railroad system.

(continued)

Table 6.1. (*continued*)

Entity/Agency	Relevant Responsibilities
III. CONSEQUENCE ASSESSMENTS	
Information Analysis and Infrastructure Protection Directorate (IAIP)/DHS	Identify critical infrastructure assets (Unified National Database of Critical Infrastructure), including cyber security.

Sources: Creating a Trusted Network for Homeland Security (New York: Markle Foundation: 2003), Appendix B; Transportation Security Administration, *Fiscal Year 2004 Budget Briefing* (Washington, DC, February 3, 2003); http://www.whitehouse.gov/omb/budget/fy2005/ homeland.html; Federal Transit Administration, *Briefing: Update on the Status of FTA Security Initiatives*, http://transit-safety.volpe.dot.gov/Security/Default.asp; Department of Homeland Security, *Preserving Our Freedoms, Protecting Our Nation—Strategic Plan* (Washington, DC, February 23, 2004); Transportation Security Administration, Internal Affairs Program Review Office, briefings for 9/11 Commission staff (Arlington, VA: September 3, 2003 and June 2, 2004); United States Coast Guard, *Maritime Strategy for Homeland Security* (Washington, DC, 2002), p. 26; and U.S. Department of Transportation, *FY 2005 Budget in Brief: Security*, http://www.dot.gov/bib2005/overview.html

intelligence network. . . . The [new] Secretary [of Homeland Security] will need to flex muscles . . . to ensure that DHS becomes more than a spectator in the detection and assessment of threats against the homeland."[37]

Furthermore, as noted earlier, *vulnerability assessment* at DHS has been largely confined to critical infrastructure, with performance information on security *layers* (conducted by DHS' Internal Affairs Program Review office [IAPR]) being very limited in both scope and distribution. Also, in the absence of MOU or other coordinating mechanisms, it is difficult to assess how well the vulnerability assessments being undertaken by components of DOT (FTA, Federal Highway Administration [FHWA], FRA) are being coordinated, either among themselves or with DHS and TSA.

DHS has begun efforts to integrate the various components of risk assessment. The Office of Domestic Preparedness (ODP) has developed a "tool kit" to assist individual mass transit and port authorities in ascertaining relative risks within their systems and prioritizing remedial measures. As of mid-2005, seven risk assessments of rail systems had been completed using the ODP system, with another twelve underway. A GAO survey reported that transit operators found the program to be "successful in helping to devise risk reduction strategies to guide security-related investments."[38]

It is TSA, however, that has primary responsibility for integrating risk assessment information and setting risk-based priorities across all transportation modes, and DHS is to establish the standards for TSA and its other agencies to use in such efforts across all sectors. In evaluating the status of these efforts as of July 2005, GAO reported:

TSA has begun to conduct risk assessments and to establish a methodology for determining how to analyze and characterize risks that have been identified but has not yet completed either effort or set timelines for doing so . . . DHS has begun developing, but has not yet completed a framework to help agencies and the private sector develop a consistent approach for analyzing and comparing risks to transportation and other sectors. Until this framework is finalized and shared with stakeholders, it may not be possible to compare risks across different sectors, prioritize them, and allocate resources accordingly.[39]

With respect to both resources and focus, DHS and TSA appear to be concentrating risk management efforts on the identification of *individual passengers or cargo* that pose the greatest risk to transportation security. For example, in its presentation on the FY2004 budget request, TSA identified a total of $120 million to be allocated for "risk management" among the following programs:

- Computer Assisted Passenger Prescreening II (CAPPS II) program, which "will seek to authenticate travelers' identities and perform risk assessments to detect individuals who may pose a terrorist-related threat or who have outstanding Federal or state warrants for crimes of violence."[40]
- "[A] risk-based air cargo screening system . . . [and] the Automated Known Shipper Database . . . which will give TSA an increased level of knowledge of each shipper in the shipper/shipment risk equation."[41]
- Transportation Worker Identification Credential (TWIC) that intends to employ biometric technology to ensure that only authorized individuals can gain access to secure areas of airports and other transportation nodes.
- Registered Traveler Initiative, which seeks to create a program to identify individuals who pose a limited risk to passenger aviation.[42]

Though CAPPS II has been subsequently replaced by the Secure Flight initiative, the focus on individual-level risk management continues.

DHS's National Targeting Center (NTC) provides "automated risk assessments for arriving international air passengers, shipments of goods to our country, and land border passenger traffic."[43] NTC's principal tool is the Automated Tracking System (ATS), which combines and sorts data derived from a number of law enforcement, customs and immigration databases (including passenger and cargo manifests), identifies high-risk targets (derived from selection "rules"), and presents the information (including targets) in a format designed to facilitate quick but thorough access by customs and border inspectors in the field.[44]

Although individual-level targeting of deployed security resources is desirable and important, confining risk management to such a level of analysis offers limited guidance for policy makers in attempting to *prioritize* resources among the large number of competing homeland security initiatives.

In a January 2005 report, GAO indicated that DHS "has not completed risk assessments mandated by the Homeland Security Act of 2002 to set priorities to help focus its resources where most needed.... DHS has not made clear the link between risk management and resource allocation." The report noted similar problems within several DHS components, including TSA, which was found to have "not fully integrated" risk management in prioritizing its efforts, and CBP, which "has not performed a comprehensive set of assessments vital for determining the level of risk for oceangoing cargo containers and the types of responses necessary to mitigate that risk."[45]

The planning process at DHS has undoubtedly been affected by the decision made at the outset of the department to not create a policy staff at the departmental level, reportedly because of White House pressure to keep headquarters staffing "lean." According to Seth Sodder, former policy and planning director at CBP, "It's very thinly staffed at the top of DHS, and there's no policy vision ... thinking through the main threats. DHS practices management by inbox, getting distracted by daily emergencies."[46]

The December 2004 Heritage Foundation/CSIS white paper similarly faulted DHS for lacking "a policy apparatus with which to lead the development of proactive, strategic homeland security policy." The report further highlighted the need for better integration of current policy efforts at the departmental level, citing the proliferation of policy offices within individual DHS components, which "has only magnified the challenge of forging coherent guidance."[47] The Administration's FY2006 budget proposal called for the creation of a DHS departmental policy planning office, combined with the department's international affairs unit.[48] The Congress subsequently approved these changes.[49]

Transportation Security Budgeting

In the FY2006 budget request for DHS, the mission of TSA was described as protecting "the nation's transportation systems to ensure freedom of movement for people and commerce," but "with a primary focus on aviation security." For the other transportation modes, the agency's role was defined as "assessing the risk of terrorist attacks ... and issuing regulations to improve the security of the modes."[50]

As carried out by TSA to date, transportation security continues to be largely passenger aviation security. In fact, this feature has been present from the agency's beginnings. In an April 2002 briefing with the President and high-level DOT officials (including Secretary Mineta) on TSA progress on passenger and baggage screening, then-OMB Director Mitch Daniels is reported to have observed that

> In terms of balancing risks against dollars—"efficient risk management"— they [TSA] were already spending too much on aviation as compared to highways, trains, and ships. "It's called the Transportation Security Administration," [Daniels] reminded them, "not the Aviation Security Administration."[51]

In fact, aviation security continues to take the lion's share of agency resources with 90 percent of the President's FY2006 budget request for TSA ($4.98 billion out of $5.56 billion) allocated for civil aviation programs. Furthermore, the $4.05 billion in the President's request (including $250 million from the Aviation Security Capital Fund for EDS installation) for aviation passenger and baggage screening alone accounted for 81 percent of TSA's aviation spending and 73 percent of its entire budget.[52] And 97 percent of TSA's total workforce is employed in aviation security.[53]

Four additional existing elements within DHS have significant transportation security functions: the Coast Guard (which received an FY06 request of $1.9 billion for port security), the Customs and Border Protection division ($138.8 million for the Container Security Initiative, $54.3 million for the Customs-Trade Partnership Against Terrorism, and $125 million for WMD detection equipment[54] in the FY06 request), the Federal Air Marshal Service (since returned to TSA, $688.9 million), and the Science and Technology unit ($110 million for counter MANPADS research and development).[55]

Under the FY2006 budget proposal, a new DHS Office of Screening Coordination and Operations (SCO) would have received a number of transportation security-related programs, to be transferred from TSA. These included:

- Aviation prescreening programs (Secure Flight/Crew Vetting, Registered Traveler, Alien Flight School Checks): $126.8 million.
- A surface transportation prescreening program for Hazardous Materials Trucker Background Checks: $44.2 million.
- Multimodal applications (Credentialing Start-up, TWIC): $264.7 million.[56]

The Administration's DHS budget also proposed to consolidate a number of existing DHS grant programs for specific transportation sectors (especially for land transportation modes such as transit and buses)[57] into a $600 million Targeted Infrastructure Protection Program (TIPP), which would aim at a more "integrated" approach, "based on relative risk, vulnerability and need." The initial focus would be "for deployment of nuclear

Table 6.2. Federal Transportation Security Spending By Mode, FY2004–2006 (in $ millions)

Agency	Program	FY04 enacted	FY05 enacted	FY06 proposed	FY06 enacted
AVIATION SECURITY					
DHS/TSA	Aviation	3,724.1	4,578.5	4,984.8	4,857.4
DHS/TSA	Secure Flight	———	———	94.3	56.7
DHS/TSA	Registered Traveler	———	———	22.5	20.0
DHS/TSA	Alien Flight School Checks	———	———	10.0	10.0
DHS/TSA	Federal Air Marshals	622.7	662.9	688.9	686.2
DHS/TSA	Crew Vetting	———	———	———	13.3
DHS/S&T	MANPADS R&D	———	61.0	110.0	110.0
DHS/S&T	Air Cargo Screening Pilot Project	———	———	———	30.0
DOT/FAA	Aviation Security	230.6	171.5	181.0	167.9
SUBTOTAL AVIATION		4,577.4	5,473.9	6,091.5	5,951.5
Percentage of Total		*70.4%*	*70.9%*	*64.9%*	*69.9%*
MARITIME SECURITY					
DHS/TSA	Maritime Security Grants	231.0	———	———	———
DHS/ODP	Port/Ferry Security Grants	———	145.9	———	175.0
DHS/CG	Port, Waterway, Coastal Security	1,265.0	1,501.0	1,900.0	1,562.0
DHS/CBP	Container Security Initiative	101.0	133.4	138.8	138.8
DHS/CBP	C-TPAT	23.0	46.1	54.3	54.3
DHS/ODP	Operation Safe Commerce	17.0	0.0	0.0	0.0
DOE/NNSA	Megaports Initiative	13.0	15.0	73.9	73.9
SUBTOTAL MARITIME		1,650.0	1,841.4	2,167.0	2,004.0
Percentage of Total		*25.4%*	*23.9%*	*23.1%*	*23.5%*
LAND TRANSPORTATION SECURITY					
DHS/TSA	Land Transportation	105.8	115.0	32.0	36.0
DHS/ODP	Rail and Transit Security Grants	49.7	150.0	———	150.0
DHS/ODP	Intercity Bus Security Grants	10.0	9.7	———	10.0
DHS/ODP	Trucking Security Grants	———	5.0	———	5.0
DHS/TSA	HAZMAT Background Checks	———	———	44.2	50.0
DOT/FHWA	Highway Security	0.0	13.0	13.0	14.9
DOT/FMCSA	Highway Security	0.0	7.8	7.8	8.0
DOT/FTA	Transit Security	37.8	37.8	36.6	42.1
DOT/FRA	Railroad Security	0.7	0.7	0.7	0.7
DOT/SLSDC	St. Lawrence Seaway Security	0.0	0.3	0.3	0.3
SUBTOTAL LAND		204.0	339.3	134.6	317.0
Percentage of Total		*3.1%*	*4.4%*	*1.4%*	*3.7%*

(*continued*)

Table 6.2. (continued)

Agency	Program	FY04 enacted	FY05 enacted	FY06 proposed	FY06 enacted
MULTI-MODAL SECURITY					
DHS/SLGCP	Targeted Infrastructure Protection	——	——	600.0	0.0
DHS/S&T	Radiation Detection Equipment	57.8	50.0	125.0	125.0
DHS/TSA	TWIC	——	——	244.7	100.0
DHS/TSA	Prescreening Administration	——	——	20.0	5.0
DOT/OST	Security	14.2	14.8	8.7	8.9
SUBTOTAL MULTI-MODAL		72.0	64.8	998.4	238.9
Percentage of Total		*1.1%*	*0.8%*	*10.6%*	*2.8%*
GRAND TOTAL		6,503.4	7,719.4	9,391.5	8,511.4

Notes:

Secure Flight, Registered Traveler and Alien Flight School Checks included in TSA Aviation totals for FY2004 and 2005.

HAZMAT Background Checks and TWIC included in TSA Land Transportation totals for FY2004 and 2005.

DOT Crisis Management Center included in DOT/OST Security account ($1.6 million in FY04, $2.4 million in FY05, $1.9 million in FY06).

Sources:

Office of Management and Budget, *Budget of the United States Government Fiscal Year 2005*, "Appendix: Homeland Security Mission Funding by Agency and Budget Account."

Office of Management and Budget, *Budget of the United States Government Fiscal Year 2006*, "Appendix: Homeland Security Mission Funding by Agency and Budget Account."

U.S. Department of Energy, *FY2006 Congressional Budget Request*.

Department of Homeland Security, *DHS Budget In Brief—Fiscal Year 2005*.

Department of Homeland Security, *DHS Budget In Brief—Fiscal Year 2006*.

Department of Homeland Security, Office for Domestic Preparedness Grants, *2004 UASI Transit Security Grants Program*, April 1, 2004.

Department of Homeland Security, Office for Domestic Preparedness, Centralized Scheduling and Information Desk, e-mail to author, May 25, 2005.

Department of Homeland Security, "U.S. Department of Homeland Security Announces Over $141 Million in Grants to Secure Transit, " news release, April 12, 2005.

Department of Homeland Security, "U.S. Department of Homeland Security Announces Over $9.5 Million in Grants to Secure Intercity Bus Programs," news release, April 22, 2005.

Department of Homeland Security, "U.S. Department of Homeland Security Announces Over $140 Million in Grants to Secure Ports," news release, May 13, 2005.

Department of Homeland Security, United States Coast Guard, http://www.uscg.mil/hq/g-cp/comrel/factfiles/fastcards/BudgetStatistics.html

U.S. Department of Transportation, *Overview, US DOT FY 2005 Budget In Brief*.

U.S. Department of Transportation, *Overview, US DOT FY 2006 Budget In Brief*.

Transportation Security Administration, *FY2006 TSA Budget Request*.

U.S. House, *Conference report to accompany HR 2360, Making appropriations for the Department of Homeland Security for the fiscal year ending September 30, 1996*, 109th Congress, 1st session (Washington, DC, 2005), H. Report 109-241.

U.S. House, *Conference report to accompany HR 2419, Making appropriations for energy and water development for the fiscal year ending September 30, 1996*, 109th Congress, 1st session (Washington, DC, 2005), H. Report 109-275.

Department of Transportation, Office of the Secretary, e-mails to author, January 31, 2006 and February 3, 2006.

Office of Management and Budget, *Budget of the United States Government Fiscal Year 2007*, "Appendix: Department of Homeland Security."

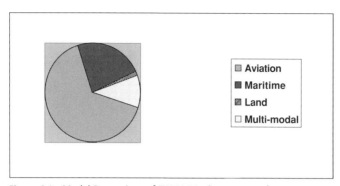

Figure 6.1. Modal Proportions of FY2006 Budget Request for Transportation Security. (*Source*: Reproduced by permission of the publisher from Bill Johnstone, *New Strategies to Protect America: Terrorism and Mass Transit after London and Madrid* (Center for American Progress: 2005), p. 7.)

and chemical detection capabilities and security investments,"[58] with priority given to "ports and other transportation facilities where people and cargo enter the United States."[59]

In action on the FY2006 DHS Appropriations bill, both houses of Congress rejected the proposed creation of the SCO because of concerns that the Administration had not adequately explained how the new office would interact with TSA so as to not disrupt progress on the included programs. Instead, the Congress moved to create a new Transportation Vetting and Credentialing Office within TSA that would "integrate" the transportation prescreening programs.[60] The House and Senate also blocked the Administration's proposed TIPP and retained separate grant programs for port ($175 million), rail and transit ($150 million), intercity bus ($10 million), and trucking ($5 million) security.[61]

Outside of DHS, DOT's modal administrations retain some security responsibilities and associated budgeting, including FAA ($181 million for security programs in the FY06 request), FHWA ($13 million), the Federal Motor Carrier Safety Administration (FMCSA; $7.8 million), FTA ($36.6 million), FRA ($700,000), the St. Lawrence Seaway security program ($300,000), and the Office of the Secretary of Transportation (OST, $9 million).[62] The Department of Energy's Megaports Initiative provides and installs radiation detection equipment at key overseas ports to screen transiting cargo containers for nuclear or radioactive materials ($74 million in the FY06 request).[63]

If these various programs are sorted by transportation mode, the prevalence of aviation security once again is demonstrated, though Coast Guard funding for port security and inclusion of multi-modal programs (such as TIPP and TWIC) does somewhat spread the federal security investment.

Granted that state, local, and private entities play a larger role here, the lack (and, indeed, *declining* level) of federal funding for the land modes (highways, rail, transit) is striking. And though the proposed TIPP program could have, *if* enacted, fully funded, and properly targeted, redressed some of this imbalance, given its relatively small size and initial focus on ports, it was unlikely to do much to significantly boost the very limited federal investment in land transportation security.

It is difficult to square the persistent lopsided distribution of federal attention and resources, demonstrated in Table 6.2 and Figure 6.1, with the DHS Strategic Plan's stated objective of "directing our resources toward . . . priority risks."

7 The Current State of Transportation Security

Overview

We now turn to an examination of what the unprecedented levels of policy attention and funding have produced in the nation's post-9/11 transportation security system.

Under the Homeland Security Act, the organizational fate of TSA may be revisited after November 2004,[1] and DHS officials have been notably reticent in discussing the agency's long-term future.[2] In addition, certain actions, such as moves to consolidate almost all of TSA's research and development component with its departmental counterpart[3] and to consider a similar consolidation of TSA's intelligence unit, have cast doubt about TSA's survival as a separate entity. Under these circumstances, the question of agency morale inevitably arises and may be related to the significant number of departures by former FAA officials who had transferred to TSA.

Furthermore, though ATSA gave TSA responsibility for the security of all modes of transportation, actions (and inaction) since the 2001 law have either eroded that role or failed to clarify the agency's position. The 2002 Homeland Security Act gave the Coast Guard the paramount role in maritime security,[4] and the absence of memoranda of understanding (or the Transportation Sector Specific Plan) have left the nature and extent of TSA's involvement in land transportation unclear. And on at least two occasions, TSA has lost out in turf battles with other DHS agencies, with Information Analysis & Infrastructure Protection (IAIP) prevailing within DHS in a dispute concerning jurisdiction for securing hazardous materials on trains, and CBP winning responsibility for tracking people and cargo at ports of entry.[5]

Even in aviation security, aside from the federalization of the check-point and checked baggage screening workforce, little has been done to strengthen TSA's hand. One former FAA security component, the Federal Air Marshal Service, was actually removed from TSA in late 2003 and transferred to DHS' Bureau of Immigration and Customs Enforcement (ICE),[6] though it was returned to TSA in July 2005.[7] Other than these changes, the organization of aviation security has been little revised from FAA days, with airlines and airports largely retaining their traditional positions within the system of divided responsibilities.

The aforementioned loss of former FAA personnel, and with them their "institutional memory," combined with the overwhelming organizational and budgetary focus on aviation screening has led some to question TSA's capacity for handling its inherited regulatory and enforcement functions. This is particularly significant when it is recalled that the current concept is for the agency to discharge its responsibilities for the nonaviation modes by "issuing regulations to improve the security."[8]

Questions about TSA's future again arose in February 2005 with the release of the FY2006 Bush Administration budget request, which would have transferred most of TSA's prescreening programs—including Secure Flight (the successor to the CAPPS program), Registered Traveler (a pilot program under which individuals who voluntarily undergo background and identity checks and thereby are shown to be low risks receive expedited security processing at airports), the Transportation Worker Identity Credential (TWIC, another pilot program that seeks to verify the identity and background of transportation workers), crew vetting, Hazardous Material (HAZMAT) Trucker Background Checks, and Alien Flight School Checks—to a new Screening Coordination and Operations (SCO) office.[9]

The SCO office, which would have been placed within DHS' Border and Transportation Security Directorate, was designed to eliminate duplication and overlap and allow for better integration of the various programs "by comprehensive coordination of procedures that detect, identify, track, and interdict people, cargo, and conveyances."[10] In addition to the transportation-related programs, SCO would also absorb customs and border prescreening programs, including US-VISIT, Free and Secure Trade (FAST), and NEXUS/Secure Electronic Network for Travelers Rapid Inspection (SENTRI). All told, the consolidated programs would receive an additional $344 million (to a total of $847 million) under the FY2006 budget proposal.[11]

The notion of integrating the various prescreening programs within DHS into a comprehensive system "addressing common problems and setting common standards with system-wide goals in mind" was endorsed by the 9/11 Commission.[12] However, the timing and manner of its presentation in the FY2006 budget proposal, with little advance public discussion or debate, led a *Washington Post* reporter to characterize the transfers as "a large scale dismantling that would strip the TSA of its biggest and most high-profile programs and leave it largely as a manager of 45,000 security screeners at a time when airports may now elect to replace the federal screeners with those employed by private companies."[13] Worried about coordination problems between TSA and the new SCO, both houses of Congress largely rejected the administration proposal in action on the FY2006 DHS Appropriations bill. While a small screening coordination office was established (with funding of $4 million), none of the prescreening programs themselves were transferred to it.[14]

The April 2005 announcement by David M. Stone—TSA's third head in its brief three-year history—of his intention to depart the agency in June continued a pattern of high turnover in top TSA positions and added further doubts about the agency's future as well as its effectiveness.[15]

Another DHS component with important responsibilities with respect to transportation security is the IAIP directorate, which "merges the capability to identify and assess a broad range of intelligence and information concerning threats to the homeland, to map threats against the nation's vulnerabilities, to issue timely warnings and advisories, and to recommend and take appropriate preventative and protective actions against any threats."[16]

The Homeland Security Act gave IAIP significant responsibilities for the collection and especially the sharing of information on the terrorist threat to the United States. As part of that role, "not just Congress, but officials both internal and external to DHS, anticipated that in this context DHS would play a lead role in terrorist watch list consolidation."[17]

The DHS Inspector General reported in August 2004 that

> IAIP has not provided the leadership of the watch list consolidation effort that is needed. Specifically, DHS is not carrying out significant responsibilities assigned to it under the Homeland Security Act. . . . Instead, other federal entities that have traditionally collected, analyzed, and disseminated watch list information continue to conduct these efforts under the auspices of two newly created interagency organizations: the Terrorist Threat Integration Center (TTIC) and the Terrorist Screening Center (TSC).[18]

The Inspector General found that both DHS and IAIP lacked sufficient infrastructure, resources, staffing, and classified information management capability to fulfill the originally assigned watch list consolidation role. It was in part for these reasons that TTIC was established on May 1, 2003, and placed under the auspices of the Central Intelligence Agency rather than DHS, with the mission of merging, analyzing, and disseminating terrorist information.[19]

According to a Markle Foundation report, "TTIC's creation has caused confusion within the federal government, and among state and local governments about the respective roles of the TTIC and DHS."[20] In January

2004 testimony to the 9/11 Commission, TTIC's Deputy Director stated, "With respect to TTIC itself, there is a degree of ambiguity between our mission and some other analytic organizations within the government...[over] how much should be handled at the departmental level [and] how much should be done within TTIC."[21]

The TSC was created, under the FBI, on September 16, 2003, to consolidate the federal government's terrorist screening activities, including the watch list. DHS officials indicated to the Inspector General that the creation of TSC was "the most expeditious way to proceed," but their expectation was that "eventually" the unit would be transferred to DHS, thus allowing the Department to fulfill its original assignment in this regard.[22]

The Inspector General called for DHS to play a more "robust" role in watch list consolidation than at present, and observed that such action would assist the Department in fulfilling its statutory information coordination function, "better ensuring that the ad hoc watch list management pattern of the past is not continued."[23] The 9/11 Commission similarly called on TSA to take prompt action to ensure that the "no fly" list for civil aviation is able to make use of the maximum number of terrorist names identified by the federal government.[24] The Commission's successor, the 9/11 Public Discourse Project, observed that "few improvements have been made to the existing passenger [pre]screening system since right after 9/11," and gave TSA an "F" for its progress to date.[25]

Aviation Security

According to a March 2005 story in the *New York Times*, a joint assessment by the FBI and DHS concluded that, "the aviation industry [is] perhaps the prime target for another major attack because of the spectacular nature of such strikes." The assessment reportedly singled out general aviation aircraft, such as helicopters and chartered planes, as particular targets "because they are less well-guarded than commercial airlines."[26]

As displayed in Table 7.1, Federal funding for aviation security moved upward somewhat after the 1995 Bojinka plot, then skyrocketed in the aftermath of 9/11, and has sustained that higher plateau up to the present.

As previously stated, the major concentration, by far, of TSA's efforts and funding has been on civil aviation, where TSA has almost exclusive federal responsibility (with the FAA retaining the mission of securing the national air space and its own air traffic control and other facilities).

Prior to 9/11, as well as today, aviation security is based on the notion of a system of layered defenses, which included, then and now: (a) intelligence, (b) airport access control, (c) passenger prescreening, (d) passenger checkpoint screening, (e) checked bag and cargo screening, and (f)

Table 7.1. Federal Funding for Civil Aviation Security FY1995–2006 (in $ millions)

1995	1996	1997	1998	1999	2000	2001	2002	2003	2004	2005	2006
65	66	73	98	123	139	139	5,100	4,516	4,577	5,474	5,952

Notes: FY2004 total includes aviation security funding for TSA, FAM, and FAA. FY2005 total includes same as FY2004, plus Counter-MANPADS R&D. FY2006 total includes same as FY2005, plus aviation-related programs of SCO.

Sources: For FY1994-FY2003: Bart Elias, *Budget History of Aviation Security Program* (Washington, DC:Congressional Research Service, March 25, 2003). For FY2004–FY2005: Department of Homeland Security, *DHS Budget in Brief—Fiscal Year 2005* (Washington, DC: 2004), p. 29; and Department of Homeland Security, *Fact Sheet: Department of Homeland Security Appropriations Act of 2005* (Washington, DC, 2005). For FY2006: Department of Homeland Security, *DHS Budget in Brief—Fiscal Year 2006* (Washington, DC, 2005), pp. 21, 40; and U.S. House, *Conference report to accompany HR 2360, Making appropriations for the Department of Homeland Security for the fiscal year ending September 30, 1996*, 109th Congress, 1st session., (Washington, DC, 2005), H. Report 109-241; pp. 49–57.

onboard security.[27] The operational theory was that with redundant measures if one layer failed, another would support or replace it in thwarting an attack.[28]

Intelligence

With respect to *intelligence*, TSA's Transportation Security Intelligence Service (TSIS) appears to be better "connected" and more relevant to its agency leadership and decision-making process than its predecessor within the FAA. Specifically, the unit provides regular briefings to top agency officials, and it interacts more effectively with both the operations and performance testing divisions. However, though it is now twice as large as its FAA predecessor, TSIS remains significantly understaffed (in part because of the post-9/11 competition for experienced intelligence analysts among a number of federal entities[29]), and its agents are now spread much thinner with responsibilities for all transportation modes, not just aviation. Furthermore, the previously cited departure from TSA of former FAA personnel has hit TSIS particularly hard, and a shift in focus whereby TSIS analysts are now to function as transportation generalists rather than modal specialists[30] has the potential to diminish expertise with respect to aviation security.[31]

Airport Access Control

Airport perimeter and access controls were apparently not implicated in the 9/11 attacks,[32] but as noted earlier, shortcomings in this defense layer had been repeatedly reported, especially by the Department of Transportation

Inspector General. After 9/11, ATSA called for the strengthening of perimeter security, and progress has been reported in a reduction in the number of airport access points, an increase in surveillance of individuals and vehicles entering airports, and some improvement in airport employee background checks. On this latter point, TSA had been developing a Transportation Worker Identification Credential, which would use biometric data to validate the identity of airport workers in order to keep unauthorized people out of secure areas at airports.[33] However, TWIC and all other credentialing efforts were a relatively low priority for TSA,[34] with all such programs receiving a combined $92 million (less than 2 percent of the agency total) in the FY2005 Administration budget request,[35] and the FY2006 request proposed increasing funding and transferring them to a new DHS office of Screening Coordination and Operations.[36]

More fundamental, little has been changed with respect to the old system's divided responsibilities for access control, with the federal government, airport authorities, and to a lesser extent the airlines, all having a role. On the key question of worker credentialing, for example, federal agencies have control of the intelligence and law enforcement information that is the basis for the evaluation of the worker application but the airport authorities retain the responsibility for issuance or denial of the credential. And related to the question of who is responsible for perimeter security is the issue of who pays for it. As in the pre-9/11 system, the continuing dispersal of responsibilities can diminish accountability and produce delays in implementation of security measures.[37]

Passenger Prescreening

Another aviation security layer is *passenger prescreening*, which consists today, as it did on 9/11, of two primary components that are both aimed at keeping dangerous people and/or their weapons off of commercial aircraft—the terrorist watch list and CAPPS.

The most basic, and in some ways essential, prescreening element for civil aviation security is the terrorist watch list, which is to supply the names of government-identified or suspected terrorists to aviation authorities for the "No Fly" list that is used to prevent them from boarding commercial aircraft, and the "Automatic Selectee" list that subjects them to additional security scrutiny.[38]

The number of names currently on these lists (reportedly around 70,000[39]) is orders of magnitude greater than the twelve No Fly names and the even smaller number of Automatic Selectees in effect on 9/11.[40] Yet the August 2004 DHS IG report on "DHS Challenges In Consolidating Terrorist Watch List Information" documents a number of problems that have inhibited the effort, including a lack of strategic planning and centralized oversight, inadequate staffing and budgeting, interagency coordination difficulties, and privacy concerns.[41] These problems, combined with the intelligence community's concern about sharing sometimes highly classified names on the terrorist watch list with the private airlines that still implement the No Fly and Automatic Selectee programs, have dramatically limited the usefulness of the watch list to civil aviation applications, with many identified terrorists still not appearing on either aviation security list.[42]

The TSC's consolidated watch list of known and suspected terrorists, which is to serve as the basis for the No Fly and Automatic Selectee lists, was found, as of the end of 2004, to still be missing key information, most important, the omission of the names of some known terrorists.[43]

The second prescreening component is a TSA-approved and airline-implemented computerized system, which, based on past experience, utilizes ticketing information to identify passengers who might pose a threat to civil aviation. The system in use today is largely the same as the Computer Assisted Passenger Prescreening System (CAPPS) that selected ten of the hijackers on 9/11,[44] but with the added consequence of subjecting the selectee to a physical search of their person and carry-on bags, on top of the previous requirement that their checked luggage be screened for explosives. This change in consequence, a direct response to the 9/11 attacks, is an obvious improvement from the old system, but because of public and Congressional concerns about privacy issues,[45] TSA officials have shelved plans for a follow-on CAPPS II system, which they had originally seen as a necessary means to "greatly enhance TSA's ability to prevent terrorists from boarding commercial airplanes."[46] Thus, the CAPPS system itself has been only marginally improved since 2001.

In September 2004, TSA announced that after review of the original plans for CAPPS II, and "consistent with a recommendation of the National Commission on Terrorist Attacks Upon the United States (9/11 Commission)," the agency would move forward with testing "a next generation system of domestic passenger prescreening, called 'Secure Flight,' which will prescreen airline passengers using information maintained by the Federal Government about individuals known or suspected to be engaged in terrorist activity." More specifically, Secure Flight is to compare passenger information already collected by airlines in the ticketing process (passenger name record, or PNR) against the consolidated watch lists of known or suspected terrorists maintained by the TSC. A second stage of the testing would involve TSA making limited use of commercial data to help correct inaccurate PNR information and thereby verify the identities of individuals selected as matches for terrorist suspects. Once the testing is successfully completed, TSA would be able to take over from the airlines the implementation of the No Fly and Automatic Selectee lists.[47]

Because of continuing privacy and other concerns about the prescreening process, Congress included, as part of the FY2005 Homeland Security Appropriations Act, a requirement that GAO assess and report on ten aspects of the development and implementation of Secure Flight:

1. Stress test the system and demonstrate its efficacy and accuracy.
2. Assess accuracy of databases.
3. Implement modifications with respect to intrastate travel to accommodate states with unique air transportation needs (such as Alaska).
4. Establish internal oversight board.
5. Establish effective oversight of system use and operation.
6. Install operational safeguards to protect system from abuse.
7. Install security measures to protect system from unauthorized access.
8. Examine life-cycle costs and expenditures.
9. Address all privacy concerns.
10. Create a redress process for passengers to correct erroneous information.[48]

In a March 28, 2005, report to Congress, GAO indicated that

> Overall, TSA is making progress in addressing key areas of congressional interest . . . However, TSA has not yet completed these efforts or fully addressed these areas. . . . Specifically, initial tests have only recently been completed and key policy decisions—including what data will be completed and how it will be transmitted—have not yet been made. Until requirements are fully defined, operating policies are finalized, and testing is completed—scheduled for later in the system's development—we cannot determine whether TSA will fully address these areas of interest.[49]

Of the ten items on the congressional list, GAO found that only the internal oversight board issue had been addressed, with action on all others "under way."[50] In response, TSA indicated that the GAO findings largely reflected the status in the eighth month of a planned fourteen-month process, and that the agency still expected to be ready to pilot test Secure Flight with two unidentified airlines in August 2005.[51] After missing that deadline (in part because TSA ignored the recommendation of the 9/11 Commission to focus on watch list screening by combining that function with a "streamlined version" of CAPPS and the use of commercial data to verify passenger identities),[52] TSA indicated that the test would begin by the end of 2005 or early 2006.[53]

Privacy groups remain concerned about the potential impact of the program, describing it, at the first meeting of the DHS advisory panel on privacy rights in April 2005, as "an unprecedented government role, designating citizens as suspect," and criticizing TSA for being "incredibly resistant" to providing the public with necessary information.[54] In its

September 2005 report, the group called on Congress to "prohibit live testing of Secure Flight" until DHS provides more adequate information and "there has been adequate time to review, comment and conduct a public debate on the additional documentation."[55]

Indicating "TSA has failed to provide a fully justified cost estimate for this program for fiscal year 2006 or achieve initial operational capacity with two airlines . . . as originally planned," and that the agency still lacked "a revised schedule and milestones," the House and Senate Appropriations Committees imposed a substantial cut in the administration's FY2006 budget request for Secure Flight and imposed additional controls on its future development.[56] And, as previously noted, the 9/11 Public Discourse Project graded TSA progress in this area as an "F."[57]

While Secure Flight is under development, difficulties continue to be reported with respect to current prescreening programs, particularly in regard to international flights to the United States. DHS officials have cited late notice from the airlines of passenger manifests, and the carriers pointed to their lack of access to the full, up-to-date watch list names. The result, according to federal authorities, is that the "No-Fly list has shortcomings that could allow suspected terrorists and people with ties to terrorism to board U.S. airplanes from overseas." Such concerns led the federal government to order seven incoming international flights to be diverted between September 2004 and May 2005.[58]

To remedy such problems, DHS had initially sought to require airlines to provide it with passenger manifests at least sixty minutes prior to departure, rather than within fifteen minutes after takeoff as at present. In response to strong concerns expressed by U.S. and European air carriers, who were worried about the disruptions to their flight schedules, the Department withdrew the plan,[59] thereby providing another illustration of where finding the proper balance between security and a competing priority—this time an economic one—continues to be unresolved.

The Registered Traveler program, which promised expedited processing to passengers who submit to digital fingerprinting, an iris scan, and a background check to verify their "low-risk" status, has also run into problems. As of February 2005, the program was confined to 9,000 participants and five airports (Boston, Houston, Los Angeles, Minneapolis, and Washington Reagan National), with only one airline per airport. Among the factors that impeded further progress were the lack of technical standards, questions about its integration with other border and transportation prescreening programs, and whether the government or a private contractor will retain the identities database.[60]

Becoming tired of waiting on TSA's slow pace of implementation, a number of airlines and airports formed the Registered Traveler Interoperability Consortium, which seeks to develop its own standards to enable all airports to offer the program in the near future. Although TSA did not endorse the effort, the agency indicated that it would "help move the system forward."[61] In late September 2005, TSA announced that it was ending the pilot program amid indications that the agency had no plans to proceed further with the concept.[62]

At the beginning of 2006, TSA reported that

> The Registered Traveler [RT] programs will be market-driven and offered by the private sector. Individual participation ... will be entirely voluntary, with prices established by private sector providers. TSA will mandate a core RT security assessment for each applicant.... If RT providers undertake more in-depth security background checks (e.g., by using commercial data specifically authorized by customers, or by other voluntary means), TSA will offer a variety of enhanced or time-saving participant benefits at passenger screening checkpoints.[63]

This new version of the Registered Traveler concept is to become operational by late June 2006, but the tying of expedited checkpoint processing—the key benefit for many potential subscribers—to the possible use of commercial data has raised privacy concerns similar to those that have stymied progress on the Secure Flight program.[64]

Passenger Checkpoint Screening and Checked Bag and Cargo Screening

The next two aviation security layers—*checkpoint screening of passengers* and *checked baggage screening*—have been the chief focus of post-9/11 security efforts. Deeming these two layers to be in most urgent need of repair in the immediate aftermath of 9/11, the Aviation and Transportation Security Act of 2001 set forth specific, ambitious goals for checkpoint and checked bag screening, including the establishment of a federalized screener workforce at all but five of the nation's 429 commercial airports by November 19, 2002,[65] and the installation of explosives detection equipment to screen all checked baggage by December 31, 2002.[66]

Perhaps understandably in view of ATSA's stringent statutory mandates, TSA struggled to meet the legislated objectives for creation of the screener workforce and deployment of explosives detection equipment. Particular problems occurred with respect to timely completion of background checks on the 45,000 screeners ultimately hired and of the placement of explosives detection machines "in-line" with baggage conveyors and sorting facilities (rather than in airport lobbies, for instance) at commercial airports. In the first instance, it was clear that TSA would have been unable to meet the November 19, 2002, deadline if it had required thorough background checks to have been completed on the entire workforce, and in the latter the high costs and physical limitations at many airports, not to mention the largely unanswered question of who was to pay, seriously impeded achievement of the statutory mandate. Subsequently, TSA pledged to make continuous progress in eliminating the screener background check backlog, and Congress provided, in the Homeland Security Act of 2002, relief from the explosives detection requirement by extending the deadline until December 2003 and by allowing alternative means of checked baggage screening (including trace-detection machines, explosives-sniffing dogs, and physical searches by hand) for another year beyond that.[67]

Today, the federalized screener workforce is unquestionably more numerous, better paid, more experienced (because of a dramatic drop in the astronomical pre-9/11 turnover rate), and the recipient of better training than its pre-9/11, private contractor counterpart. All of the background checks have been completed, and those employees with problematic histories have been removed.[68]

Yet, in spite of the large expenditure of money and the undoubted upgrade in the "caliber" of the screener workforce, major questions remain as to the extent of the improvement in that workforce's actual performance in detecting potential weapons or other threat objects. A GAO report cited a July 2003 screener performance analysis by TSA, "which identified numerous performance deficiencies, such as inadequate staffing and poor supervision of screeners. These deficiencies were in turn caused by a lack of skills and knowledge, low motivation, ineffective work environments, and wrong or missing incentives."[69]

Ongoing covert testing audits by the DHS IG have demonstrated the persistence of shortcomings in checkpoint screening. In April 2004 testimony to Congress, DHS Inspector General Clark Kent Ervin reported that his office's audits revealed poor performances by both the federalized screeners and the private contract screeners at the five pilot test airports.[70] That finding was reaffirmed in an October 2004 report, which also indicated that the screener workforce suffered from low morale, understaffing, and excessive overtime requirements.[71] And a March 2005 follow-up observed that, "despite the fact that the majority of screeners with whom our testers came in contact were diligent in the performance of their duties and conscious of the responsibility those duties carry, the lack of improvement since our last audit indicates that significant improvement in performance may not be possible without greater use of technology."[72]

With respect to checked bag screening, an investigation by the DHS IG found that by the latter part of 2003 all checked bags were being screened for explosives, compared to just 5 percent at the time of the 9/11 hijackings,[73] though, because of shortages of equipment and screener personnel as well as maintenance and repair requirements, not all of this screening was being done via explosive detection equipment as mandated by ATSA, with canine bomb-sniffing teams, manual bag searches, and positive passenger bag match being used as substitutes.[74] (By the end of 2005, the DHS IG reported that TSA had been "largely successful" in implementing the ATSA mandate.)[75]

The Intelligence Reform and Terrorism Prevention Act of 2004 (Public Law 108-458) required DHS to develop and deploy effective checkpoint explosives and weapons of mass destruction (WMD) detection equipment, and to screen all selectees and their carry-on property for explosives.[76] TSA has deployed explosives trace detection devices at all airports to examine selectees' carry-on items, and installed explosives detection trace portals ("puffers") at seventeen airports (with seven more airports due for installation in the near future) to scrutinize the persons of selectees.[77] After the suicide bombing of a Russian commercial aircraft in August 2004, TSA stepped up the use of "pat-down" searches for explosives, but after privacy-related protests, it took steps to reduce the "intrusiveness" of these searches.[78] Given that the currently deployed portals cover only a small portion of the nation's 441 commercial airports, and that significant problems continue to exist with respect to the capabilities of checkpoint screeners, there is obviously still much need for improvement with respect to the detection of explosives at the checkpoints.

Concerns also continue to be expressed about the capabilities of the existing certified bulk explosives detection equipment (called "large, slow and . . . [with] a high false alarm rate," in an October 2003 report by the House Subcommittee on Aviation[79]) and especially about the deployment of many of these machines in airport lobbies, rather than "in-line" with baggage conveyor systems within the baggage handling area. Such placements increase the labor-intensity of the baggage screening process, introduce additional potential sources of human error into the process, and impede efficient use of the lobby space.[80] Once again the obstacle to full use of in-line screening, which would increase both the effectiveness and efficiency of baggage screening and enhance the safety and security of both passengers and screeners,[81] has been the failure to address the question of who will pay the multibillion-dollar price tag.

Because it illuminates some of the most fundamental problems confronting efforts to significantly improve transportation and homeland security, it is worth considering the "in-line" baggage screening issue in somewhat greater detail. The FAA Reauthorization Act of 2004, also referred to as Vision 100—Century of Aviation Reauthorization Act,[82] created a capital fund to help finance the deployment of "in-line" explosives detection systems (EDS).[83] But whereas Vision 100 authorized $500 million a year for this purpose, only $250 million was requested by the Administration and appropriated by Congress in both FY2004 and FY2005, and the same amount was requested by the Administration for FY2006. (Congress ultimately provided a total of $295 million for FY2006.)[84] With an estimated total price tag of over $4 billion to complete "in-line" installation at all airports, at the current pace completion would obviously take a number of years. To try to accelerate this timetable, Congress attached language to an appropriations bill[85] authorizing TSA to issue Letters of Intent (LOI) to airports as a means of leveraging the limited annual level of federal funds for EDS deployment by stretching out the payment over five to ten years. However, thus far, the Administration has used the LOI program solely to reimburse select airports for expenses as they are incurred.[86]

The net result of all of this was that, as of July 2004, only nine of the country's 441 commercial airports had converted to full in-line EDS systems for baggage screening, while another three airports had partially converted and nineteen had begun installation. And in spite of the fact that airport operators have stated that they need federal assistance to be able to afford in-line installation and that TSA has reported that twenty-seven additional airports will need to have such systems in place in order to comply with the statutory mandate requiring the physical screening of all checked bags for explosives, neither TSA, nor the Bush Administration, nor the Congress have provided funding for further in-line deployment beyond the eight airports[87] that have already received LOIs.[88]

A related issue is that of cost sharing. Currently, the first $250 million made available for "in-line" EDS installation comes from aviation security fees collected from the airlines and airline passengers. Because this amount was the total funding in FY2004 and FY2005, the federal share has, effectively, been zero for the last two years.[89] Furthermore, the Administration proposed and the Congress adopted, as part of the FY2005 Homeland Security Appropriations bill, that the airport share of "in-line" costs be significantly raised from the proportion specified in Vision 100 (10 percent for large and medium-size airports, 5 percent for small airports) to 25 percent for large and medium airports and 10 percent for small facilities.[90]

In response to these facts, and to hearing from virtually everyone who was asked that "in-line" screening would improve both baggage screening security and efficiency, the 9/11 Commission called on TSA to "expedite the installation of advanced (in-line) baggage screening equipment," with industry paying a "fair share" of the costs.[91] Finding that "improvements have not been made a priority by the Congress or the administration," the 9/11 Public Discourse Project gave a "D" to the federal government's implementation of this recommendation.[92]

House Aviation Subcommittee Chairman John Mica (R-FL) observed that the current baggage screening program is "a hodgepodge system that employs trace explosive detection devices [and] has a poor performance record."[93] The DHS Inspector General found current problems with explosives detection back-up systems and pointed to a remaining need for: (1) deployment of EDS equipment at the airports where alternative screening methods are still employed, (2) placement of EDS systems "in line," and (3) "using research and development to develop and deploy more effective and economical equipment to address current and future threats and risks."[94]

TSA has been seeking to significantly upgrade future screening performance through research and development programs. However, these efforts have not necessarily been afforded a high priority within the agency, as evidenced by the fact that in FY2003, TSA reallocated $61 million, out of a total Congressional appropriation of $110 million for TSA R&D, to fund other TSA programs viewed as higher priorities. GAO reported that, "As a result, TSA had to delay several key research and development projects, including developing a device to detect weapons, liquid explosives, and flammables in containers found in carry-on baggage or passengers' effects, and further development and testing of a walk-through chemical trace detection portal for detecting explosives on passengers."[95] (The Administration's FY2006 budget proposed the transfer of almost all of the TSA research and development unit to the DHS Science and Technology division,[96] and the Congress accepted this recommendation.[97])

A December 2005 DHS IG report succinctly summarized the current state of affairs with respect to passenger and baggage screening as follows: "Improvements are needed in the screening process to ensure that dangerous prohibited items are not being carried into the sterile areas of heavily used airports or do not enter the checked baggage system." The report pointed to problems in a whole range of areas, including "training; equipment and technology; policy and procedures; and management and supervision.[98]

Onboard Security

The *onboard security* layers underwent the most immediate transformation after the events of 9/11 with all U.S. airlines and international airlines flying to the United States having installed reinforced and bulletproof cockpit doors;[99] the "Common Strategy" training program for flight crews, which as of 9/11 had called for accommodation with presumed nonsuicidal hijackers, having been revised and broadened to take into account the 9/11 tactics;[100] and the number of Federal Air Marshals (FAMs) having been increased dramatically, with its agents now assigned to domestic as well as international flights.[101]

Deficiencies have been noted in each of the onboard security measures, however. Concerns have been expressed that the effectiveness of the newly hardened cockpit doors has been compromised by crew failures to secure the door throughout a flight.[102] Although the old "Common Strategy" paradigm has certainly been removed,[103] the quality of the new training, especially for flight attendants, has been questioned, with flight attendant representatives indicating that "we still have not been trained to appropriately handle a security crisis or terrorist attack onboard our airplanes,"[104] that the current training does not provide instruction "even in the fundamentals of self-defense," that the new system's requirement for such training can be met by an airline showing a single videotape on self-defense techniques once every thirteen months,[105] and that TSA has "continued to stonewall efforts" to provide improved security training.[106]

A September 2005 GAO report on flight and cabin crew security training found that, although TSA has "enhanced guidance and standards," the agency "has not established strategic goals and performance measures for assessing the effectiveness of crew member security training, nor required air carriers to do so." TSA's advanced voluntary training program for pilots and flight attendants was reported as suffering from "the lack of recurrent training, the lack of a realistic setting in which to conduct the training, and instructors' lack of knowledge of crew members' actual work environment."[107]

Though the FAM program has been greatly enlarged from the thirty-three agents in place on 9/11,[108] that rapid expansion itself has produced several operational and management problems, including an abbreviated training curriculum. Furthermore, budget constraints, caused in part by departmental funding shifts from the FAM program to other DHS accounts, have "delayed completion of [advanced] training . . . not permitted the Service to reach its target staffing levels and are delaying efforts to develop its field location infrastructure and its automated system to schedule air marshal missions."[109]

Additionally, serious concerns were raised during the summer of 2004 by some air marshals, law enforcement officers, airline pilots, flight attendants, and members of Congress that the operational policies of DHS were "endangering the lives of federal air marshals by making them conspicuous to terrorists." Specifically, the Department's dress code for air marshals reportedly required that they have neatly trimmed hair and be clean-shaven, and some of the air marshal field offices mandated that the agents wear dress clothing, including ties for the male agents.[110] (In April 2005 the FAM dress code was modified, largely eliminating the complaints that had been raised.)[111]

The November 2003 transfer of the air marshal program to DHS' Bureau of Immigration and Customs Enforcement (ICE) presented new challenges for TSA as to the scheduling of what flights would be covered by air marshals, and for ICE's immigration and customs components as to how cross-training and possible deployment as air marshals would impact their agents' current responsibilities and workload.[112] Such concerns were behind the July 2005 decision by DHS Secretary Chertoff to restore the FAM program to TSA "to increase operational coordination."[113] It remains to be seen what impact this latest shift will have on FAM morale and on interagency coordination between TSA and ICE.

Finally, in spite of the significant post-9/11 expansion in the number of air marshals, it has been reported that less than 5 percent of all U.S. flights are actually covered by the marshals at present.[114]

Non-Passenger Aviation

Turning to the non-passenger aviation sectors, little has been done post-9/11 to enhance security for either *general aviation*[115] or *air cargo*, and these remain "gaping holes" in U.S. aviation security efforts.[116]

ATSA contained some broad guidelines with respect to general aviation and flight schools,[117] and some limited, largely voluntary actions have been taken post-9/11 to improve security in these areas. Background checks have been enhanced for foreign nationals applying to flight schools or for U.S. pilot certificates. "Best practices" guidelines have been issued for flight schools and general aviation airports.[118] And TSA is in the process of increasing the number of air cargo security inspectors, to a total of 200 by the end of March 2005.[119] In the FY2006 DHS appropriations bill, Congress provided funding for an additional 100 inspectors and for "three cargo screening pilot programs testing different concepts of operation."[120]

Overall, however, general aviation security has not been substantially upgraded, with neither pilots, passengers, baggage, nor cargo subjected to any security screening whatsoever. Furthermore, threat and vulnerability assessments have yet to be undertaken for most general aviation airports.[121] A December 2004 Congressional report criticized TSA for failing to understand the potential risks from small private planes, provide useful threat information to general aviation airports, and enforce security compliance by charter airlines and flight schools.[122]

Similar shortcomings continue to exist in air cargo security. For example, approximately 22 percent of all air cargo is currently transported onboard passenger flights, and although, as noted earlier, all checked bags on such aircraft are now being examined in some fashion, the vast majority of the accompanying cargo is not subject to any inspection.[123] In fact, reportedly only 5 percent of all air cargo is currently screened, and the GAO has stated to Congress that aircraft carrying cargo continue to be highly vulnerable to terrorist sabotage.[124]

In a November 2004 proposed rule making, TSA unveiled an air cargo security plan, which included background checks for cargo handlers, restrictions on access at cargo airport facilities, increased security responsibilities for freight forwarders, and preboard screening for all those who board cargo aircraft.[125] However, the plan, which has yet to make much progress through the regulatory process, contains few details on how the freight industry, which is expected to implement and pay for it, is to accomplish these objectives.[126]

Maritime Security

Concerns about the potential vulnerability of the U.S. maritime sector to terrorist attacks predated the events of 9/11. A federal Interagency

Commission on Crime and Security in U.S. Seaports reported in the fall of 2000 that, though the FBI then considered the terrorist *threat* to American ports to be low, these ports were highly *vulnerable* to any such attack.[127] More specifically, al Qaeda has had a history of maritime assaults and is known to have had possession of a manual on how to attack ships.[128] Moreover, a number of independent analyses have calculated that the closure of U.S. seaports resulting from terrorist action would produce substantial damage to the entire American economy, with one estimate placing the costs at up to $1 trillion.[129]

Port Security

As previously discussed, the Maritime Transportation Security Act (MTSA) was adopted in late 2002 to address vulnerabilities at U.S. *port and shipping facilities*. However, unlike ATSA, which mandated a number of very specific actions with deadlines for implementation of aviation security measures, MTSA contained few such deadlines, and most of these have not been fully met.[130] For example, according to a September 2004 GAO report, the vulnerability assessments undertaken by the Coast Guard at the nation's fifty-five most important ports had been subject to a number of "missteps" and changes in implementation, with the result that few such assessments had been completed and further progress was still "at risk." The assessments that have been finished have revealed inadequacies in access controls, unavailability of patrol boats and law enforcement personnel, and security vulnerabilities of fuel and chemical storage depots.[131]

MTSA mandated that all U.S. ports, facilities, and vessels develop and submit for Coast Guard approval comprehensive security and incident response plans, based on the Coast Guard's vulnerability assessments and security recommendations.[132] Though, as just mentioned, there have been problems with the vulnerability assessments, DHS has indicated that "over 99 percent" of the port and facility security plans have been received,[133] totaling 9,000 domestic vessel security plans and 3,200 domestic facility plans by the end of 2004. The Coast Guard has also "verified security plan implementation" for 8,100 foreign-flagged vessels.[134]

As of February 2005, the Coast Guard had developed forty-eight Area Maritime Security Plans, as required by MTSA, that "define the roles and responsibilities of the local, state and federal government to protect the critical infrastructure in our ports," and that supplement the individual vessel and facility security plans.[135]

The National Maritime Security Plan called for by MTSA, retitled the National Strategy for Maritime Security, was finally issued in September 2005, and eight supporting plans were announced the following month.[136] These documents resemble the previously described National Infrastructure Protection Plan and National Strategy for Transportation Security in containing laudable general principles and objectives but very few policy specifics. (One exception is a provision in the "Maritime Commerce Security Plan" calling for DHS to "pursue a regulatory requirement that loaded containers being transported to the U.S. be secured (at a minimum) with a high-security mechanical seal."[137])

Though the content of the port and vessel security plans varies, among the reported security enhancements made to date are the following: increased identification checks on crewmembers and visitors; additional canine bomb detection teams; increased passenger and baggage screening; enhanced perimeter fencing, with surveillance cameras; greater restrictions on access to secure areas of ports; deployment of X-ray machines on all large cruise ships; additional security training for workers; and increased security patrols.[138]

The effectiveness of these measures was addressed in a recently published report on maritime security.

> A compressed and disjointed timeline for implementing the act has definitely affected what the MTSA has actually accomplished. . . . It remains to be seen whether or not the thousands of facility security plans, scores of area plans and an overarching national plan collectively have achieved unity of purpose and coherent operational procedures for preventing attacks on the maritime transportation system. . . . Overall, too many facility plans are little more than lists of activities that individually and collectively fall far short of the goals set by MTSA.[139]

The Coast Guard estimated that the first year costs for implementing MTSA as well as the International Maritime Organization security code would be approximately $1.5 billion, with a ten-year total of $7.3 billion.[140] Through FY2005, only $560 million had been specifically awarded by DHS for these purposes in the form of direct federal grants for 1,200 projects involving physical and operational security upgrades at American ports.[141] Furthermore, because these grants may be used only for capital expenses (such as the purchase of equipment) whereas MTSA implementation costs are primarily operational ones (salaries and maintenance), it has been estimated that less than 10 percent of federally mandated port security enhancements are eligible for federal funding.[142]

In December 2004, the DHS IG reported that "the Coast Guard budget requests during FY2003–2005 did not include adequate funding for the re-capitalization of critical infrastructure . . . [which] could be a major detriment to the Coast Guard's ability to perform both its legacy and homeland security missions."[143] The Commandant of the Coast Guard, Admiral Thomas Collins, noted in his 2004 "State of the Coast Guard" address that "mission growth" had "out-stripped, in many ways" the growth in funding for the Coast Guard.[144] And in May 2005 testimony to Congress GAO reported, "Our reviews indicate that funding is a pressing challenge to putting effective seaport security measures in place and sustaining these measures over time."[145]

Also in May 2005, the DHS IG reported that the Coast Guard was faced with three major "barriers" to its ability to perform both its homeland security and "legacy" missions:

- The lack of a comprehensive performance management system.
- The declining experience level of agency personnel.
- A high operations tempo, which "will tax the Coast Guard's infra-structure including its aging cutter and aircraft fleet."[146]

Another DHS Inspector General report, in January 2005, indicated that DHS' port security grants program was being hampered by a number of factors. Most important, "the program's strategic effectiveness is hindered mainly because it is attempting to reconcile three competing approaches: the competitive program mandated by Congress, MTSA's grant authority, and risk-based decision making." Furthermore, the program was not well-coordinated with IAIP and lacked an adequate evaluation process, which resulted in awards being made to lower priority projects, and those projects not being sufficiently monitored to ensure they achieve the stated security objectives.[147]

Container Security

Although the Coast Guard has been assigned the lead role in federal maritime security efforts, the Customs and Border Protection division of DHS has responsibility for the related field of *container security*. Given the key role in global commerce performed by cargo containers, and their inherent vulnerability to tampering, efforts have begun to identify high-risk containers and bar them from entry into the United States. One such effort, the Container Security Initiative (CSI) that started in February 2002, employs an automated system to identify and prescreen high-risk containers bound for the United States from the largest ports outside the country. A second initiative, called the Customs-Trade Partnership Against Terrorism (C-TPAT) and begun in April 2002, creates government–industry partnerships that offer expedited customs processing for shipping companies that reduce their security vulnerabilities. A third program, Operation Safe Commerce initiated in November 2002,[148] seeks to verify the contents of seaborne containers where they are loaded, prevent tampering in transit, and track their movement through to final destination.[149]

By the end of 2003, all of the twenty largest ports had agreed to participate in the CSI and 4,600 importers, ocean carriers, and freight forwarders had submitted applications to join C-TPAT. By the end of 2004, CSI was operational in thirty-four overseas ports in Europe, Asia, and Africa, and C-TPAT enrollment stood at just over 4,000 certified partners.[150] But homeland security expert Stephen Flynn reported in his book, *America the Vulnerable*:

> The Customs and Border Protection Service lacks the manpower and re-
> sources to adequately staff the Container Security Initiative, to review the
> applications of companies who wish to participate in C-TPAT, and to move
> away from error-prone cargo manifests that remain the cornerstone of its tar-
> geting system . . . . And none of these programs address the core cargo security
> imperative of confirming that the goods loaded into a container from the start
> are indeed legitimate and that the container has not been interrupted and
> compromised once it is moving within the transportation system.[151]

Recent GAO reports have generally confirmed Flynn's evaluation with respect to inadequacies in staffing for CSI and C-TPAT and noted shortcomings in these programs' performance measurement and strategic planning as well.[152] More specifically, it was discovered that, while the CSI program has improved the information flow between United States and foreign customs officials, staffing difficulties have resulted in 35 percent of U.S.-bound shipments not being subjected to its prescreening targeting, and 28 percent of those containers identified by such targeting as high-risk and referred by the CSI program to host governments for inspection were not subsequently physically searched.

With respect to C-TPAT, GAO reported that participants have been receiving the promised benefits (in the form of a reduced probability of inspection) prior to CBP's having validated their security measures. Moreover, the validation process itself was found to possess several flaws that compromise its effectiveness, including a lack of rigor in its procedures and a slow pace, that has resulted in only 11 percent of certified members having been validated thus far.[153]

An August 2005 audit by the DHS Inspector General found that the Automated Tracking System—the cornerstone of the container prescreening program—needed improvement with respect to both its targeting rules and its physical controls over containers selected for examination.[154]

Operation Safe Commerce, which had received $75 million in FY2002–2004, did not receive any funding in the Administration's subsequent budget requests.[155] The bottom line is that, with all of the efforts made since 9/11, just 6 percent of all containers currently entering the United States receive any physical inspection.[156]

CBP also seeks to secure American ports of entry (land, sea, and air) through use of Non-Intrusive Inspection (NII) technology to detect weapons of mass destruction (WMD). More specifically, CBP is in the process of deploying personal radiation detectors (PRDs), radiation portal monitors (RPMs), and radioisotope identifier devices (RIIDs) to detect nuclear and radiological materials arriving at the ports.[157] A few more than 400 RPMs had been deployed by the beginning of 2005, with 900 more to be in place by the end of the year.[158] As of early 2005, these deployments re-sulted in only two seaports having the capability to non-intrusively screen all incoming cargo for radiological or nuclear material,[159] with a third, the nation's busiest port (Los Angles/Long Beach, CA), due for complete coverage by the end of 2005.[160]

The Department of Energy's (DOE) Megaports Initiative also aims at detecting nuclear and radiological materials at key foreign ports by pro-viding the host governments with radiation detection equipment to screen shipping containers transiting through the ports. Begun in 2003, the Ini-tiative has had, in the words of GAO, "limited success" thus far, with completed deployments at only two ports (Piraeus, Greece and Rotter-dam, the Netherlands)[161] and continuing problems in reaching agree-ments with key countries, most notably China. Furthermore, as with the CBP radiation detectors, the DOE-supplied equipment has been faced with a number of technical and operational problems that have limited its effectiveness.[162]

And once again to look at the bottom line, despite all of these efforts (or at least the ones in place as of September 2003), on two occasions (the first and second anniversaries of the 9/11 attacks, in September of 2002 and 2003), representatives of ABC News succeeded in smuggling a depleted uranium cylinder into the United States. Although CBP's Automated Targeting System identified the container carrying the cylinder as high-risk in both cases—resulting in physical inspection by CBP personnel each time—the depleted uranium was not detected by the searches and the cargo was permitted to enter into the United States. Subsequent investigation by the DHS Inspector General found several weaknesses in CBP protocols and procedures that allowed the uranium cylinder to avoid discovery.

According to a May 2005 DHS IG report, "CBP has since enhanced its ability to screen targeted containers for radioactive emissions by deploy-ing more sensitive technology at its seaports, revising protocols and proce-dures, and improving training of CBP personnel."[163] However, no unclas-sified information has been presented to demonstrate the effectiveness of these improvements in media or "Red Team" tests like the aforementioned ABC instances.

Reportedly, the currently deployed radiation detection equipment can be foiled by a variety of means and produces a large number of false pos-itives because it has difficulty in distinguishing between highly enriched uranium, which would pose a security threat, and common household products that include trace amounts of radiological material.[164] Addi-tionally, the NII equipment utilized in the CSI program was found by GAO to be of variable quality and not subject to any minimum technical requirements.[165]

In June 2005, Representatives Edward Markey (D-MA) and Bennie Thompson (D-MS) released the results of an analysis they had requested by the American Association for the Advancement of Science's (AAAS) Center for Science, Technology, and Security Policy. The AAAS report concluded that the kind of test object employed by ABC would still "likely" evade detection by the existing portal detectors and procedures and that the detectors continue to be limited in their ability to identify radioactive sources and thereby to distinguish between naturally occurring and potentially hazardous materials.[166]

In September 2004, officials from the Ports of Tacoma and Seattle issued preliminary results from the Operation Safe Commerce pilot program at their ports, which included findings that

- In many cases, the [cargo] origination point lacked access control and general security.
- In other cases, the integrity of container seals was not verified at each point in the supply chain. Finding out that the seal has been compromised when it arrives here is too late.
- The identity of the drivers used to transfer the containers between supply points is not always easily verified.[167]

A November 2004 independent analysis of the nation's maritime cargo supply chain, conducted by Forrester Research, found that the maritime sector was "still vulnerable" and that current programs to improve security are "rife with weaknesses." Among the flaws cited by the report were the voluntary nature of the programs and the absence of federal funding for security measures, both of which limited adoption of the recommended measures, and reliance on a company's self-reported security procedures and a one-time government inspection in certifying freight as low-risk. Forrester analyst Noha Tohamy stated, "Where I see the government in need of taking a firmer stand is in minimum mandatory requirements that would be applicable to all companies. The federal government has to shoulder more of the cost of the investment in these initiatives. This isn't just the cost of doing business; this is about the security of the U.S. population."[168]

Maritime Domain Awareness

In addition to port and container security, maritime security efforts include activities to improve *maritime domain awareness*, which is defined as "the understanding by stakeholders involved in maritime security of anything associated with the global maritime environment that could adversely affect the security, safety, economy, or environment of the United States."[169]

Maritime domain awareness efforts include the Automatic Identification System (AIS) for tracking vessels; Maritime Intelligence Fusion Centers; Field Intelligence Support Teams; Area Maritime Security Committees, which serve as forums for federal, state, local, and private stakeholders "to gain a comprehensive perspective of security issues" at a given seaport; and Interagency Operational Centers, which provide 24/7 information and involve relevant federal and nonfederal agencies.[170]

GAO found that the forty-three area maritime security committees have "improved information sharing among seaport security stakeholders, including the timeliness, completeness, and usefulness of the information shared." However, the watchdog agency also reported that maritime information sharing has been hampered by difficulties experienced by nonfederal participants in obtaining the security clearances necessary to receive key federally generated intelligence information. For example, as of February 2005, only twenty-eight out of 359 nonfederal area maritime security committee participants had been able to submit the necessary paperwork for the requisite background check.[171] In addition, shortcomings were discovered in the execution of seaport security exercises, including difficulties in communications with first responders, inadequate facilities or equipment, differing response procedures, and inadequate training for joint agency response.[172]

Summary

As with most homeland security efforts, the question of how security costs should be allocated looms large in the maritime sector. Although "skeptics of additional [government] spending argue that taxpayers should not provide funds to large and profitable corporations to secure infrastructure that is in their own financial interest to do so,"[173] as Flynn has observed, "for most U.S. companies, security investments in the absence of federal support or a government mandate are not in the cards."[174] And GAO testified that, given current economic difficulties among state and local governments, as well as within the private sector, it is "unclear" where necessary funding for maritime security will come from.[175]

The unresolved questions of roles and missions, and of financing sources have undoubtedly hampered maritime security. A February 2003 analysis found that "maritime security currently remains wholly inadequate. Multiple vulnerabilities remain that could easily be exploited by terrorists to attack vessels, port facilities, or coastal infrastructures."[176] In April 2003 testimony to the 9/11 Commission, the GAO indicated that, "an effective port security environment may be many years away."[177]

A comprehensive assessment of maritime security by GAO, presented in May 2005 testimony to Congress, found "the main challenges" to be

> Failure to develop necessary planning components to carry out the programs; difficulty in coordinating the activities of federal agencies and port stakeholders to implement programs; and difficulty in maintaining the financial support to continue implementation of security enhancements.[178]

Land Transportation Security

As one analysis of transportation security put it, with respect to land transportation, "The least emphasis has been placed on this area because it was perceived as least pressing, and also because it is hardest to protect."[179]

Though resource allocation decisions and various publicly reported threat assessments have prioritized aviation and, to a lesser extent, maritime security, land transportation systems have been a frequent terrorist target around the world, accounting for 42 percent of all terrorist attacks from 1991 to 2001.[180] From 1998 to 2003, an estimated 181 attacks on rail transportation resulted in 431 deaths, and 293 such attacks on buses produced 467 fatalities.[181]

A TSA presentation to a panel of bridge and tunnel security experts[182] noted that land transportation systems are particularly vulnerable because they are easily accessible; their associated infrastructure is generally fixed, and unguarded; they present attractive targets for terrorist attacks; and such attacks require only a small, well-directed force but can cause serious injuries and other damage. Furthermore, an al Qaeda training manual found in England included instructions for missions to destroy bridges.[183] And in February 2005 testimony to Congress, Deputy DHS Secretary James Loy reported, "We think we are most likely to be attacked with a vehicle borne improvised explosive device,"[184] in other words, a car or truck bomb.

Though ATSA gave it security responsibility for all modes, including land transportation, TSA sees its role as that of "manager" of the security risk for modes other than aviation,[185] to be carried out by

> developing best practices, standards, and regulations to protect the transportation infrastructure; conducting inspections to monitor and enforce compliance with standards and regulations; designing and implementing vulnerability assessment models for all land transportation modes; and strengthening industry stakeholder partnerships through sustained information sharing.[186]

With a proposed FY2006 budget of just $32 million, and with only 100 security inspectors (all assigned to rail and transit security),[187] TSA and DHS land transportation efforts continue to be minimal, and the various Department of Transportation (DOT) land transportation modal agencies have retained substantial security roles.

Rail and Transit Security

In the aftermath of 9/11, a variety of actions were taken by federal and nonfederal entities to shore up *rail and transit* security.

- The Association of American Railroads, which represents the freight rail industry, prepared a classified analysis of risks and countermeasures.

- The Federal Railroad Administration (FRA) commissioned a systematic review by the RAND Corporation of Amtrak's security posture and current programs.
- Amtrak received $100 million for safety and security enhancements of rail tunnels in the New York City area.
- State and local transit agencies utilized federal transit grant funds and technical assistance to conduct emergency drills, increase employee security training, complete vulnerability assessments, and determine and implement security measures, including perimeter barriers, increased security patrols, increased usage of canine bomb detection teams, use of security alert announcements to passengers, and increased video surveillance.
- DOT coordinated rail security-related projects, including responding to bomb and other security threats, monitoring incident reports on acts of sabotage and vandalism, and serving as the liaison to rail operators concerning terrorist threats.
- The DHS Information Analysis and Infrastructure Protection (IAIP) unit and TSA worked with the Federal Railroad Administration and the Federal Transit Administration to conduct vulnerability assessments of rail and transit networks in heavily populated areas.
- DHS provided $115 million in grants for urban rail and transit security.
- TSA joined the Surface Transportation Information Sharing and Analysis Center (ISAC), managed by the Association of American Railroads and designed to facilitate the sharing of security and threat information.
- TSA conducted rail security training exercises.
- DHS' Federal Law Enforcement Training Center provided security training for rail personnel.
- DHS' National Targeting Center and border inspectors prescreened high risk rail cargo entering the United States.
- DHS assisted in the deployment of biological and radiation detectors by certain local transit systems.[188]

Continuing terrorist interest in land transportation attacks, and the vulnerability of these systems to such attacks, were gruesomely demonstrated by the bombings of commuter trains in Madrid, Spain, on March 11, 2004,[189] and of London's mass transit system on July 7, 2005.[190]

Repeating a pattern often seen in aviation security, the 2004 Madrid bombings led to a scramble by government officials to devise an effective response. DHS' reaction was outlined in a post-Madrid "fact sheet" prepared by the department (perhaps notably rather than by TSA) and that indicated, again in words reminiscent of civil aviation security—pre- and post-9/11—that "the responsibility of securing our nation's rail and mass transit systems is a shared one," involving DHS, the Department of Transportation, and unnamed other federal agencies "in partnership with the public and private entities that own and operate the nation's transit and rail systems."[191]

The DHS post-Madrid rail and transit security effort was described in four parts:

1. Leadership, under which DHS is to "engage the industry and state and local authorities to establish base-line security measures based on current industry best practices . . . [which] could be adjusted . . . in response to higher threat levels or specific threats." (Note the similarity to the pre-9/11 aviation security alert system.) DHS is also to have the responsibility to "ensure compliance" with the security standards, to identify any security gaps (with DOT), and (through TSA) to provide technical assistance and training.[192]
2. Threat response capability, including the development of a "rapid deployment" canine bomb detection capability to be drawn from current DHS resources, and a Transit Inspection Pilot program to test the feasibility of screening baggage for explosives at train stations and on trains.
3. Education and awareness activities, under which DHS and TSA are to work with industry, the Federal Transit Administration (FTA), and local rail and transit authorities to develop, implement, and integrate passenger and employee awareness and security training programs.
4. Future technological innovations, which at present are focused on biological, chemical, and high explosives weapons countermeasures.[193]

Grants have been the primary means by which DHS has assisted rail and transit security, with much of the impetus coming from Congressional appropriations action. Under the Urban Area Security Initiative (UASI), $67.8 million was distributed to the largest transit systems in FY2003, and another $50 million was provided in FY2004.[194] Congress appropriated $150 million for this purpose in FY2005,[195] but as of April 2005, only $136.6 million had been allocated by DHS.[196] Funding for intercity bus security grants amounted to $5 million in FY2003, $10 million in FY2004, and $9.7 million in FY2005.[197] The FY2006 DHS appropriations bill provided another $150 million for rail and transit, and $10 million for intercity bus security grants.[198]

The Federal Railroad Administration (FRA) and FTA have been the lead agencies within DOT for rail and transit security, respectively. With a proposed FY2006 security budget of $700,000, FRA is to coordinate rail security projects, respond to notifications of bomb and other security threats provided by the National Response Center, and provide security-related information to railroad operators. FTA, which received $36.6 million in the President's FY2006 budget proposal, is to assist local transit agencies with respect to security, emergency preparedness, employee security training, and public awareness.[199]

An April 2004 survey of mass transit systems by their trade association (the American Public Transportation Association) reported $6 billion in unmet security needs, including $5.2 billion in capital investments and $800 million in annual personnel and other security-related operating expenses. The survey detailed a number of areas in which transit operators felt that federal funding was "very important," including security personnel and training, communications and monitoring equipment, and WMD detection devices.[200]

The "evolving" federal transit security role was described in a September 2002 GAO report that highlighted a number of potential obstacles posed by uncertainties in that role, including the limited authority of FTA, the failure of TSA to assume its presumed statutory responsibilities, and the accompanying coordination problems between the two agencies as well as with state and local transit authorities. At the time of the report, it was hoped that a "memorandum of understanding" (MOU) between the two agencies would resolve such difficulties by clearly defining the security roles and responsibilities of each.[201] An MOU was completed in September 2004, but it only delineated very broad areas of responsibility at the departmental level (between DHS and DOT), leaving the articulation of "specific security-related roles, responsibilities, resources, and commitments for mass transit, rail, research and development, and other matters" to subsequent annexes.[202] As the House Committee on Transportation and Infrastructure commented one month later:

> The roles and responsibilities of TSA, other offices within DHS, and the Department of Transportation (DOT) regarding public transportation security implementation and oversight have not been clearly defined by the administration. As a result, there is a strong sense among the transit community and other stakeholder groups that there is not consistent, risk-based management of public transportation security issues, particularly in the allocation of security improvement grants funding.[203]

The muddled picture as to the federal role in rail and transit security was a major contributing cause of the fact that less than half ($115 million) of the DHS rail and transit grants had actually been expended as of August 2005.[204] New York City's Metropolitan Transportation Authority (MTA), by far the largest transit system and recipient of federal transit security grants, has spent only 5 percent of the $600 million it has received for security. In the absence of clear federal agency leadership, MTA balked at "wasting money on unproven technology," and pursued an ultimately fruitless effort to contract with the U.S. Army to help secure its facilities.[205] (On August 23, 2005, MTA announced that it was awarding a $212 million contract to the Lockheed Martin Corp. to provide monitoring, surveillance, access control, intrusion detection, and response capabilities for New York City's subway and commuter rail systems, and the associated bridges and tunnels. Deployment of the system is expected to take three years.)[206]

In May of 2004, TSA issued Rail Security Directives setting security standards, which are to serve as "a formal baseline and standardize protective measures for all passenger rail assets."[207] These mandates, with no federal funding included, require rail and transit system operators to deploy a number of protective measures derived from existing best practices. Among the specified measures are increasing the number of security personnel, utilizing canine explosives detection teams, and removing or securing station trash cans. Compliance is to be ensured via TSA's aforementioned total of 100 rail and transit security inspectors.[208]

Shortly after the announcement of the Security Directives, a representative of the local transit systems that are charged with implementing the measures raised serious questions about their effectiveness because of the difficulty the systems were likely to have in funding them in the absence of federal support, and of the belief that TSA had not sufficiently involved these key stakeholders in the planning process.[209] A September 2005 GAO report commented, "it is unclear how TSA developed the required measures contained in the directives, how TSA plans to monitor and ensure compliance with the measures, and which entities are responsible for their implementation."[210]

In another example of the pace and scale of federal transit security efforts, TSA announced in September 2005 that it was at last "expanding the canine [explosives detection] program to mass transit and commuter rail systems" via the deployment of thirty dogs to ten different U.S. transit systems.[211] (To put this into perspective, there are 2,872 mass transit stations around the country.)[212]

The report accompanying the final version of the FY2006 DHS appropriations bill by members of the House and Senate Appropriations Committees indicated they "are very disappointed with TSA's reluctance to quickly hire rail inspectors and deploy canine units at transit systems nationwide. Although these activities were funded in fiscal year 2005, TSA does not have a full contingent of rail inspectors on board and only announced the deployment of canine teams on September 27, 2005. This is unacceptable."[213]

It is instructive to compare these federal responses with the recommendations presented to the Congress in the immediate aftermath of the Madrid bombings by the RAND Corporation, based in part on the work it had been doing for the freight rail industry.

There is a need for a coordinated federal policy on rail security, encompassing freight, passenger, and commuter rails. Compared to other transportation sectors, decision-making appears to be quite de-centralized between a number of federal, state, local, and private concerns. A coordinated approach for counter-terrorism measures in the rail transportation system should undertake three tasks. First, it should define the federal role in preventing or mitigating such attacks. Second, it should prioritize investments needed to prevent attacks against rail transportation systems with those needed to prevent attacks against other transportation systems. Third, it should define the roles and responsibilities of federal, state, and local agencies, transportation companies, and passengers and freight shippers in preventing terrorist attacks against rail systems and in responding to their consequences. Given the magnitude of the recent attacks in Spain, it would be prudent to undertake such planning steps in the near future.[214]

With the efforts to date, it is perhaps not surprising that security experts have cited continuing vulnerability and limited improvement in transit security. Juliette Kayyam of Harvard University stated that the transit sector is currently "about as vulnerable as it always has been," with security measures "pretty piecemeal—not part of any comprehensive effort."[215]

The absence of federal leadership in rail security was at the heart of an April 2005 ruling in the United States District Court for the District of Columbia that allowed the city of Washington to proceed with its own ban of hazardous material from being transported within the zone, including the U.S. Capitol and other key government facilities.[216]

> The [federal government] has the ultimate authority and responsibility to provide a safe, secure and efficient rail transportation system in the United States and to formulate an effective and coordinated response to the threat of terrorism.... The District Act will stand only so long as there is a gap in federal coverage.... All parties believe it is in everyone's best interests to have one consistent and comprehensive federal policy addressing the risk of terrorism on our interstate rail system.[217]

Highway, Bridge, and Tunnel Security

If anything, the picture with respect to the federal role in *highway, bridge, and tunnel security* is even less clear than it is in rail and transit. The Department of Transportation's Federal Highway Administration (FHWA) has taken the federal lead in this area. It received $13 million for various security activities, including vulnerability assessments, countermeasures, and emergency operations, preparedness, and response, in the Administration's budget request for FY2006 (the same amount appropriated for FY2005).[218] DHS and TSA have played a minimal role to date in this entire area.

This modest federal effort stands in contrast, not only to the previously cited DHS belief that the most likely future terrorist attack is in this sector, but also to the findings of the Blue Ribbon Panel on Bridge and Tunnel

Security established by the American Association of State Highway and Transportation Officials (AASHTO) and FHWA, which pegged the potential consequences of the loss of a critical highway bridge or tunnel at "hundreds or thousands of casualties (and) billions of dollars worth of direct reconstruction costs," and indicated that "The highway infrastructure has vulnerabilities, which must be addressed. This is important enough to be a matter of national security policy." The panel's recommendations included *improved coordination* among FHWA, AASHTO, TSA, and other highway system stakeholders; *clarification of legal responsibilities* of state and local transportation authorities concerning their obligation to act on the results of risk assessments of their facilities; and *provision of new funding sources* "beyond and outside of current federal-aid highway funding sources."[219]

In what would appear to be an indication of some unavoidable federal responsibility in this sector, containers transported by truck from Canada over border-crossing bridges are not currently being subjected to security screening because of unresolved negotiations at the national level on inspection procedures and criminal enforcement standards.[220]

Pipeline Security

TSA is supposed to be the lead federal agency for *pipeline security*, though because of the close relationship of security and safety (which appears to be more acknowledged here than in other transportation sectors), the Office of Pipeline Safety (OPS) within the Department of Transportation is also involved. TSA issued general pipeline security guidelines in 2002 and plans to issue more binding regulations at some point. In 2003, the agency inspected twenty-four of the largest pipeline operators and found that almost all had met or exceeded the minimum security guidelines. (OPS participated in approximately one-third of these inspections.) TSA is also in the process of developing self-assessment tools for pipeline operators to use in identifying critical facilities and conducting vulnerability assessments.

As is the case for other sectors, questions have arisen about funding and roles for pipeline security operations. The Administration's FY2005 and FY2006 budget requests for TSA did not include a line item for pipeline security, which was to be provided for out of the agency's general operations budget, and TSA's current limited capacity for pipeline security inspection and enforcement is likely to continue. Concerns have also been raised about overlapping and potentially conflicting regulatory policies between TSA and OPS, which has continued to assert a security role. In spite of that, no formal agreement specifying security responsibilities has been reached between the two, and reportedly neither agency believes such a document is necessary.

Finally, the general security responsibilities of the federal government with respect to pipelines have been questioned by pipeline operators, many of whom have cited a need for more specific threat information and a clearer definition of what assets are "critical" and therefore require special attention.[221]

Summary

It is noteworthy that, although there have been some useful surveys of land transportation operators,[222] compared to the other transportation modes, very little security system performance data is available for the land sector. Thus, evaluations of these systems have tended to be little more than "bean counts" of inputs (money spent, cameras deployed, etc.) rather than an analysis of their effectiveness.

Summing up the current state of land transportation security efforts, a February 2003 assessment by the Dartmouth Institute for Security Technology Studies reported that, "A non-prohibitive, cost efficient security strategy for surface transportation has yet to be developed," and "efforts to secure surface transportation systems have only minimally reduced the risk of terrorist attacks."[223] The DHS IG reported in December 2004 that TSA "is moving slowly to improve security in the surface transportation modes,"[224] and reaffirmed that finding at the end of 2005.[225] Writing shortly after he left the job of DHS Inspector General, Clark Kent Ervin was more direct in noting, "too little attention has been paid and too few resources devoted to modes of transportation other than aviation."[226]

Part Three: Where Do We Go From Here?

8 "Looking Back to Look Forward": The Post-9/11 Policy Failure of Transportation Security

The primary failure on 9/11 was a systemic one involving the institutions and defenses responsible for U.S. civil aviation security. That failure was, in part, the product of the system's history, as well as the specific circumstances surrounding the 9/11 hijackings. Furthermore, all elements of the system, including not only the FAA and the airlines but also the Congress and other key elements of the executive branch, participated in and contributed to the failure.

In spite of the massive increase in attention and resources devoted to transportation—especially aviation—security in the wake of the 9/11 catastrophe, in spite of some improvements in areas such as checked bag screening, onboard aircraft security procedures, the conduct of threat and vulnerability assessments (of variable quality) for a variety of transportation modes and assets, and a start to better air and maritime cargo security, many of the 9/11 systemic weaknesses continue.

- *Reactivity and incident-driven decision making still predominate in transportation security*, evident in the ongoing focus on passenger aviation, the (short-lived) priority afforded to rail and transit security after the 2004 Madrid and 2005 London bombings, the limited use of rule making in making permanent revisions in the transportation security "baseline," and the absence of strong policy planning.
- *The clash of security with other societal imperatives, including consumer convenience, citizen rights, and taxpayer and shareholder satisfaction*, continues to strongly influence the performance of the transportation security system. Although there is no formal "dual mandate" for TSA, countervailing pressures can still be seen within the current aviation security program, whether in the form of arbitrary Congressional

limits on the screener workforce driven by budgetary pressures, or the abandonment of the more ambitious CAPPS II airline passenger prescreening system in the face of strong opposition from privacy advocates. Outside of aviation, the Customs and Border Protection division, the Coast Guard, and the various land transportation modal authorities face their own dual mandates in trying to balance the newly received security mission with their older, more established, and far better funded "legacy" or core missions.[1]

- *The system of shared responsibilities and dispersed accountability that marked the 9/11 aviation security system remains in force today for all transportation security efforts.* For land transportation, this model has been explicitly adopted and numerous "gray areas" of uncertain jurisdiction continue to exist in the other modes. Even in passenger aviation, the one area where the federal government has accepted primary responsibility, clearly paralleling pre-9/11 FAA attitudes, "TSA views the individual air carriers as responsible for establishing performance goals and measures for their (crew member security) training programs, but has not required them to do so."[2] The apparent abandonment of ATSA's vision of TSA as *the* federal agency responsible for, as its name indicates, transportation security, as well as the loss by DHS of certain intelligence coordination functions envisioned for it in the Homeland Security Act, has actually led to a post-9/11 proliferation of federal agencies responsible, and presumably accountable, for discrete elements of transportation and homeland security. Furthermore, as before, all elements of the system—including federal agencies, the White House and OMB, the Congress, and state, local and industry stakeholders—continue to share in contributing to its weaknesses.

- *The layered approach to transportation security, under which the failure of a single component does not lead to a systemwide failure, that was the goal of both the pre- and post-9/11 aviation security systems[3] and is a key attribute of effective transportation security in general[4]continues to be honored more in the breach than the observance.* Such layers are either flawed (still the case with all of the aviation security layers), incomplete (for example, air cargo is largely reliant on industry-funded and implemented security, just like pre-9/11 passenger aviation security, and container security—perhaps the single most important component of maritime security—is overwhelmingly reliant on a single security layer: prescreening of cargo) or virtually nonexistent (with respect to all land modes with the partial exception of mass transit).

- *As was true on 9/11, security is still not being engineered into and integrated with basic transportation operations.* A 2002 report from the National Research Council of the National Academies of Science highlighted the importance of both the preceding point (on layering) and this one:

> Transportation security is best-achieved through well-conceived security systems that are integrated with transportation operations.... Moreover, layered security features that are well integrated with operations and confer multiple benefits, such as enhanced safety and operating efficiency, are likely to be maintained and improved over time.[5]

Although evidence for such integration is lacking for aviation and maritime security as well, the most glaring example is to be found in land transportation. Remembering that the proposed FY2006 federal budget for securing this entire mode totaled $135 million (1.4 percent of all federal transportation security spending), it is noteworthy that the legislation to reauthorize the single largest federal investment in transportation—grants for highway construction and safety, and public transit—contains almost nothing in the way of security design or performance standards. The land transportation legislation, signed into law by the President on August 10, 2005, authorizes grants totaling $286 billion through 2009,[6] of which a little more than $30 million is statutorily required to be spent for security purposes (1 percent of the Urbanized Formula Grant for mass transit systems).[7]

- *Transportation security is not being handled as a national security issue.* In its Final Report the Gore Commission observed that terrorists "know that airlines are often seen as national symbols. When terrorists attack an American airline, they are attacking the United States." For these reasons that Commission stated that the federal government should consider aviation security as a "national security issue."[8] The level of funding and policy approach previously described clearly indicate that as of September 11, 2001, this goal had not been achieved, and, aside from checkpoint and baggage screening, there is little indication, in the form of either resource allocation or policy attention, that the federal government is currently treating either aviation security or transportation security as a whole as matters of national security, and deserving of priority attention.

In spite of its proposed increase in funding for aviation and maritime security, the Administration's FY2006 budget was reminiscent, in a number of respects, of the pre-9/11 mindset. Thus, "In protecting America, the Federal Government must defeat terrorism before it reaches our shores,"[9] indicating the focus is "over there." Or, "Private owners remain responsible for security" of most critical infrastructure.[10] And, finally, even in the case of aviation, the one area of transportation where the federal government has accepted primary responsibility, the budget reaffirms the pre-9/11 philosophy that system users rather than the general treasury should shoulder most of the burden for financing security measures, specifically by more than doubling (from $2.50 to $5.50) the typical fee on aviation passengers.[11]

Thus, the systemic flaws of pre-9/11 transportation security efforts have persisted, but with one important difference. It was asked earlier whether more security-conscious leadership could have been able to improve civil aviation defenses sufficiently to have thwarted the 9/11 hijackings. The FAA's Baseline Working Group (BWG), which in 1996 called for a quantum increase in federal aviation security activities, was cited as just such an opportunity. But in the pre-9/11 world, the BWG was doomed to fail, with neither the White House, nor the Congress, nor the American public prepared to accept the financial costs and inconveniences its recommendations would have entailed.

However, 9/11 was a watershed event, and in its aftermath there was a sea change in attitudes toward the terrorist threat and the priority to be attached to homeland security. And the national leadership has responded with a multibillion-dollar increase in federal expenditures, and a raft of policy initiatives, including the Aviation and Transportation Security Act of 2001, the Maritime Transportation Security Act of 2002, the Homeland Security Act of 2002, the creation of the National Commission on Terrorist Attacks Upon the United States also in 2002, and, most recently, the Intelligence Reform and Terrorism Prevention Act of 2004. It has clearly become possible to do much more to bolster transportation security than was ever the case prior to 2001.

If significant systemic problems persist in aviation and transportation security, as the available evidence indicates, the post-9/11 failure is, then, one of policy and national policy makers.

9   Key Questions, Hard Choices

The terrorist threat was not, and is not, only "over there." In February 2005 testimony to Congress, FBI Director Robert Mueller indicated that transportation systems and nuclear power plants continue to be major targets for al Qaeda and that his top concern is "the threat from covert operatives who may be inside the U.S."[1] At the same hearing, acting DHS Deputy Secretary Loy testified, "We realized that an attack here could come in any form, at any place, on any timetable."[2] And the anthrax attacks in the fall of 2001 not only highlighted the nation's vulnerability to biological weapons, but also demonstrated that a major terrorist act need not involve a sophisticated organization but could be carried out by a single, unaffiliated individual.[3] No matter how successful our preventive or preemptive military actions abroad, we will have to expend considerable effort and resources here at home, and our policies and institutions must be adjusted accordingly.

Much as our history, between two great oceans, and our institutions—which have evolved in a manner that makes a sharp distinction between "national defense" and "homeland security" and between "law enforcement" and "counterterrorism"—may predispose us to focus our attention overseas, with less attendant disruption in the daily lives of American citizens and less cost to American taxpayers and businesses, the realities of the terrorist threat of the twenty-first century would seem to dictate that this conflict must be waged every bit as aggressively and with at least as much commitment (financial and otherwise) on the home front.

To truly be successful in avoiding the mistakes of the past and preparing to meet an unknown future, any plan for improving transportation security, whether from TSA or DHS, the Congress, or any outside source, must face up to and provide appropriate answers for three fundamental policy questions. Without better guidance as to their authorities, roles, and funding sources, neither DHS, nor TSA, nor the other components of transportation security will be able to succeed, regardless of the best efforts of their workforces.

Balance

The first key policy question is, *how is security to be prioritized, and balanced with other societal imperatives, including fiscal responsibility, economic efficiency, and civil liberties?*

Homeland security is unquestionably a preeminent priority for any national government and, perhaps, should be the single highest priority. But, whatever the political rhetoric, it cannot be, and certainly is not now for the U.S. government, the sole priority whose pursuit overrides all competing claims.

Before 9/11, many, many other values were allowed to outweigh security considerations with respect to aviation security. For example, prior to 9/11, the CAPPS program was a prime means for targeting limited security resources on airline passengers who posed the greatest potential risk. However, the consequences for selection by CAPPS were limited to inspections of checked bags and, thus, totally ineffective against hijacking because they provided for no additional scrutiny of a selectee's person or carry-on items, in large part because passenger convenience was afforded the higher priority by the FAA, the Congress, the airlines, and the flying public. In the final analysis, it was easier to compromise security than to engage in a difficult national debate on the hard, but achievable, task of simultaneously protecting lives and civil liberties.

Although in the immediate aftermath of 9/11, it was perhaps true that the country and its leaders were willing to subordinate other competing budgetary and policy priorities to homeland security needs, with the passage of time and in the absence of further incidents, these other claims have predictably, and necessarily, reasserted themselves. As Stephen Flynn observed, security measures "are not sustainable if they clash with the freedoms of the populace or work in direct opposition to the imperatives of the marketplace."[4] It is worth remembering "the steady bleeding of the U.S. economy is one of al Qaeda's main objectives in its war against America."[5]

Thus, TSA has had to back away from the more ambitious CAPPS II program for targeting aviation security resources and continues to stumble in its attempts to move forward with the scaled-back Secure Flight program, because of its inability to successfully address public and Congressional concerns about the program's impact on civil liberties. Congress has limited TSA spending on, and deployment of, checkpoint screeners and the installation of in-line explosives detection equipment has slowed because of competing budgetary priorities.

A further problem here is what GAO has found to be a "lack of performance measures to determine what [homeland security] activities are intended to achieve and measure progress toward these goals,"[6] thus making it difficult to ascertain exactly how much actual security current efforts have produced.

All of this highlights the fundamental need to debate fully the costs and benefits of proposed security measures and, through our democratic institutions, to determine the proper balance among security for the society, individual rights, personal convenience, and financial cost. There are no easy answers here, and to pretend otherwise, or even worse, to ignore such a need, was an invitation for disaster on 9/11, and continues to be so.

Organization

The second fundamental issue is, *how is transportation security to be organized: who is to be responsible for what?*

One facet of the 9/11 aviation security failure was the lack of accountability afforded by the system of divided responsibilities. Unfortunately, for the most part, little has been accomplished post-9/11 to clarify the situation. In particular, other than for passenger aviation, the security roles and responsibilities of federal, state, local, and private entities over the whole range of transportation modes have gone largely undefined.

The February 2005 Interim National Infrastructure Protection Plan began its very general and nonspecific chapter on the subject by indicating that its "proposed roles and responsibilities . . . are intended to be a starting point for further discussion and engagement" with the various federal and nonfederal stakeholders.[7]

The importance of the private sector "in the design and implementation" of transportation security measures has been acknowledged and cited by TSA officials who describe, à la the Gore Commission, security as a "partnership," under which the agency holds private stakeholders "responsible for their contribution to security."[8]

Yet, the Congressional Budget Office (CBO) found that, based on the limited data available, "relatively little additional [security] spending has come from the private sector." Among the possible explanations for this is the concept of "moral hazard," which describes a situation under which businesses are reluctant to undertake protective measures that are in their own interest because of a belief that someone else will ultimately pay for any damages that are incurred. According to CBO, "In the case of homeland security, the prospect of moral hazard can create a gap between social and private costs if, for example, businesses expect the government to compensate them for major losses from an attack."[9] As former DHS Inspector General Ervin has stated: "Eighty-five percent of America's critical infrastructure is owned by the private sector, which has been reluctant to protect itself (and which the government has been reluctant to prod into protecting itself)."[10]

The preceding survey of the current state of transportation security is full of examples where large questions remain unanswered about the nature and extent of the federal role, including airport access, general aviation, port security, and the entire realm of land transportation.

In addition, important decisions have yet to be made as to how certain transportation security functions are to be handled within the federal government, many of them centering on the future of TSA:

- What is TSA's role vis-à-vis the Coast Guard and the Customs and Border Protection division with respect to maritime security?
- How are land transportation security responsibilities to be divided between TSA and the various DOT modal administrations?
- What is the security role of the DOT Office of Pipeline Safety?
- How will TSA ensure that the research and development resources transferred from it to DHS' Science and Technology directorate remain focused on applied research that takes into account both the security and operational realities and needs of transportation systems?
- How is DHS to be involved, with the Terrorist Screening Center and the Terrorist Threat Integration Center, in the terrorist watch list process?
- And, perhaps above all, what is TSA's long-term organizational future?

As discussed earlier, there have been a number of indications that TSA may be eliminated or, at the very least, severely restricted in size and scope. To be sure, the agency was created in haste, in the immediate legislative reply to the 9/11 hijackings, and little thought was given as to how it would, or should, fulfill its responsibilities for the security of nonaviation modes. Even so, there were (and are) good arguments to be made for the original goal of uniting all federal transportation security efforts under one roof.

A single transportation security agency offers, in principle, the opportunity for comprehensive assessment of risks and assignment of priorities not only across the various modes, but also including the numerous, and often vital, intermodal connections among them. It affords (or *could* afford) the chance for clarification of the federal role and closer coordination of federal transportation security efforts. By being an agency whose primary mission is quite clearly security, it avoids the problem faced by the pre-9/11 FAA, or indeed by the Coast Guard and land modal administrations today, of seeing security subordinated to other objectives, including passenger convenience or competing organizational priorities. And, by being focused on transportation, it has the potential for developing the kind of expertise in transportation systems and operations that would allow it to best find the proper, and sustainable, balance between security and efficiency. Finally, a single agency allows for clearer accountability in placing full responsibility for transportation security performance in one place.

The fact that TSA has not, to date, achieved, or even approached achieving, any of these attributes, does not mean that they are unattainable or should be shunted aside without further effort. But even if that were the case, the issue of how to optimize the organization of federal transportation security efforts should receive full and open debate in public and within the halls of Congress.

It was hoped that the transportation security plan called for by the 9/11 Commission and mandated by the Intelligence Reform and Terrorism Prevention Act of 2004 would answer such questions. That was clearly the Commission's intent when it recommended, "The plan should assign roles and missions to the relevant authorities (federal, state, regional, and local) and to private stakeholders."[11] However, whereas most of the strategic plan components advocated by the Commission were retained in the new law, this element was modified so that the plan now, "sets forth the agreed upon roles and missions of federal, state, regional, and local authorities and establishes mechanisms for encouraging private sector cooperation and participation in the implementation of such plan."[12] In the absence of more detailed guidance than was contained in the National Strategy for Transportation Security unveiled in September 2005 as to how the governmental roles are to be "agreed upon," or of how the private sector *role* will be defined, it therefore remains to be seen whether this document will significantly clarify the current muddle.

In the end, the key measure of the effectiveness of the strategic plan, or any other effort to delineate responsibilities for transportation security, will be the extent to which the federal role is detailed. The other governmental and private stakeholders can, and likely will, adjust their approaches once the federal government indicates what it will, and as importantly, what it will not do with respect to transportation security. The federal government cannot, and should not, be expected to "do it all," but the following pre-9/11 comments with respect to aviation security, penned by Israeli security expert Ariel Merari, are relevant to today's situation in transportation security as a whole:

> To put the burden of security on the shoulders of the airline companies is bureaucratically an easy solution, which is a recipe for the perpetuation of the existing unsatisfactory state of affairs. Governments must recognize their comprehensive responsibility for aviation security and shoulder their task.[13]

Funding

The final key question is, *how are security measures to be funded: who will pay?*

Of all of the impediments to improved security, this one appears particularly intractable under current circumstances. Perhaps foremost among these is a likely federal budget crunch. CBO's "Budget and Economic Outlook: Fiscal Years 2006 to 2015," issued in January 2005, reported that, leaving aside uncertain funding levels for operations in Afghanistan and Iraq, "the total deficit projected for the 2005–2014 period has grown by more than $500 billion." Furthermore, to achieve even this result, the CBO estimates assumed that discretionary spending, under which almost all homeland security spending falls, will decline from 7.6 percent of Gross Domestic Product (GDP) in 2005, to 5.6 percent by 2015. (Mandatory programs, such as Social Security and Medicare, were projected to grow from 54 percent of total federal spending to 62 percent over that same time frame.) And the CBO projections assumed that the tax cuts currently scheduled to expire in 2010 will not be extended and made permanent, as requested by the President.[14]

In an update to Congress two months later, a CBO witness testified that if the President's tax and spending proposals as contained in the FY2006 budget request were adopted, the ten-year deficit for FY2006–2015 would be $2.58 *trillion*, or $1.6 *trillion* above the level that would occur otherwise.[15] A further CBO update in August 2005 forecast that higher than anticipated revenues would likely reduce the previously predicted deficits in the short run, but "the fiscal outlook for the coming decade remains about the same" as in the earlier estimates.[16] And this was before the September 2005 announcement by President Bush of a massive reconstruction plan to help Louisiana and Mississippi recover from the severe damage caused by Hurricane Katrina. Although the President did not cite the anticipated cost, other officials estimated the price tag at over $200 billion, which will produce much larger deficits over the next few years.[17]

The private sector faces its own challenges in finding the resources to pay for security measures. For example, the airline industry has still not recovered financially from the aftermath of the 9/11 attacks. Certain smaller, low-cost airlines like Southwest or JetBlue have posted positive earnings, but the larger companies continue to run in the red.[18] And these losses have persisted up to the present, with the industry as a whole projecting a shortfall of $9 billion to $10 billion in 2005.[19]

GAO set forth the broader problem facing all transportation modes in May 2005 testimony to Congress.

> Where the money will come from is unclear. In our 2002 statement on national preparedness, we highlighted the need to examine the sustainability of

increased funding . . . for homeland security efforts. . . . The current economic environment makes this a difficult time for private industry and state and local governments to make security investments and sustain increased security costs. According to industry representatives and experts we contacted, most of the transportation industry operates on a very thin profit margin, making it difficult to pay for additional security measures.[20]

From the pre-9/11 aviation security system where documented screening performance shortcomings went unfixed and mandated explosives detection systems went undeployed in large part because of the unresolved question of how those measures should be financed, all the way through to the November 2004 legislation implementing the 9/11 Commission recommendations, which deleted the Commission's requirement that the national transportation security plan provide a means for adequately funding its security measures,[21] this particular "hard question" has not so much been poorly answered as *ignored* by federal policy makers. Even today, the primary federal security efforts for air cargo, ports, and mass transit are little more than unfunded mandates.[22]

As demonstrated over and over again in the survey of the current state of transportation security, failure to address the problem does not make it go away. In the absence of clear cost-allocation decisions by the federal government, efforts to increase security investments in airport access control, airline flight crew security training, general aviation, port security, rail transportation, mass transit, highways, bridges, tunnels, and pipelines will continue to be deferred and/or denied.

In the final analysis, a failure to make a formal decision on who pays for security is, in fact, a decision that no one will have to pay. And the failure of the federal government to assume a significant share of transportation security costs other than for passenger aviation is a telling indicator of the actual priority attached to such efforts.[23]

10 Principles for Action

Unless these foregoing fundamental questions are effectively addressed, transportation security efforts are doomed to flounder. But, though they are a necessary prerequisite for better security, they alone are not a sufficient guide to policy makers. For that, it is useful to look at the lessons learned and the policy recommendations made by the many commissions and other organizations that have examined aviation and transportation security in recent years.

National Security

Transportation security must be regarded as a national security issue. The Pan Am/Lockerbie and Gore Commissions, among others, highlighted the national security dimensions of civil aviation. Most of the factors underlying that judgment apply to the other transportation modes as well. Terrorists have demonstrated both the interest in and the capability of attacking maritime and land modes; and the economic, psychological, and other consequences of such attacks could certainly be national in impact. The federal government has seemingly accepted such logic via the creation of TSA and DHS and their mandate to secure all modes of transportation.

But the available facts would appear to contradict the notion that transportation security is actually being treated as a matter of national security, whether viewed in terms of budgetary priority or the continuing failure to address the three fundamental policy questions just posed.

This treatment of homeland security as something distinct from "national defense" only reinforces the impression that, apart from speechmaking, homeland security measures are still not being treated as matters of real national security. The $29 billion in the Administration's FY2006 budget proposal for the Department of Homeland Security represented only 3.5 percent of the total federal budget for discretionary spending.[1] Though significantly more than pre-9/11 funding levels for these programs, it stands in sharp contrast to the $400 billion allocated to the Department of Defense, and is more in line with the amounts budgeted for the Departments of Housing and Urban Development ($32 billion) and Veterans Affairs ($31 billion).[2]

Several of the recommendations of the 9/11 Commission's aviation and transportation security staff dealt with this national security issue. One in particular (Recommendation 1.2, Appendix A) indicated that, "Both the legislative and executive branches of the federal government should ensure that transportation security receives the appropriate share of homeland/national security spending—resources that should be allocated based on what is necessary to maximize the security of the American people against the most serious threats."

If transportation security is, in fact, a *national security* issue, it is imperative that the artificial budget and policy distinctions between "national defense" and "homeland security" be eliminated so that security and counterterrorism efforts at home and abroad can be better integrated and that a more comprehensive assessment can be undertaken as to the optimum allocation of roles and resources to best secure the people of the United States.

Risk Management

Risk management must guide decision making. It is certainly true that, based on historical experience, civil aviation seems likely to remain *one* of the major targets for terrorists and, thus, should command some degree of prioritization with respect to policies and resources. However, one need look no further than the 2004 terrorist attack on commuter rail in Spain—which produced high consequences from many different perspectives—or indeed to the September 11, 2001, suicide hijackings in the United States—which represented a new tactic in scope and methodology—to discern the dangers of invoking historical precedent as the only guideline in prioritizing efforts against nonstate terrorist adversaries. As has been shown, focusing on the most recent incident was, and is, a hallmark of the civil aviation security system, up to and after 9/11/01.

Under these circumstances, it is imperative that TSA and DHS develop a sound approach for making appropriate decisions with respect to setting priorities, both budgetary and otherwise. With all due respect, and taking into account the enormous start-up challenges facing both of these entities, this is one requirement that should not be allowed to slip. In its absence, which the foregoing analysis of current transportation security policy making suggests is most definitely the case at present, neither the agencies, nor the Administration, nor the Congress, nor the public can properly evaluate critical decisions that are being made every day with respect to the large increase in federal funding that has been made available—for now at least—to support homeland security. Questions such as the optimum number (and therefore cost) of airport checkpoint screeners, or Federal Air Marshals, or port security assessments, or canine teams for mass transit, or transportation security intelligence analysts should not be made in isolation. Yet, at present, there does not appear to be any more of a basis for TSA to prioritize across all transportation modes than there was for FAA to do so within aviation security. This is where risk assessment is supposed to come in.

The GAO has been at the forefront of organizations urging federal agencies, especially within the Departments of Defense and Homeland Security, to move toward more comprehensive risk management principles. GAO's testimony to the 9/11 Commission at its very first public hearing in New York City on April 1, 2003, indicated that

> To achieve transportation security as well as homeland security, it will be important to effectively manage the risks posed by terrorist threats and direct national resources to the areas of highest priority. We have advocated the use of a risk management approach to better prepare for and withstand terrorist threats.[3]

Risk management in the field of security is comprised of three main elements:

- *Threat assessment*, which "identifies and evaluates potential threats on the basis of factors such as capabilities, intentions, and past activities."
- *Vulnerability assessment*, which "identifies weaknesses that may be exploited by identified threats and suggests options to address those weaknesses."
- *Criticality (or consequence) assessment*, which "evaluates and prioritizes assets and functions in terms of specific criteria, such as their importance to public safety and the economy."[4]

Although threat assessment is, of course, a key component, as the GAO pointed out in testimony to the Congress, "We will never know whether we have identified every threat, nor will we have complete information about the threats we have identified. Consequently, we believe the other two elements of the [risk management] approach, vulnerability assessments and criticality assessments, are essential and required to prepare better against terrorist attacks."[5] Additionally, threat assessment by itself does not offer decision makers the full range of information necessary to make appropriate decisions on resource allocation and priority setting.

More troubling than the absence of a fully deployed, across-the-board risk management system, an achievement that may indeed be years in the making, is the apparent inability of DHS and TSA to take even modest steps in that direction. For example, in early 2002, Congress mandated that DHS develop a plan for devising a national risk assessment of critical infrastructure, with a reporting deadline of December 15, 2003. Not only was this deadline missed, but, with the issuance of HSPD-7 in December of 2003, the Administration extended it to the end of 2004 (a deadline that was also missed). When a draft final plan was at last produced in November 2005, it contained few specifics and merely aimed at establishing "the risk management framework."[6] A DHS official testified to Congress that the actual infrastructure analysis could take up to five years to complete.[7]

Furthermore, as was discussed earlier, TSA does not seem to be working toward any kind of risk assessment that will allow it to prioritize investments and countermeasures across transportation modes, preferring instead to focus on assessments of individual risk within a given component of the transportation sector (Secure Flight, TWIC, "known shipper," etc.). Although the latter is very valuable in its own right with respect to allocating a given level of screening resources, for example, it does not assist with the larger question of prioritizing allocations among competing countermeasures (or agencies).

The 2002 Report of an Independent Task Force Sponsored by the Council on Foreign Relations (Hart–Rudman Task Force), entitled "America—Still Unprepared, Still in Danger," included as one of its "Key Recommendations" a charge to the federal government to "Recalibrate the agenda for transportation security; the vulnerabilities are greater and the stakes are higher in the sea and land modes than commercial aviation."[8] While there may be merit to the substance of this argument, the bigger point at present is that DHS and TSA lack, and seemingly will continue to lack for the foreseeable future, the ability to address such a charge, or to argue convincingly for the current allocation, which weights one layer of one mode (screening of civil aviation passengers and baggage) well above all other layers and all other modes.

As summarized by the December 2004 joint white paper by the Heritage Foundation and CSIS:

> In the three years since the September 11 attacks, our nation has created the third largest bureaucracy in the federal government and spent close to $100 billion on efforts to secure the homeland from further attack. Yet we still have not completed a threat/vulnerability assessment that can help to develop strategy, set priorities, and guide spending.... Many officials have

recognized the need for such an assessment and it has been promised for years. The latest DHS estimate is that such a study will be completed by 2008, but America cannot wait that long.[9]

Two examples from December 2005 illustrate both the persistence and consequences of the continuing inadequacies in federal risk management for homeland security. On December 2, TSA announced that, after a "risk-based" assessment of its airport checkpoint priorities, the agency had decided to devote "more focus on higher threat areas, like explosives" in part by permitting scissors and certain sharp tools onto planes while stepping up random physical searches of passengers.[10] The appropriateness of this policy change was quickly challenged by flight attendants, representatives of the families of victims of the 9/11 attacks, and members of Congress who expressed concern that TSA had failed to adequately factor in the impact on the safety of passengers and cabin crew.[11]

Later in the month, the agency unveiled an ambitious pilot program to deploy "Visible Intermodal Protection and Response" (VIPER) teams, which would include federal air marshals and canine explosives detection units, at a small number of select rail and ferry systems.[12] However, the effort was scaled back almost immediately in the face of concerns about coordination with local officials and the effects on aviation security. This led one transportation security expert to comment that, in the continued absence of a completed comprehensive risk assessment of all transportation modes, "we really don't have a good idea how much we ought to be allocating to air versus rail versus other modes of transportation."[13]

Comprehensiveness

All transportation modes and intermodal connections must be addressed. The ability to look at and systematically plan for securing all modes is a vital, but yet-to-be-realized, aspect of homeland security if TSA and DHS are to succeed in developing the kind of layered security system called for by the Hart–Rudman Task Force "that focuses on the entire logistics and intermodal transportation network rather than an unintegrated series of tactics aimed at addressing vulnerabilities" in individual components of the transportation system.[14]

The Transportation Research Board of the National Academies of Science described the state of affairs after the passage of ATSA:

> The advent of TSA should be helpful in increasing the attention paid to security within the transportation community, but perhaps not in overcoming the bias of viewing transportation assets and operations within functional domains.... A broad-based understanding of terrorist threats that involve transportation and its intersection with other domains is clearly needed if the

transportation community is to do its job in keeping its systems from being exploited again [by terrorists] to such tragic effect.[15]

If anything, the moves to reduce the role of TSA would appear to take us even further from achieving the comprehensive approach called for by the Hart-Rudman Task Force and the Transportation Research Board. The de facto current arrangement, under which TSA is primarily responsible for passenger aviation security, the Coast Guard and CBP share responsibility for port security, and state, local, and private stakeholders play the predominant part in all other modes, means that some entity has to play a strong coordinating role to set and enforce priorities and to make sure that nothing falls between the intermodal "cracks." If TSA is not to fulfill this mission, apparently it will be left to DHS, which, as we have seen, has experienced many problems in exercising policy coordination even among its existing responsibilities.

Attempting to fix the "top" of the policy chain with respect to cross-modal coordination and priority setting is key, but so is renewed recognition of the FAA's 1996 Baseline Working Group recommendation that the civil aviation security system should

> develop a comprehensive "team" approach to security that treats aviation industry employees as team members with a stake in promoting aviation security, emphasizing that employees are the first line of defense . . . [and that security training programs should strive] to keep employees involved in, and informed of, aviation security and build a better understanding of the system.[16]

The 9/11 Commission aviation and transportation security staff recommended that such a team perspective should be adopted for the other modes as well (Recommendation 3.4, Appendix A), and that

> TSA should ensure that all transportation workers receive training in how to recognize, report and respond to suspicious activity and terrorist attack. Such training should include behavior pattern recognition. More specifically and as a start, TSA should design, develop and begin implementation of mandatory, comprehensive, industry-wide anti-terrorism and basic self-defense training for all flight attendants. Because the agency and air carriers have thus far failed to do so, despite the urging of legislation, if TSA does not take such action by December 31, 2004, Congress should consider transferring jurisdiction for this program to the Justice Department, with a statutory mandate to implement this training requirement by April 1, 2005. Furthermore, because such anti-terrorist training is, inherently, a matter of national security, the federal government should assume a fair share of the cost. (Recommendation 3.4.1, Appendix A)

Security training has come to be recognized as a necessary component of many transportation security programs. However, in spite of a number of complaints about the content and quality of this training, including for flight attendants and transit security employees,[17] with the exception of the extensively studied training of airport checkpoint screeners, little has been done to evaluate its effectiveness. That needs to change.

Sustainability

Security measures must be sustainable. In its "Security Manual for Safeguarding Civil Aviation Against Acts of Unlawful Interference," the International Civil Aviation Organization (ICAO) identified sustainability, which it defined as "a State having the political will and accompanying capability to maintain appropriate reliable security measures," as an important aspect of viable aviation security, and noted further that "Without the commitment to sustain effective aviation security measures, the efficacy of the other principles is diminished."[18]

The entire history of civil aviation security has demonstrated how difficult it has proven to adhere to this principle. The pattern of incident, followed by response with heightened attention, followed by gradual diminution of perceived threat and security effort, is almost certain to be repeated as the events of September 11 recede in memory. As one analyst put it, "This [current] zero-risk mentality is as unsustainable as our pre-September 11 no-security policy. Eventually, Congress and the American public will be forced to confront the fact that there simply isn't enough money to fund every security program, nor is it possible to completely eliminate the risk of another terrorist attack."[19]

When faced with a similar quandary after the foiling of the Bojinka plot in 1995, when the civil aviation security system had become increasingly reliant on ad hoc, "temporary" Security Directives and Emergency Amendments to the air carrier and airport standard security programs, and when significant increases in security measures required the all too hard to come by "specific and credible" intelligence threat reports, the FAA created the Baseline Working Group (BWG) to try to raise the standard, "baseline" security level that would be obtained systemwide in the absence of specific threats or disasters. Though, as discussed previously, the BWG was overtaken by events (the crash of TWA 800, the appointment of the Gore Commission, and the determination by NTSB that the TWA 800 crash was likely to have been the result of accidental equipment failure), the concept of an unexceptional baseline standard of security—which all users of the system can rely on—continues to be a sound one, not only for aviation, but for all transportation modes. Only such an approach will be effective and sustainable over time.

Although one cannot fault calls, such as the one Admiral James Loy made to the 9/11 Commission, that "we find a way to hold a sense of urgency, to sort of keep the edge,"[20] it is not sound policy to depend on extraordinary levels of alert and their corresponding security measures to provide for the nation's security. To do so would be to pin one's hopes on changing the nature of human beings and institutions. As a practical matter, no individual, institution, or system can sustain themselves at high alert indefinitely, and if expected to, the high alert level necessarily abates. Over the long haul, when people, institutions, and systems are maintained at extraordinary levels of alert without an incident, the risk of complacency actually increases.

But how does one simultaneously defeat these seemingly contradictory enemies, and avert both complacency and unsustainable high alert? I believe the answer lies in two steps: 1. Establishing and maintaining a reasonable but constant security "baseline." 2. Providing realistic threat and vulnerability information to key stakeholders and the public, in a regular and effective manner, allowing both government and people to make more realistic risk assessments (to be discussed in the following sections).

In the long run, and unfortunately there is nothing to indicate that the fight against the terrorists will be anything but a long-term struggle, the United States must put its faith and efforts in building an adequate "ordinary" security baseline, one that encompasses all transportation and related infrastructure modes, and not just aviation security.

The elements of such a baseline can be found in the 2002 National Research Council (NRC) report, *Making America Safer*. Though the NRC presented these comments in the context of providing principles for use in deploying science and technology on behalf of homeland security, they offer a useful blueprint for the kind of comprehensive transportation security baseline envisioned here.

- Identify and repair the weakest links in vulnerable systems and infrastructures.
- Use "circuit-breakers" to isolate and stabilize failing system elements.
- Build security into basic system designs where possible.
- Build flexibility into systems so that they can be modified to address unforeseen threats.
- Search for technologies that reduce costs or provide ancillary benefits to civil society to ensure a sustainable effort against terrorist threats.[21]

The NRC report elaborated on the last point.

By working with transportation system owners, operators and users in exploring alternative security concepts, TSA will be better able to identify opportunities for conjoining security with other objectives, such as improving shipment and luggage tracking. Such multiuse, multibenefit systems have a greater chance of being adopted, maintained and improved.[22]

The number of potential "ancillary benefits" is quite large in the realm of transportation security, ranging from improving the physical safety and security of transportation system employees and customers against nonterrorist criminal acts, to reducing the opportunities for cargo theft across all transportation modes. For example, in the case of mass transit, "since fear of crime is among the most often reported reasons for not using transit, any personal crime reduction is likely to far outweigh security benefits" of security measures.[23]

The 9/11 Commission aviation and transportation security staff made a series of proposals for building security into transportation systems, including the issuance of standards by DHS or TSA "to ensure that new and remodeled transportation facilities, equipment, and related infrastructure are designed, constructed, operated, and maintained to promote security and minimize the adverse consequences of terrorist attack" (Recommendation 3.6, Appendix A), and the empanelment of transportation security experts "to develop and prioritize appropriate design criteria to promote security of passengers, conveyances and facilities" (Recommendation 3.6.1, Appendix A).

In addition, the Commission staff specifically addressed the previously cited security-enhancing opportunity afforded, but not yet realized, in the reauthorization of surface transportation grant programs.

> Congress should consider amending the surface transportation reauthorization bill to add the promotion of homeland security into the basic purposes of the law; requiring the states to submit (in a reasonable time frame) their plans for beginning to "build" security into their surface transportation programs; and/or authorizing certain high priority security-related proposals. We recognize that the surface transportation reauthorization bill is well along in the legislative process and that comprehensive revision as recommended would be difficult. However, given that the bill provides the largest single federal investment in transportation infrastructure; that it is multi-year and will not be due for re-authorization for five years; and that it covers transportation modes that are not the focus of current federal transportation security efforts, it represents an opportunity that we cannot afford to miss. (Recommendation 3.6.3, Appendix A)

Last, there are indications that TSA has provided insufficient attention to its regulatory and enforcement duties,[24] which were for FAA and are and will be for TSA or any successor, a linchpin of "ordinary" security measures. Although transfers and other program changes make exact year-to-year comparisons difficult, it would appear that the TSA budget for airport regulation and enforcement suffered an actual decline in funding between FY2004 and FY2005.[25] Furthermore, the Congress has placed an even lower priority on these functions. For example, in action on the FY2006 DHS Appropriations bill, both houses made cuts in the Administration's request for funding and staff levels for aviation regulation and enforcement, and airport management.[26]

This lack of focus is especially troubling given that TSA was explicitly provided with expedited rule-making authority under ATSA,[27] an authority that has been little used since its establishment. Furthermore, under current plans for nonaviation modes, rule making is to be the key component of TSA's and DHS' security efforts.[28] Therefore, TSA (and the Congress) should devote more attention and resources to improving the agency's regulatory and enforcement capabilities.

Information Sharing

Information sharing must be improved. Reports by both the Markle Foundation[29] and the Century Foundation,[30] the January 2005 designation by GAO of homeland security information sharing as "high risk,"[31] and the December 2005 finding by the DHS IG that "creating a single infrastructure for effective communications and information exchange at various classification levels within the Department remains a major management challenge for DHS,"[32] document a continuing unmet need to improve the flow of information in the field of homeland security, including transportation systems. On the one hand, this is perhaps not surprising given the complexity of the task. On the other hand, the clearest, and most unchallenged, lesson growing out of the 9/11 disaster was in this very area.

FAA security and intelligence officials told the 9/11 Commission, as well as the special Congressional Joint Committee on Intelligence Community Activities Before and After the Terrorist Attacks of September 11, 2001 (also known as the Joint Inquiry), that the intelligence community did not share important information with them, especially with respect to domestic threats. The leadership of the FAA and the airlines indicated that they lacked specific threat information upon which policy could be changed and security tightened.[33]

The January 2005 GAO report cited continuing problems in homeland security information sharing, including inadequate planning by DHS and the absence of clear procedures for disseminating necessary information to the private sector, and concluded "a great deal of work remains to effectively implement the many actions called for to improve homeland security information sharing."[34]

The 9/11 Commission and its staff, the Markle Foundation, and the Century Foundation made a number of recommendations to address the existing information sharing and coordination problem, that, taken together, offer a comprehensive solution to current difficulties.

1. The 9/11 Commission proposed that "the sharing and uses of information must be guided by a set of practical policy guidelines that

simultaneously empower and constrain officials, telling them clearly what is and is not permitted."[35]

2. The Markle Foundation called on DHS "to improve the two-way flow of terrorism-related information between government and industry," by expanding the scope of all industry-created Information Sharing and Analysis Centers (ISACs) "to include focus on terrorism-threat information," and encouraging the ISACs to share more information with the government and with each other.[36] The Century Foundation cited the need for DHS to "take the lead establishing clear procedures for providing state and local officials with better information to help guide their own homeland security decisions."[37] And the 9/11 Commission aviation and transportation security staff recommended that DHS, through TSA, work with the various transportation stakeholders, including industry and state and local authorities, to develop a standard architecture for locally generated *suspicious incident reporting* that would allow such information to be shared in a timely and effective manner with federal homeland security and intelligence officials (Recommendation 4.4, Appendix A).

The great challenge, but also the enormous opportunity, of successfully integrating the various components involved, or potentially involved, in collecting transportation security information is illustrated by the fact that apart from a single security layer of a single transportation mode (the federalized aviation passenger and baggage screening workforce), the vast majority of all individuals who are likely to see suspicious incidents, be required to implement or enforce security measures, or respond to security incidents are nonfederal workers, including airline ticket agents, baggage handlers, pilots, and flight attendants, and their counterparts in other transportation modes; local police, fire and rescue personnel; and of course the vast majority of passengers or shippers who are law-abiding and who wish to help in fighting the terrorist threat.

3. With respect to the privacy issue, the Century Foundation proposed that "Congress, the Bush Administration, and the courts need to provide clear guidance about what information can—and should—be collected, how it should be safeguarded, and how long this information should be retained."[38]

4. Per the Markle Foundation,

> Instead of a culture of classification and occasional, post-facto sanitization of classified documents, we need a culture of distribution, in which the rewards go to those whose information has been found most valuable by people across the network. . . . To some extent, this can be seen as an expansion of the current approach of some agencies to producing "tear-line" reports, in which an agency produces a classified version of information with a less classified, or unclassified, version below a tear-line. In our approach, the production of such alternate versions would be commonplace and automatic. And it would be a top priority.[39]

The tear-line was the standard practice with FAA civil aviation security intelligence, though many of those on the receiving end (airlines, airports, local authorities) told the Commission that what they received was neither as frequent nor as detailed as they felt they needed.[40] Although there is some indication that this has improved,[41] it is essential in the transportation arena that a mindset like the one described by the Markle Foundation be fostered and implemented within DHS and TSA.

To address the need for improved dissemination of sensitive information, DHS is in the process of implementing the Homeland Secure Data Network (HSDN), which aims at streamlining and merging the disparate existing systems for sharing classified information into a single, integrated network. HSDN is to "become the major secure information thoroughfare joining together intelligence agencies, law enforcement, disaster management, and front-line disaster response organizations."[42] The new system was supposed to begin operations by the end of 2004, but it was not activated until April 2005. In addition the network is currently operational only within a few DHS agencies and at a total of three nonfederal sites, and under existing plans will not fully connect with state and local authorities for a number of years.[43]

In an April 2005 report, the DHS IG found that the Department "has taken a number of key steps toward the implementation of HSDN," but because of an accelerated deployment schedule, users were not sufficiently involved in defining security requirements and implementation plans, and essential testing was not completed on schedule. As a result, the IG found that DHS does not have assurance that HSDN will be able to satisfy user needs or adequately protect classified information,[44] presumably the most critical missions of the new system.

The Congress too has expressed concerns "that because of insufficient management controls, information that should be in the public domain may be unnecessarily withheld from public scrutiny." The FY2006 DHS appropriations bill required DHS "to provide clear guidance as to what is SSI [Sensitive Security Information, which is withheld from public disclosure] material and what is not."[45]

A distinction must be made, however, between the necessity for facilitating a better flow of *threat-related* information to the various components of the U.S. transportation system, and the equal necessity of preventing the public disclosure of specific *vulnerability* information, which could be exploited by terrorists and others who seek to bring harm.

The major information problem, as documented by the 9/11 Commission, the Joint Inquiry and other reports, was *too little* information being shared with *too few* of the components of the civil aviation system. However, there were (and are) instances of *too much* information being shared with *too many* people (including our terrorist adversaries).

Simply stated, we know that the terrorists watch our transportation systems closely, looking for exploitable vulnerabilities. Some of this is in the form of direct observation of operations, in the form of surveillance or "practice runs."[46] But some of it comes from their searching of publicly available sources, including governmental reports, for signs of security weaknesses.[47]

The problem of too much sharing of security vulnerabilities also appears to have persisted. There has not been a significant change in how the executive branch, the Congress, or the news media approach the issue of security vulnerability disclosure. The December 2004 Heritage Foundation/CSIS report noted that the federal effort to protect "unclassified but security-relevant information" suffers from "no usable definition, no common understanding about how to control it, no agreement on what significance it has for U.S. national security, and no means for adjudicating concerns regarding appropriate levels of protection."[48]

However, in seeking to cloud terrorist awareness of specific security measures and vulnerabilities, policy makers must not take action that would lessen effective oversight and accountability of transportation security policies and personnel. As with privacy and security, reconciling the necessary, but sometimes conflicting, goals of effective oversight and operational security is difficult but must be done.

The 9/11 Commission aviation and transportation security staff made several recommendations on this point, including the following:

> Each House of Congress should designate one Committee or Subcommittee with expertise in transportation security policy to be kept "fully and currently" informed of the status of the transportation security system, including up-to-date information on threats, vulnerabilities, consequences and system performance. This arrangement could follow the model established between the Congressional intelligence oversight committees and the Intelligence Community. In implementing this recommendation, in many cases this Congressional oversight should be conducted in closed sessions. Committees which maintain jurisdiction over non-security aspects of transportation should be routinely updated on security issues, by the Intelligence Committees and the panels with jurisdiction over transportation security to integrate vital security information and considerations into overall policymaking. (Recommendation 5.5, Appendix A)

Public Information

More accurate risk information must be provided to the public. A vital, if sometimes overlooked, part of the utilization of risk management techniques is the effective communication of the process to the ultimate stakeholders, who in our democracy are the people of the United States. In the final analysis, they (and their elected representatives at the federal, state, and local levels) must determine the acceptability of a given risk, which in turn should drive the decision-making process with respect to whether a given countermeasure proceeds. Thus, it is imperative for homeland security policy makers to make sure the public's perceptions of risk (including acceptability levels) are well informed.[49]

The importance of effective communication is especially acute with respect to terrorist threats like the 9/11 attacks. Dennis Mileti, former head of the National Hazards Center at the University of Colorado, observed, "They [the public] delegate the problem of low-probability, high consequence risks to their government. This seems to make sense—until the government fails" to take steps to address such threats.[50]

Carnegie Mellon University sponsored a study of the psychological impact of the 9/11 attacks, based on a survey of a representative sample of 973 Americans taken just after the attacks and then a year later. The results underscore the centrality of risk communication in dealing effectively with the "terror" of terrorism, which is, by definition, a primary goal of terrorists.

- Americans "wildly overestimated" the risk of terrorism right after the 9/11 attacks, with individuals estimating a 20 percent chance that they themselves would be directly affected by a terrorist attack in the next year, and a 48 percent chance that "average Americans" would be affected. As one of the researchers observed, for even the 20 percent estimate to be accurate, the country would have had to encounter a 9/11 attack "every day and then some."
- Those respondents who reported being primarily "angry" about the attacks (the more prevalent response) were more optimistic that future attacks could be prevented, that most Americans faced a low risk of injury from terrorism, and that they personally would be safe.
- Those who were identified as primarily "fearful" were pessimistic about the risks of future attacks, and of their own safety.
- In summary, the researchers indicated that their findings suggested that the government and the news media can, wittingly or not, alter risk perception by making people either fearful or angry. Furthermore, that connection can be employed to better convey the real degree of risk.[51]

The effective communication of risk must, therefore, be made a top priority. The system in use at the present time almost always issues general warnings to the American public at-large, based on limited information, the "mere volume of terrorist communications," and guesswork. Given its nonspecific nature, it provides limited guidance as to what the proper response should be at the local level. (Under these conditions, the State of Arizona announced that its state and local response agencies will not take action based simply on the national threat warning level.)[52]

At a December 2004 meeting of the Homeland Security Advisory Council—created to advise the Secretary of Homeland Security—Secretary Ridge indicated, "We need clearly to take a look at what kind of information do we need to give to the public," as part of the national warning system. Ridge's former chief of staff, Bruce Lawler, stated that the current color-coded alert system has "credibility issues" and may have outlived its purpose. Participating in the same meeting, Massachusetts' Republican Governor, Mitt Romney, criticized the federal government for providing confusing and sometimes conflicting warnings to state and local authorities.[53]

A January 2005 news report observed, "The shift in rhetoric about the dangers posed by terrorists during the inauguration marks the latest retreat from last year's terrorism warnings which, in retrospect, were based largely on faulty intelligence, dated information or—as with the inauguration— an educated guess."[54] And a May 2005 Congressional Research Service report noted, "A perceived lack of coordination in the federal government's warning notification process and inconsistent messages regarding threats to the homeland have led to an erosion of confidence in the information conveyed to the nation."[55]

Furthermore, although the current approach appears to have generated additional public reporting of suspicious incidents—with unclear actual contributions to security—it runs a grave risk of leaving the public unprepared for, and thus exacerbating the consequences of, a future terrorist attack. Defeating the terrorists over the long haul will require not only "hardening" of physical targets, but of the "psychological targets"—the American people—as well.

Figure 10.1 shows that, with the exception of a few occasions when the national threat level was raised to "Orange" (High), the nation has been kept on "Yellow" alert ever since the federal threat advisory system was established in 2002. Not a single day has been classified as "Green" (Low), "Blue" (Guarded), or "Red" (Severe).

The announced intention of DHS to revise its current system to a more targeted approach is a step in the right direction because, otherwise, a permanent, national "Code Yellow" will, inevitably, in time become no more effective or sustainable than was the FAA's long-standing "AVSEC Level III." Disturbingly, the move to make such a change appears to have stalled, and it is important that it be accomplished as expeditiously as possible.[56]

The Heritage Foundation and CSIS called for scrapping the existing system in favor of "regional alerts and specific warnings for different types of industries and infrastructure."[57]

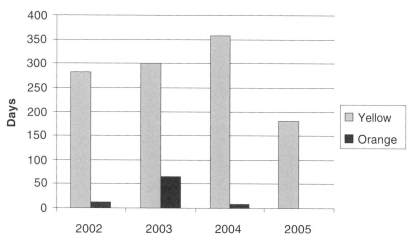

LEGEND:

Yellow = Elevated Threat Level; Orange = High Threat Level

Figure 10.1. Number of Days at Various Nationwide Threat Advisory Levels (March 12, 2002–December 31, 2005)

Notes: 1 Since the federal terrorist advisory system was established in March of 2002, the nationwide threat level has never been set at either the lower (Green=Low, Blue=Guarded) or highest (Red=Severe) ends of the scale. For 98 days (August 1, 2004–November 10, 2004) financial institutions in New York City, Washington, DC, and parts of New Jersey were placed on Orange alert, while the rest of the nation remained at Yellow. Starting on the day of the London subway and bus bombings (July 7, 2005) and continuing for thirty-six days (until August 12, 2005), mass transit systems were placed on Orange alert. These are the only instances to date where the advisory system has given targeted, rather than nationwide, alerts.

Sources: Congressional Research Service, *Homeland Security Advisory System: Possible Issues for Congressional Oversight, Table 2. Homeland Security Advisory Threat Level Changes* (Washington, DC: February 16, 2005), pp. 16–17; and Spencer S. Hsu and Dan Eggen, "Terrorism Alert Level Lowered for Transit," *Washington Post*, August 13, 2005.

The 9/11 Commission transportation security staff recommended, "DHS should develop a comprehensive communication plan to share accurate transportation security risk information with state, local, and tribal authorities, stakeholders, Congress, and the public" (Recommendation 2.6, Appendix A), and that such plan should incorporate the proposal by the National Research Council that, "Appropriate and trusted spokespeople should be identified and trained now so that, if a terrorist attack occurs, the government will be prepared to respond not only by supplying emergency services but also by providing important, accurate, and trustworthy information, clearly, quickly and authoritatively" (Recommendation 2.6.1, Appendix A).[58] Finally, the Commission staff indicated that, "Given the integral role of the news media in disseminating information to the public about threats, attacks and responses involving transportation, emergency exercises at the federal, state and local levels should include news media reporters as active participants whenever possible" (Recommendation 2.6.2, Appendix A).

DHS has moved to address some of these issues. The National Incident Management System (NIMS), which was launched by DHS in March 2004 to create "a unified structure for federal, state, and local lines of government" for response to terrorist attacks, natural disasters and other major emergencies, includes the establishment of Joint Information Systems (JIS) to "provide the public with timely and accurate incident information and unified public messages."[59]

The Department also initiated, with the Ad Council, the Ready Campaign "to educate and empower American citizens to prepare for and respond to potential terrorist attacks and other emergencies" by urging individuals to assemble an emergency supply kit, create a family emergency plan, and "be informed about the different types of emergencies that could occur and their appropriate response."[60]

Last, DHS has held a series of training exercises with news media representatives around the country, in partnership with the National Academy of Sciences and the Radio-Television News Directors Association.[61]

However, notwithstanding the contributions some of these initiatives may make to public education efforts, on the fundamental issue here— improving the accuracy of the risk information transmitted to the public— all of these potential reforms, including possible revision of the current national alert system and the NIMS program, rest on completion of the planned, but not yet finished, DHS risk assessment of the entire country. As the Heritage/CSIS white paper noted, this analysis would be most useful if it would address "criteria such as population, threat assessment, number of important sites, and level of vulnerability, and then classify each area as low, medium, or high risk."[62]

Response and Recovery

Response and recovery measures must be prioritized. We cannot afford to repeat the old system's mistaken faith in the invincibility of the presumed deterrent by counting on an unachievable "perfect" prevention. Therefore, it is imperative that we give priority attention to developing means to mitigate the damage from any attacks and to "recovering" as quickly as possible. As Flynn noted in *America the Vulnerable*:

> Recall that in the case of 9/11, nineteen men armed with box cutters were able to accomplish what no other world power could dream of achieving by conventional means. Within hours of the attacks, our government severed

our transportation umbilical cord with the world. As a result, we effectively imposed a blockade on our own economy.[63]

In other words, our response vastly exacerbated the impact of the attacks themselves, and contributed substantially to the terrorists' success.

Indications are that detailed recovery plans have not been prepared for the transportation sector. For example, on the maritime side, "if the U.S. government decided to close our seaports following a terrorist attack, agencies still have no plan for how they would get traffic moving through ports once they elected to open them up again."[64] Under the December 2004 Homeland Security Presidential Directive 13, which outlined the Administration's "Maritime Security Policy," a Maritime Infrastructure Recovery Plan was to be developed by June 21, 2005.[65] An initial version was presented in October 2005, but the Plan is still undergoing internal review "to incorporate lessons learned from Hurricanes Katrina, Rita and Wilma,"[66] and one port security analyst has concluded that, although the effort itself represents an advance, its approach fails "to address major issues related to security and continuity of operations" and "to fully integrate security and recovery into a unified concept emphasizing continuity of operations."[67]

The DHS approach to security has focused overwhelmingly on prevention of terrorism through enhanced screening of goods and individuals, better coordinated intelligence, and improved border and immigration enforcement.[68] Response and recovery has clearly been secondary. For example, the FY2006 budget proposed $20 million for "catastrophic incident response and recovery planning and exercises," by DHS' Federal Emergency Management Agency (the federal organization long responsible for dealing with natural disasters that was transferred to DHS by the Homeland Security Act), which represented 0.4 percent of FEMA's proposed budget.[69]

TSA officials indicated to 9/11 Commission staff that, because of Congressional mandates and other priorities, the agency had not been able to concentrate as much on recovery planning as they would have liked.[70]

FEMA has seen its disaster mitigation programs reduced substantially since 2001.[71] Furthermore, the transfer to DHS diminished the agency's clout within the federal bureaucracy, eliminating its Cabinet-level status under which its leadership directly reported to the President. A February 2004 survey of FEMA employees conducted by the American Federation of Government Employees found that 80 percent felt FEMA had become a "poorer agency" under DHS, and 60 percent indicated they would move to another agency if they could retain their current pay and grade.[72]

In a 2003 report on "Best Places to Work in the Federal Government," compiled by the Partnership for Public Service and American University's

Institute for the Study of Public Policy Implementation based on a survey of 150,000 executive branch employees, FEMA ranked last among all departments and independent agencies. In the follow-on 2005 report, it tied for last among the 220 "subcomponents and small agencies" evaluated.[73]

Predictably, the loss of resources and status and the lowered employee morale has been accompanied by the departure of a large number of experienced FEMA personnel.[74] As of September 2005, five of the top eight positions in FEMA were filled by individuals with little or no previous experience in disaster management, and "experts inside and out of government said a 'brain drain' of experienced disaster hands throughout the agency, hastened in part by the appointment of leaders without backgrounds in emergency management, has weakened the agency's ability to respond to natural disasters."[75]

In summary, Professor I. M. "Mac" Destler of the University of Maryland's school of public policy observed in September 2005, in the wake of Hurricane Katrina, that FEMA "has gone downhill within the department [of Homeland Security], drained of resources and leadership.... The crippling of FEMA was one important reason why it failed."[76]

A key objective in transportation security response and recovery must be to improve the resiliency of our transportation systems. As part of a comprehensive effort to combat the terrorist threat, it makes sense to reduce the "benefits" to the terrorists (by reducing casualties, disruptions and economic costs) as well as to raise their "costs" (by preemptive attacks and improved defenses). And enhanced resiliency is one of those aforementioned "multibenefits," in upgrading the ability of transportation systems to withstand and quickly recover from the far more frequent natural disasters.

As noted previously, the 9/11 Commission staff recommended that transportation security plans "should include the establishment of damage mitigation and recovery plans designed to expedite the "restart" of key transportation systems after any future terrorist attack" (Recommendation 1.1.3, Appendix A). The Congress added such a requirement to the transportation security strategy plan mandated by the Intelligence Reform and Terrorism Prevention Act of 2004.

Accountability

The transportation security system must be made accountable. The 9/11 Commission received many communications from 9/11 victims' families, disillusioned former civil aviation security employees, and others who believed strongly that accountability must be enforced with respect to the events of 9/11, and that such accountability can only be carried out through "naming names" and seeking disciplinary actions against particular individuals who they hold to be responsible. In principle, the Commission agreed and conducted its investigation with an eye toward making any necessary findings and recommendations with respect to implementing it. However, before proceeding in this vein, it was necessary to determine what standards would be employed and what evidence would be used to arrive at such conclusions of culpability.

In seeking to assign individual accountability with respect to the events of 9/11, the Commission sought answers for a number of questions. Was the given individual in a position to materially affect the outcome of 9/11 by his or her action or inaction? Would substituting another individual, perhaps one with a different approach or qualifications, have changed that outcome in a significant way? Was the individual (or organization for that matter) demonstrably less capable or less effective with respect to security than similarly placed individuals (both others in place on 9/11 and predecessors in relevant positions)?

After going through this exercise, it was my view that, although it is always possible to conjecture what-if scenarios, there is no clear-cut, unequivocal case that replacement of any one particular individual, whether screener, airport authority leadership, airline executive, or senior FAA official would have made a significant difference in preventing the disaster of 9/11. What was documented by the 9/11 Commission was a systemic failure in which *many* were culpable both inside and outside the civil aviation security system.

For these reasons, the Commission investigation was unable to single out "villains" among the civil aviation security system's leadership, but it revealed few heroes either, and the only significant heroic actions on that day belonged to front-line employees like the flight attendants, pilots, and passengers of the hijacked aircraft, who rewrote the Common Strategy on their own, without requiring rule making or a Security Directive to do so.

Although the aviation security system was seriously flawed and demonstrably failed to protect the country from the 9/11 plot, the Commission investigation found that the vast majority of individuals working to operate the civil aviation system and those striving to protect that system from violence were dedicated, well-meaning, and, in many cases, very talented individuals working hard to do an extremely difficult job. These findings apply to the current transportation security workforce as well.

The cause of truth would be poorly served by the pretense that the 9/11 attacks were inevitable and could not have been stopped by a better, more rational, and disciplined civil aviation security *system*. It would be equally erroneous to pretend that the cause of that failure was broad-based individual malfeasance. It is, in any case, clear that the civil aviation security system's methods of accountability were themselves seriously flawed, for a number of reasons.

- The division of security responsibilities that left no one organization or individual clearly responsible.
- The "dual mandate" of the FAA to both regulate and promote civil aviation.
- A regulatory environment dominated by a rule-making process that offered multiple, largely obscured from public view, opportunities for delay.

And it should be noted that, although there have been marginal changes, most notably with checkpoint and checked baggage screening clearly made a federal responsibility, all of these forces that inhibited accountability in the pre-9/11 system are to a large extent still present today. For example, though TSA has certainly been given a clearer security focus, its mission statement calls for the agency to protect transportation "to ensure freedom of movement for people and commerce."[77]

Similarly, the Congressional portion of the transportation security system has been little changed since 9/11. The 9/11 Commission noted that DHS faced oversight by eighty-eight Congressional committees and subcommittees,[78] and that an independent expert had cited this particular factor as "the single largest obstacle impeding the department's successful development." The Commission, therefore, recommended that each house of Congress "should create a single, principal point of oversight and review for homeland security."[79]

Two subsequent reports have made similar findings and recommendations. According to a white paper jointly produced by the Center for Strategic and International Studies and Business Executives for National Security:

> Congress has failed to remove a major impediment to effective homeland security: the balkanized and dysfunctional oversight of the Department of Homeland Security (DHS). While Congress worked with the Executive Branch to create the DHS, it has done almost nothing to match this important reorganization with a parallel initiative to put its own house in order. Instead it has protected prerogative and privilege at the expense of a rational, streamlined committee structure. The result is a Department of Homeland Security that is hamstrung by a system of Congressional oversight that drains departmental energy and invites managerial circumvention.[80]

The George Washington University Homeland Security Policy Institute Steering Committee, comprised of a number of former high-ranking national security officials, echoed these sentiments.[81] Both groups recommended the establishment of single homeland security oversight committees in the House and Senate.

Congress also bears a significant portion of the responsibility for the apparent allocation of homeland security resources based more on political connections than risk-based need. For example, the well connected but presumably "target poor" states of Wyoming and Alaska have received far more homeland security funding per capita ($28 and $25, respectively) than New York ($15.50) or California ($8).[82] The 9/11 Commission opined, "Homeland security assistance should be based strictly on an assessment of risks and vulnerabilities.... Congress should not use this money as a pork barrel."[83]

The 9/11 Commission staff for aviation and transportation security submitted a number of recommendations for TSA to "continuously and vigorously test and hold accountable each critical element of the U.S. transportation system in order to promote its effectiveness in preventing, responding to and recovering from terrorist attacks" (Recommendation 5, Appendix A), including by

- Providing for "continuous and independent testing of civil aviation and transportation security systems, such as security checkpoints. Such testing should include the simulation of terrorist tactics in order to identify vulnerabilities and assess performance." (Recommendation 5.1, Appendix A)
- Establishing "performance goals for each element of the U.S. transportation security system." (Recommendation 5.2, Appendix A)
- Considering the issuance of "general security performance 'Report Cards' measuring the relative performance of transportation security components." (Recommendation 5.7, Appendix A)
- Establishing "policies to assure that following any terrorist attack on transportation, comprehensive after-action reports are produced by responsible agencies to ascertain the facts and circumstances surrounding the attack, and to identify lessons learned about the prevention, response to and recovery from the attack." (Recommendation 5.9, Appendix A)
- Devoting "sufficient attention and resources to facilitating the oversight of their operations." (Recommendation 5.13, Appendix A)

The Commission staff called on Congress to take certain accountability-enhancing steps as well, such as "creating a presidentially-appointed and Senate-confirmed Transportation Security Oversight Board to receive and assess reports on the performance of the various components of the transportation security system, and to recommend remedial measures and initiatives" (Recommendation 5.6, Appendix A), establishing a security counterpart to the National Transportation Safety Board to perform independent investigations of terrorist attacks on transportation (Recommendation 5.10, Appendix A), creating "independent 'Red Teams' outside of TSA and DHS for the covert testing of all modes" (Recommendation 5.12, Appendix A), providing the DHS Inspector General's office "with the manpower and resources commensurate with both the size of the agency and the importance of its responsibilities" (Recommendation 5.13.1, Appendix A), and moving to protect the rights of whistle-blowers (Recommendation 5.13.2, Appendix A).

11 Reassessment and a Test

The DHS "Second Stage Review Agenda"

On July 13, 2005, DHS Secretary Michael Chertoff outlined the results of the "Second Stage Review" he had ordered to evaluate "the Department's operations, policies and structures" and to "recommend ways that DHS could better manage risk in terms of threat, vulnerability and consequence; prioritize policies and operational missions according to this risk-based approach; and establish a series of preventive and protective steps that would increase security at multiple levels."[1]

Coming on the heels of widespread negative assessments of DHS' performance to date (for example, the previously cited December 2004 report of the DHS Inspector General, "Major Management Challenges Facing the Department of Homeland Security," and the joint analysis by the Heritage Foundation and the Center for Strategic and International Studies, also released in December 2004, "DHS 2.0: Rethinking the Department of Homeland Security"), Secretary Chertoff's presentation of his new agenda contained a host of worthwhile concepts and good intentions.

It is difficult to find fault with any of the Secretary's broad "Six Imperatives":

1. Increased preparedness, especially for events with catastrophic consequences.
2. Strengthened border security and immigration enforcement.
3. "Hardened" transportation security "without sacrificing mobility."
4. Enhanced information sharing with state, local, and tribal governments, and with the private sector.

  5. Improved management.
  6. A "realigned" organization "to maximize mission performance."

Many of the accompanying principles Chertoff set forth are sound and
important ones. Homeland security policies should be based on risk assessment, with particular attention to the most consequential risks. Security
measures must be "maximized," but be consistent with other key national
values including "freedom, prosperity, mobility, and individual privacy."
Although the federal government owns or controls only a small fraction
of potential terrorist targets, it has the responsibility of setting a "clear
national strategy" and designing "an architecture in which separate roles
and responsibilities for security are fully integrated among public and
private stakeholders."[2] And to prevail over the terrorists in the long run,
"resiliency" must be built into our defenses.[3]

As indicated previously, from the beginning, the Department of Homeland Security and its components have faced enormous managerial and
coordination challenges. Furthermore, not all of the current problems in
homeland security have been caused by the actions or inactions of the
executive branch. The Congress continues to resist calls by the 9/11 Commission and others to streamline its oversight of DHS and to remove the
pork barrel from homeland security spending.

But granting these challenges and fully allowing for the sincerity of Secretary Chertoff's pronouncements, the American public should evaluate
the proposal from the bottom-line standpoint of its likelihood of actually
improving homeland security.

The July 13 initiative was clearly premised on the notion of setting priorities based on risk management where attention and resources are directed
at the most serious threats and vulnerabilities. However, that has been the
stated objective of DHS from its very beginning. (See, for example, the 2004
DHS "Homeland Security Strategic Plan."[4]) And in spite of the expressed
commitment to this principle by former DHS Secretary Ridge and all other
top officials within the Department, it remains an unrealized objective
as indicated by a number of independent analyses by the Government
Accountability Office,[5] the Heritage Foundation, the Center for Strategic
and International Studies,[6] and the 9/11 Commission,[7] among others.

Secretary Chertoff's strong support for risk management is laudable.
However, more than two years into the operation of DHS, it is appropriate
to demand concrete actions to implement the high-sounding rhetoric. For
starters, DHS should revise and dramatically improve the existing national
infrastructure protection plan and the National Transportation Security
Strategy, both of which were supposed to specifically define risk-based
priorities but are at present little more than sets of general principles. In
the words of the 9/11 Public Discourse Project, "It is time that we stop
talking about setting priorities, and actually set some."[8] Most important,

the next DHS budget must be reoriented to reflect a risk-based perspective so that there is not a repetition of all previous DHS budget submissions, including the one for FY2006, which concentrated more than two-thirds of the Department's transportation security spending on one mode (aviation), with two-thirds of that total going to passenger and baggage screening alone. Although it is perhaps possible to conclude that such allocations do reflect appropriate priorities, the budget submission has never sought to justify them as such. Risk-based decision making must be made explicit in the FY2007 budget, and the allocations adjusted accordingly.

Another key component of Secretary Chertoff's presentation was the importance of resilience. The Secretary's prepared remarks and the accompanying DHS fact sheets did not utilize this term, but it was employed by Mr. Chertoff in his response to questions,[9] and in his meeting with *Washington Post* editorial personnel.[10] For analysis, it is useful to break this concept down into two parts: the resilience of protective systems and the resilience of potential targets, especially the human ones that are the main focus of al Qaeda-inspired terrorism. On the former, what Mr. Chertoff had in mind seems to be exemplified by his calls for improving DHS preparedness to "prevent, protect against, and respond to acts of terror or other disasters." To do so, he called for better planning (including the establishment and use of a threat/target matrix "to identify and remedy current gaps in preparedness"), the consolidation of all DHS preparedness activities—including those currently performed by FEMA—within the Information Analysis and Infrastructure Protection division (which is to have its analysis and operations components moved to another division and is to be renamed the Directorate of Preparedness), and the "focusing" of FEMA on response and recovery efforts.[11] Congress concurred with these changes in its action on the FY2006 DHS appropriations bill.[12]

As with risk management, the effort to add the capability of rapid recovery to our homeland security efforts is very worthwhile, and indeed essential. But as with the former, the usefulness of the concept will lie in the actions implementing it rather than oratory alone. A threat matrix can be a useful analytical tool, and the 9/11 Commission transportation staff team called for such action in the recommendations it submitted to Congress in September 2004 (Recommendation 3.2.1, Appendix A). The Congress added this requirement to the aviation sector security plan mandated in the Intelligence Reform and Terrorism Prevention Act of 2004.[13] But as with any tool, the key will be in how it is designed and when and how it is utilized. More specifically, the public should watch how this approach is employed in producing the heretofore lacking detailed recovery plans for "restarting" the various transportation modes and critical infrastructure in the aftermath of a terrorist attack.

Although the creation of a unified "preparedness" office might improve the coordination of these activities, their separation from "response and recovery" raises new issues about the integration of preparedness, mitigation, and recovery efforts. Rep. Chris Van Hollen (D-MD) is reported to have observed, "that's a bit like having one squad practice and another play the game."[14] (Then-FEMA Director Michael Brown had written in a September 2003 memo to DHS Secretary Ridge, "FEMA learned the hard way that disjointed efforts between preparedness and response create significant problems in effectively managing disasters.")[15]

Furthermore, the placement of this responsibility with IAIP, an entity that has experienced a number of problems in its short history, rather than with FEMA, which had enjoyed a relatively good reputation prior to its absorption into DHS, is open to serious question. With respect to FEMA, its ability to handle its new role will be determined by the quality of the leadership it is provided, the level of funding it is provided, and the organizational priority it is afforded, all of which appear to have been lacking since its transfer to DHS.

The director of the State of Washington's emergency management department wrote, in the wake of Hurricane Katrina in late August 2005, that the latest changes for FEMA will result in the agency's being "systematically downgraded and all but dismantled by the Department of Homeland Security." He elaborated:

> This year it was announced that FEMA is to "officially" lose the disaster preparedness function that it has had since its creation. The move is a death blow to an agency that was already on life support. In fact, FEMA employees have been directed not to become involved in disaster preparedness functions, since a new directorate (yet to be established) will have that mission. . . . Those of us in the business of dealing with emergencies find ourselves with no national leadership and no mentors. We are being forced to fend for ourselves, making do with the "homeland security" mission. Our "all-hazards" approaches have been decimated by the administration's preoccupation with terrorism.[16]

The "hardening" of human targets seemed to be Chertoff's chief reference point in his favorable remarks on resiliency, given his repeated use of the concept in terms of the ability of Londoners to avoid panic and recover quickly from the July 7 bombings.[17] It is difficult to discern related policy commitments in the Secretary's remarks, though the accompanying DHS fact sheet did indicate a plan to "refine the Homeland Security Advisory System."[18]

Shortcomings in that system have been widely reported, and upon taking office, Secretary Chertoff was reportedly given a number of options for replacing it. With all of this lead-up, the continuing absence of action in changing the current system and the implication of marginal "revisions" in the offing, are disturbing. Although Secretary Chertoff appears to realize the critical importance of helping the public to become more resilient in facing the long-term terrorist threat, his actions do not yet reflect this understanding.

A third laudable element of the Secretary's July 13 announcement was the notion that security cannot be pursued "at any price" but must be made consistent with "Americans' freedom, prosperity, mobility, and individual privacy."[19] This represents a long overdue emphasis on one of the key questions in transportation security that the foregoing analysis suggests must be successfully addressed if sustained progress is to be made. Once again, though, the absence of specific policy proposals, plus DHS' less than stellar record in this regard to date (especially with respect to reconciling airline passenger prescreening with privacy concerns), necessitates a certain degree of skepticism.

Somewhat more specifically, Secretary Chertoff also stated that

> The more comprehensive and efficient passenger screening system that DHS must develop will give us the ability to automatically clear low-risk travelers. By clearing [them], TSA can reasonably focus on a smaller and more distinct pool of passengers that might pose a threat to aviation. The result: less frustration; faster service; better security. Better forms of screening will also promote privacy, because they will reduce the number of mistakes or unnecessary interventions that annoy travelers.[20]

These are worthy sentiments, but they are also the same ones that underlie the CAPPS I and abortive CAPPS II efforts The intentions are yet again the right ones, but "the devil is in the details," which again are lacking at this point.

But perhaps more important than concerns about the translating of the commendable principles of the Chertoff agenda into real improvements in security are critical omissions on the other two fundamental issues that have plagued federal homeland security efforts from the beginning, and will continue to do so unless effectively addressed.

Whereas Secretary Chertoff devoted a great deal of attention to the question of DHS' internal organization (including the return of the Federal Air Marshal Service to TSA),[21] except for an otherwise unexplained reference to the need for DHS to "design an architecture in which separate roles and responsibilities for security are fully integrated among public and private stakeholders,"[22] there was no apparent attempt to answer or clarify the fundamental matter of how homeland security is to be organized among these different entities and what the federal role (especially the TSA role) is to be beyond the realm of passenger aviation.

Finally, the new DHS agenda is largely silent on the question of how security measures are to be financed, calling into question not only *when* but also *if* the accompanying principles will ever be translated into better security. Secretary Chertoff did reiterate the Administration's support for increased user fees to fund aviation security enhancements,[23] but this request had already been rejected by both houses of Congress in action on the FY2006 DHS appropriations bill.[24] Furthermore, nowhere in the new agenda was it indicated how the numerous existing transportation security funding shortfalls previously identified, including the unfunded federal mandates for air cargo, port, and rail and transit security, are to be addressed.

The current capabilities of DHS were put to their most severe test to date in little more than one month after Secretary Chertoff's speech.

Hurricane Katrina

At 6:10 a.m. local time on August 29, 2005, Hurricane Katrina made land-fall near Buras, Louisiana, with winds measured at 145 miles per hour. Adjoining coastal regions of Louisiana and Mississippi were devastated. Later that night, two levees protecting the city of New Orleans broke, and by the next day 80 percent of the city was covered by water, which rose to a height of 20 feet in some areas.[25] As of mid-September, the confirmed death toll stood at more than 900, with one million people displaced as a result of the storm.[26]

Almost immediately, the Department of Homeland Security and its FEMA component came under a barrage of criticism for their handling of the emergency. As reported by *The Washington Post*, "Despite four years and tens of billions of dollars spent preparing for the worst, the federal government was not ready when it came at daybreak on Monday, according to interviews with more than a dozen current and former senior officials and outside experts." Former DHS Inspector General Clark Kent Ervin called the response a "devastating indictment of this department's performance four years after 9/11."[27] Former Speaker of the House Newt Gingrich (R-GA) stated that its response "puts into question all of the Homeland Security. . . planning for the last four years." And Senator David Vitter (R-LA) termed FEMA "completely dysfunctional and completely over-whelmed. . . . There was no coherent plan for dealing with this scenario."[28]

Once again, unanswered questions about who was responsible and how the necessary protective and recovery measures are to be paid for plagued the national homeland security effort.

DHS Secretary Chertoff initially declared that the federal response was delayed "because our constitutional system really places the primary au-thority in each state with the governor."[29] Yet under DHS' own "National Response Plan," the federal government is to provide a "proactive" re-sponse to "catastrophic events," which are defined as "any natural or manmade incident, including terrorism, that results in extraordinary levels of mass casualties, damage, or disruption severely affecting the population, infrastructure, environment, economy, national morale, and/or government functions."[30]

The potential for precisely such consequences from an event like Hurricane Katrina were long known. For example, an article entitled "Drowning New Orleans" appeared in the October 2001 edition of *Scientific American*, which was out in newsstands at the very time the 9/11 hijackers struck:

> A major hurricane could swamp New Orleans under 20 feet of water, killing thousands.... New Orleans is a disaster waiting to happen. The city lies in a bowl bordered by levees that fend off Lake Pontchartrain to the north and the Mississippi River to the south and west.... A direct hit is inevitable. Large hurricanes come close every year.[31]

Under the National Response Plan, in the event of a "catastrophic event" the "proactive federal response" is to be governed by a number of principles, including the following:

- The primary mission is to save lives; protect critical infrastructure, property, and the environment; contain the event; and preserve national security.
- Standard procedures regarding requests for assistance may be expedited or, under extreme circumstances, suspended in the immediate aftermath of an event of catastrophic magnitude.
- Notification and full coordination with States will occur, but the coordination process must not delay or impede the rapid deployment and use of critical resources.[32]

In the immediate aftermath of Katrina, Secretary Chertoff called DHS response plans inadequate to deal with what he termed an "ultra-catastrophe... as if an atomic bomb had been dropped."[33]

As in other areas of homeland security, the lack of clearly defined roles and responsibilities (including confusion within the federal government itself as to its own role) in responding to Hurricane Katrina led to "the inability of the federal, state and local governments to work together in the face of disaster long foretold.... Confusion reigned at every level of officialdom, according to dozens of interviews with participants in Louisiana, Mississippi and Washington."[34]

How to pay for the projected $200 billion or more in recovery costs has also raised a number of concerns. President Bush pledged that the federal government would take the lead in assisting with the rebuilding of storm-damaged parts of Louisiana and Mississippi, but he neither provided a cost estimate nor indicated how the recovery programs are to be financed. Reaction to this lack of specificity was particularly pronounced among Congressional Republicans, who "were annoyed by the lack of concrete ideas for paying the Hurricane Katrina bill."[35]

12 Priorities

In my view, one of the reasons why much of the attention as to the causes of and remedies for the 9/11/01 security failures has focused on the intelligence realm is precisely because to do so largely avoids the hard policy questions posed earlier.

Intelligence operations are largely "over there" and/or directed at non-U.S. citizens. They do not raise nearly as many questions about the impact on the American public, their privacy, convenience, jobs, and so forth, as would most other elements of the homeland security equation. Thus, the issue of balancing the security benefit of an intelligence measure with competing economic or civil liberties values can be more easily ignored.

Similarly, it is widely accepted that intelligence is a responsibility of the federal government, and though turf consciousness is every bit as strong within the intelligence community as it is elsewhere in the federal bureaucracy, there is little need to fight high consequence battles with respect to the roles of state and local governments or the private sector.

And the fundamental matter of who pays is essentially a settled question with respect to intelligence. Few would propose user fees, or other forms of cost sharing, or a shift in funding over to state, local, or private payers. In addition, both the direct (in the form of federal expenditures) and indirect (in the form of economic impact) costs are much smaller than, for example, the deployment of explosives detection equipment at airports or radiological detectors at the nation's seaports.

But, if we have learned nothing else from the history of aviation security before, during, and after 9/11, there are no silver bullets with respect to security—not technological improvements in explosives detection equipment as sought after Pan Am 103, nor better screening of suspect baggage pointed to by the Gore Commission, nor tighter checkpoint screening that has received so much of post-9/11 attention and resources, nor intelligence reform, which was the focal point of the legislation implementing the 9/11 Commission recommendations (appropriately titled the Intelligence Reform and Terrorism Prevention Act).

No single defensive (or offensive) measure can possibly secure the nation and the various (and evolving) targets of the terrorists. Furthermore, no such layer is, or possibly can be, 100 percent effective over time and against changing threats. Putting all one's eggs in one basket is a proven recipe for failure and disaster.

In the end, all questions of public policy come down to the setting of priorities and the making of choices among a myriad of competing claims for attention and resources. And so it is with transportation security.

At one level, there are the questions involving prioritization within existing programs and available resources. For example, how should the 45,000 federal airport screeners be optimally utilized: screening all passengers and baggage equally, screening pre-identified "high risk" people and bags more intensively, or, more likely, striking the proper balance between these two extremes? It is a question of targeting, and there are a variety of such programs already underway within DHS that aim at categorizing a passenger, or transportation worker, or baggage, or cargo as high or low risk. And although all of these efforts have run into problems that have inhibited their effectiveness, progress has been made and is likely to continue. (Recall that even the pre-9/11 CAPPS I prescreening system, with all of its own shortcomings, was perhaps the single most effective defense layer on 9/11 in targeting ten of the nineteen hijackers. The fatal flaw was in the screening of the selectees.)

Another level of priority setting is that within the entire sphere of transportation security. It involves the asking of questions on how to allocate the finite level of funding, personnel, and policy attention made available for transportation security overall across the various modes. As was made clear in Part Two, there is little evidence of significant progress on this front, with the lion's share of dollars, people, and legislation still being directed at one layer (passenger and baggage screening) of one sector (civil aviation) of transportation, and one entire mode (land transportation) being, for all intents and purposes, written off.

The proposed Targeted Infrastructure Protection grant program was supposed to begin to redress this imbalance. However, its limited size ($600 million), broad focus (everything but aviation), and poor executive branch and Congressional track records in directing such grants to areas with strong risk-based rather than political claims raised serious doubts about its ability to do so—even before its rejection by the Congress in action on the FY2006 DHS appropriations bill.

Furthermore, without a very good national infrastructure risk assessment plan, which has been long promised but still not delivered, and which may or may not be sufficient for this purpose in its current form, there will not be a comprehensive basis for Congress and the executive branch to make, and be judged on, policy allocation decisions. And with TSA playing a small and diminishing role outside of aviation, it will apparently be left up to DHS to fulfill the necessary mission of finding the proper balance among all transportation sectors. Given the Department's many other challenges and existing performance problems, it remains to be seen whether it will be capable of fulfilling this additional role.

Where DHS was presumably designed to play a major direct part was in the third, and broadest, level of priority setting: making choices among all competing governmental and societal objectives. This book has focused on transportation, but it is not the sole component of homeland security, and it ought not to be assumed a priori that it should be preeminent. For example, if one accepts the previously cited notion of a particular federal responsibility for dealing with high-consequence but low-probability events (because no one else will and failure to attend to such possibilities can produce serious and nationwide consequences if the unlikely happens, as it did in the case of the suicide hijackings on 9/11), how should the federal government prioritize airport checkpoint screening versus the Cooperative Threat Reduction and other programs designed to prevent the spread of weapons-grade nuclear materials, or public health programs designed to strengthen our capability to respond to bioterrorist attacks? It is difficult to discern where such debates are occurring currently within the federal government, and decision making seems to be taking place in the same balkanized fashion—driven by Congressional jurisdictional lines and executive branch turf wars—as it did prior to 9/11.

This last level is also the realm within which all of the previously posed "hard questions" (how to balance security with other competing societal interests, who is responsible for what, and who pays for security) properly reside. And the available evidence indicates that federal policy makers are not making much headway on any of them. DHS and TSA dropped CAPPS II rather than confront and resolve the important privacy versus security issues involved, with a result that the citizens of the country are denied a potentially powerful tool for focusing screening resources while the difficult policy debate is merely postponed until another time. Little has been done since the federalization of the airport screener workforce in the immediate aftermath of 9/11 to clarify the federal and other roles in transportation security. And by not determining whether transportation security is, in fact, a national security issue with a substantial claim on taxpayer dollars, the default position on the financing of security measures has been a return of unfunded federal mandates (for example, in air and maritime cargo) or increasing reliance on user fees (such as in civil aviation) where the higher fees are to be used not to raise security but merely to substitute for funds from the general treasury.

The very things that make transportation systems a continuing target for terrorists—their high visibility and their ubiquity, and their central economic and social roles—make the stakes for their protection extraordinarily high. The workers at DHS, TSA, and the other federal and nonfederal entities involved in homeland security are trying hard and the vast majority are, in the words of a DHS Inspector General assessment of airport screeners, "diligent in the performance of their duties and conscious of the responsibility those duties carry." But in spite of their good intentions and best efforts, the emerging security system more and more resembles pre-9/11 aviation security.

It is a system of shared and uncertain roles and responsibilities, of multiple dual mandates where agency missions and priorities repeatedly collide, of plausible deniability as to who is to implement and pay for security enhancements, of the continually dissipating impact of the elevated security of the nationwide and ever-present "Yellow Alert," and of a slow-paced air cargo security rule making that brings to mind the multiyear but never finished pre-9/11 regulatory effort to improve checkpoint screening.

Federal transportation security efforts over the past four years have been marked by frequent organizational reshuffles, multiple missed deadlines, and, in almost all cases where performance data is available, disappointing results.

The federal government has expended more than $20 billion on aviation security alone, and although the relatively inexpensive changes in onboard security systems have significantly enhanced our defenses against another 9/11-type of attack, other areas—most notably air cargo and general aviation—have seen only marginal improvements at best.

The more than $5 billion in federal funds spent for maritime security has undoubtedly upgraded the protective systems in this sector, but the pre-9/11 security system here was so low that even with the enhancements, ports and containers remain very vulnerable to terrorist attacks.

With a much smaller investment (substantially less than $1 billion in federal expenditures) and with virtually nonexistent security performance information, it is more difficult to rate the level of improvement in land transportation security, but there is little reason to believe that current efforts make U.S. land systems more prepared to prevent or respond to terrorist attacks than was the London transit system prior to the July 2005 bombings.

A consistent theme in all of this has been the absence of effective federal leadership. Moreover, given the track record and its failure to engage in the necessary debates on priorities, roles, and funding, the Administration has been left in a poor position from which to defend even potentially promising attempts to improve security performance, such as the Screening Coordination and Operations Office and the Targeted Infrastructure Protection Program, both of which were in line with recommendations of the 9/11 Commission, but both of which were rejected by the Republican-controlled Congress.

The abdication of responsibility on the part of the federal government in failing to address fundamental questions about how transportation security is to be prioritized, organized, and financed makes the country less safe and secure than it could or should be. The failure to acknowledge such abdication is perhaps even worse because it leaves everyone—state and local authorities, private stakeholders, and the general public—in the dark about what is being, or will be, done and who should be held accountable. Such issues must not be allowed to slide until after the next attack and the appointment of the next Commission.

Appendix A: Transmittal Letter and Recommendations of 9/11 Commission Aviation and Transportation Security Staff

September 1, 2004

Dear Member of Congress:

As you are aware, the final report of the National Commission on Terrorist Attacks Upon the United States presents a set of key recommendations to improve homeland security, including the transportation sector. The commissioners unanimously endorsed the panel's recommendations.

We, the undersigned, served as staff members on the Commission's aviation and transportation team. We were privileged to assist the commissioners in their vital work, including investigation of the facts and circumstances surrounding the 9/11 attacks and the development of recommendations to improve transportation security.

During our work we had the opportunity to interview many government officials, industry representatives, and outside experts about the performance of the aviation security system on 9/11, the lessons learned from the attacks, and how the nation might further improve aviation and transportation security policies and practices in light of the lessons.

The most important lessons derived from the Commission's investigation are reflected in the final report, which necessarily focused on the highest priorities. To be of further help, however, we are forwarding to you the attached list of additional proposals for the consideration of the committee's leadership, members, and staff. As you will see, the proposals are consistent with and complement the key recommendations made by the Commission. The list reflects what we learned from our interviews, our review of documents, and analysis of the facts and circumstances of the 9/11 attacks.

The recommendations are solely those of the undersigned, and have not been formally endorsed by the commissioners. However, the Commission has urged that we share our views with you to add to the debate and so that the public may take maximum advantage of our work.

As you will see, we have organized our proposals around five major principles, which we believe provide a framework for addressing vital security needs of the nation's transportation system. While not exhaustive, the specific recommendations reflect our attempt to translate these principles into important actionable policies.

We will be pleased to provide further information or to assist the Committee in any way we can. Thank you for providing us the opportunity to share our thoughts with you.

Sincerely,
Gerald Dillingham
R. William Johnstone
John Raidt

The following recommendations to improve transportation security are based on five major principles:

- Transportation security policy making is a matter of national security and requires comprehensive strategic planning to adequately protect passengers, equipment, and facilities of the various modes and their interconnections.
- Transportation security resources should be allocated based on risk assessment and management.
- Transportation security policy should be based on the establishment of appropriate goals for all modes of transportation, and the implementation of standards and best practices necessary to achieve them.
- Transportation security requires effective information sharing and coordinated teamwork among all stakeholders.
- Transportation security policies, practices, and procedures require vigorous oversight and enforcement to assure they remain current, relevant, and effective.

Recommendations

Principle 1: *Transportation security policy making is a matter of national security and requires comprehensive strategic planning to adequately protect passengers, equipment, and facilities of the various modes and their interconnections.*

RECOMMENDATION 1: The Department of Homeland Security and the Transportation Security Administration should complete comprehensive strategic plans to ensure that the nation is adequately addressing the greatest security risks to our transportation systems across all modes including aviation, maritime, and surface transportation and their interconnections. (**NOTE:** Since its inception the vast majority of TSA's resources have been devoted to aviation security measures, and to meeting important mandates imposed by Congress. Other transportation modes are at risk and have significant vulnerabilities. Congress established the agency as the "Transportation" Security Administration. DHS and TSA should be provided the guidance and resources to adequately address all modes to ensure we are dealing with the most serious security risks among and within the various modes and their interconnections.)

RECOMMENDATION 1.1: The National Infrastructure Protection Plan and the Transportation Sector Specific Plan developed pursuant to Homeland Security Presidential Directive 7, (including all of the components recommended herein) should be finalized by February 1, 2005.[1] Securing the nation's transportation system requires strategic planning. This entails identifying and prioritizing the transportation assets that require federal protection based on relative risk;[2] selecting the most practicable, cost-effective methods of protecting passengers, equipment, and facilities;[3] and developing appropriately detailed blueprints that include methods, milestones, budgets, and measures of effectiveness necessary to meet the stated goals.[4] (**NOTE:** Such strategic planning should be reflected in both the National Infrastructure Protection Plan and the Transportation Sector Specific Plan. Without identifying key transportation assets, comprehensively assessing risk to these assets, and strategically planning to protect them, policy makers may find themselves continually fighting the last war rather than anticipating and protecting the nation's transportation system against future threats.)

RECOMMENDATION 1.1.1: The National Infrastructure Protection Plan should identify each federal, state, local, tribal, and private stakeholder with responsibilities for transportation security and clearly define their roles, responsibilities, and relationships, including with foreign counterparts.

RECOMMENDATION 1.1.2: The Transportation Sector Specific Plan of the National Infrastructure Protection Plan, and its modally specific annexes, should identify each federal, state, local, tribal, and private stakeholder and clearly define their roles, responsibilities, and relationships. (**NOTE:** Many security experts interviewed by the Commission staff cited the need to provide a clear delineation of roles and missions as among the most important steps for improving transportation security.)

RECOMMENDATION 1.1.3: The Transportation Sector Specific Plan and its modally specific annexes should include the establishment of damage mitigation and "recovery plans" designed to expedite the "restart" of key transportation systems after any future terrorist attack.

RECOMMENDATION 1.1.4: The Transportation Sector Specific Plan and its modally specific annexes should include cost estimates for the protective measures and programs it identifies and should recommend to Congress how these costs should be financed, including the recommendation of funding mechanisms such as Congressional appropriations, appropriate fees, and cost-sharing arrangements.

RECOMMENDATION 1.1.5: Congress should exercise vigorous and ongoing oversight of the strategic plans to assure that each possesses the required elements and degree of specificity, and that the plans are fully implemented.

RECOMMENDATION 1.2: Both the legislative and executive branches of the federal government should ensure that transportation security receives the appropriate share of homeland/national security spending—resources that should be allocated based on what is necessary to maximize the security of the American people against the most serious threats. (**NOTE**: Security expert Stephen Flynn has recommended that the nation take a more comprehensive approach to the allocation of security resources, and that we be careful not to diminish the overall security of the nation by maintaining artificial barriers between homeland security spending and national security spending. Homeland security is a vital component of national security and should be treated as such in the budget process.)

RECOMMENDATION 1.2.1: In consultation with Congressional Budget Office, the Office of Management and Budget should establish a separate functional account for transportation security within a homeland security account in order to facilitate executive and legislative branch evaluation of such security spending and priorities.

RECOMMENDATION 1.2.2: Each house of Congress should create a standing Committee or subcommittee to provide the principal oversight of transportation security as part of the overall homeland security account, including oversight of strategic planning. (See also recommendation 5.5).

Principle 2: *Transportation security resources should be allocated based on risk assessment and management.*

RECOMMENDATION 2: DHS and TSA should continue to develop, and implement as soon as possible, a system that allows the federal government to set security priorities among the different components (air, land, and maritime, and their interconnections) of the U.S. transportation network; i.e., identify what infrastructure we need to protect most and from what kinds of attack.

RECOMMENDATION 2.1: Transportation security funds and policy attention should be allocated based on priorities identified using risk management.

Priority setting should utilize the best available risk assessment information, while continuous efforts are made to improve the quality of such information.

RECOMMENDATION 2.2: In assessing risk among and within the various modes, DHS should take into account not only the threats to transportation as identified and assessed by the intelligence community but also the system's vulnerabilities, and the negative consequences of a successful attack. (**NOTE:** Pre-9/11 the FAA's security system was primarily a threat-based system. Security measures were based mainly on the government's assessment of how terrorists might attack. This assessment was based generally on two factors: whether terrorists had used the tactic before and whether "specific and credible" evidence indicated that a particular kind of attack was in the offing. Because the United States can't always count on forewarning, risk assessment should factor in both our security vulnerabilities and the consequences of each type of possible attack, even in the absence of information that terrorists are planning to conduct a particular kind of attack.)

RECOMMENDATION 2.3: By no later than January 1, 2005, TSA should take over implementation of the "no fly" and "automatic selectee" lists from air carriers. If TSA implements the program, we can be more certain that these lists are being fully enforced. In addition, the United States government will be able to include more terrorist names on the lists, and the U.S. intelligence community can assure that foreign air carriers aren't sharing the names with terrorist organizations. (**NOTE:** In managing risk it seems prudent to begin by assuring the people known or suspected to be terrorists are not allowed to fly or, as appropriate, subject to extraordinary security screening.)

RECOMMENDATION 2.3.1: Steps should be taken as soon as possible to convert the "No-Fly" list into a "No-Transport" list that would be provided to transportation providers in addition to air carriers (starting with cruise ships and AMTRAK).

RECOMMENDATION 2.3.2: The Transportation Security Administration's "no fly" and "automatic selectee" lists should include the names and known aliases of the maximum number of individuals known or suspected by the U.S. government to be terrorists, consistent with the national security interests of the United States.

RECOMMENDATION 2.3.3: The federal government should seek agreements with countries allied in the fight against terrorism to share lists of known and suspected terrorists for purposes of transportation security (as well as immigration enforcement), consistent with the national security interests of the United States.

RECOMMENDATION 2.3.4: The federal government should ensure that state, local, and tribal law enforcement authorities, including those with transportation security responsibilities, receive appropriate access to the terrorist watch lists to enhance national efforts to locate, monitor, and apprehend these individuals. Procedures should be put in place to ensure that the appropriate federal agencies are informed when state, local, and tribal authorities, such as airport police, come into contact with listed individuals.

RECOMMENDATION 2.4: The pilot testing of a successor to the Computer Assisted Passenger Prescreening system should proceed as expeditiously as possible. Airlines and other relevant parties should submit necessary data to TSA, under appropriate safeguards, by not later than six months after implementation of the no fly and automatic selectee list by TSA as described above. The test of the system should commence as soon as possible thereafter. TSA should clearly state the goals and parameters of the program for Congress and the public, as well as publicly and credibly address privacy, fairness, and necessity concerns regarding the prescreening system prior to implementation. (**NOTE:** Because the government cannot be certain of obtaining the names of all known and suspected terrorists who could pose a threat to aircraft and other conveyances, the nation needs an appropriate, well-designed and targeted system for determining whether a passenger may be a security risk to assure such individuals receive appropriate screening. The current prescreening system does not look at factors such as a passenger's race, religion, or color. It should not. Greater emphasis should be placed, however, on improving risk identifiers and for assuring that passengers are who they say they are. This can be accomplished both by improving the integrity of identification that passengers must present at the airport such as state driver's licenses, etc. and by using improved computerized prescreening.)

RECOMMENDATION 2.4.1: As part of the effort to improve prescreening, TSA should develop standards to protect privacy, establish procedures to redress grievances with the prescreening system, and create an independent privacy oversight panel made up of appropriate experts and private citizens to oversee the development, implementation, and operation of the system. (**NOTE:** The public will not accept a more vigorous prescreening system until it is assured that privacy concerns are fully and fairly addressed. Such assurances will require that TSA fully engage the public and privacy experts in the debate from inception through implementation.)

RECOMMENDATION 2.4.2: TSA should focus the prescreening system exclusively on terrorists and other violent threats to transportation security, rather than as a law enforcement tool for tracking a wider class of criminal offenders. (**NOTE:** Permitting mission creep in the prescreening system would divert the program from its primary focus, which should be to stop terrorists, and would exacerbate privacy concerns, which could limit the program's effectiveness.)

RECOMMENDATION 2.4.3: The prescreening of passengers should be expanded as soon as practicable to include transportation modes in addition to civil aviation, starting with cruise ships and AMTRAK where appropriate.

RECOMMENDATION 2.5: DHS should bolster efforts to identify, track, and screen suspicious cargo entering the country from foreign ports, as well as assure that an appropriate number of containers are chosen at random for screening to deter the gaming of targeted screening systems.

RECOMMENDATION 2.6: DHS should develop a comprehensive communication plan to share accurate transportation security risk information with state, local, and tribal authorities, stakeholders, Congress, and the public; and submit the plan to Congress by March 1, 2005.

RECOMMENDATION 2.6.1: As part of developing a comprehensive transportation security communication strategy, DHS should implement the following recommendation made by the National Research Council: "Appropriate and trusted spokespeople should be identified and trained now so that, if a terrorist attack occurs, the government will be prepared to respond not only by supplying emergency services but also by providing important, accurate, and trustworthy information, clearly, quickly and authoritatively."[5]

RECOMMENDATION 2.6.2: Given the integral role of the news media in disseminating information to the public about threats, attacks, and responses involving transportation, emergency exercises at the federal, state, and local levels should include news media reporters as active participants whenever possible.

RECOMMENDATION 2.7: A "Registered Traveler" program should be expeditiously developed and deployed, but participants should not be exempted from "baseline" security scrutiny. Safeguards, such as biometric identification, should be built in to the system so that we can be sure that passengers identified as "registered travelers" are who they say they are.

RECOMMENDATION 2.8: TSA should accelerate its development of the Transportation Worker Identification Credential (TWIC) program to establish the necessary standards for secure identification for all 12 million transportation workers who require access to secure areas of transportation facilities.

RECOMMENDATION 2.9: All security-sensitive transportation workers, trainees, students, and operational licensees and certificate holders including pilots, hazmat drivers, etc. should be properly screened against terrorist watch lists (including the terror watch lists of allies where feasible) before receiving permission to enter specialized training, receiving professional licenses or certifications, or being hired as professionals in the field. Such names should then be rescreened regularly as watch lists are updated with additional names.

RECOMMENDATION 2.10: The federal government should work with other countries and international institutions including the International Civil Aviation Organization (ICAO) to assure that pilot training institutions and facilities abroad are overseen to prevent terrorist exploitation.

RECOMMENDATION 2.11: Federal homeland security assistance grants for transportation should be based on risk assessment information, and not on per capita or other general population or geographic factors. This should be implemented as soon as possible, but should be fully in place prior to the beginning of FY2006.

Principle 3: *Transportation security policy should be based on the establishment of appropriate goals for all modes of transportation, and the implementation of standards and best practices necessary to achieve them.*

RECOMMENDATION 3: DHS and TSA should establish a security standard (or "baseline") for the U.S. transportation security system and its associated infrastructure, based, at minimum, on: (1) a layered approach that assures effective, redundant protections, against high consequence forms of attack; (2) prioritization in the identification and repair of the weakest links in vulnerable transportation systems; and (3) building appropriate security features into the design and construction of transportation systems.

Security Standards and Guidelines

RECOMMENDATION 3.1: On or before August 1, 2005, TSA should issue enforceable performance-based standards to protect the security of critical transportation infrastructure and operations; and approve "best practice" guidelines to protect noncritical transportation infrastructure and operations. TSA should require that owners and operators of public (and where appropriate private) aviation, rail, freight, mass transit, and maritime transportation operations or facilities develop plans to achieve the applicable standards or guidelines. DHS/TSA should work with stakeholders and outside experts to develop the required security standards and best practices.

RECOMMENDATION 3.1.1: Priority for the department's establishment of standards and best practices should be assigned according to risk (taking into consideration threat, vulnerabilities, and consequences of attack). Areas that represent high consequence and relatively "weak links" should receive priority attention.

Layering Transportation Security

RECOMMENDATION 3.2: DHS/TSA should implement a layered security system to protect critical transportation infrastructure against high consequence forms of attack. (**NOTE:** Because we cannot count on any single layer of protection to be perfect, we must implement various layers to assure that a single point failure in the system is not catastrophic.)

RECOMMENDATION 3.2.1: DHS/TSA should provide to Congress documentation listing the various ways that terrorists could attack the various transportation modes, the layers in place to protect against such an attack, and the reliability of each layer. Congress should provide vigorous oversight of the documentation recommended above, to be certain it is duly comprehensive and complete. (**NOTE:** Such a "threat matrix" should be detailed regarding the various ways an attack might be launched. For instance, the matrix should consider the possibility that terrorists might try to hijack a commercial jet using an insider pilot and list the measures in place to foil such an attack. The matrix must be sufficiently comprehensive. For instance, it should consider such an attack using a domestic commercial aircraft, but also a foreign carrier that flies to the United States, the use of a cargo aircraft, charter aircraft, etc. The preparation of such a document will inevitably identify vulnerabilities that the nation should address. It might also identify vulnerabilities that will be difficult for the nation to do anything about. We recognize that there may be significant apprehension about producing such a comprehensive list because doing so will create a responsibility to act. That is a good thing. But we also believe the country should be honest about the vulnerabilities that are difficult to do anything about, at least so that proper alternative strategies can be devised.)

RECOMMENDATION 3.2.2: In cases where the possibility of consequential attacks exists but no current security measures (layers) are available to counter it, DHS/TSA should establish research and development priorities to develop such countermeasures.

RECOMMENDATION 3.2.3: To the extent possible, security measures should incorporate some element of randomness as a means of providing "unpredictability" to those who would try to defeat it. (**NOTE:** The security experts consulted by Commission staff consistently identified randomness and unpredictability as indispensable elements of sound security. For instance, passengers and cargo that are chosen at random for extraordinary screening, Federal Air Marshals that terrorists can't pick out of a crowd, and police who patrol facilities at irregular times, give pause to terrorists who are seeking predictable patterns they can learn to defeat with certainty.)

Security Checkpoints

RECOMMENDATION 3.3: TSA should continue to refine and implement a program to provide for the continual improvement of checkpoint performance, in terms of both human and technological capability. (**NOTE:** Though checkpoints should never again be relied on, as was the case on 9/11/01, as the only real defense layer against aircraft hijackings, civil aviation security checkpoints continue to play a vital role in aviation security, and their operations must be improved continuously.)

RECOMMENDATION 3.3.1: TSA should plan, develop, and deploy as soon as possible the "security checkpoint of the future" that maximizes the ability of checkpoints to detect and stop the full array of weapons and prohibited items, operate with top efficiency, and provide excellent customer service. The plan should include appropriate benchmarks and deadlines. Efforts should be made to explore the possible application of this work to modes other than commercial aviation.

RECOMMENDATION 3.3.2: TSA should conduct a detailed human factors study to improve screener performance and set measurable and attainable goals for individual screeners and security checkpoints at airports and any other transportation facilities where screening takes place. (**NOTE:** Many experts interviewed by Commission staff agreed that more pay and a better "career path" are not enough, by themselves, to increase screener performance to the level required. Other elements factor into the quality of screener performance, and these elements should be fully understood and addressed.)

RECOMMENDATION 3.3.3: TSA should move forward with efforts to assure that X-ray screening personnel are isolated in a manner that will ensure they are not influenced by the appearance of the passenger or distracted by the checkpoint environment.

RECOMMENDATION 3.3.4: Personnel and vehicles that access air operations areas (AOAs) at commercial airports should be appropriately credentialed and, where necessary, screened to assure that unauthorized people and items are not permitted access to the AOA or aircraft.

Transportation Worker Training and Regulatory Enforcement

RECOMMENDATION 3.4: TSA should take all appropriate steps to implement the recommendations of the FAA's 1996 Baseline Working Group that the civil aviation security system should "develop a comprehensive 'team' approach to security that treats aviation industry employees as team members with a stake in promoting aviation security, emphasizing that employees are the first line of defense. . .[and that security training programs should strive] to keep employees involved in, and informed of, aviation security and build a better understanding of the system."[6] This approach should be adopted for the other modes as well.

RECOMMENDATION 3.4.1: TSA should ensure that all transportation workers receive training in how to recognize, report, and respond to suspicious activity and terrorist attack. Such training should include behavior pattern recognition. More specifically and as a start, TSA should design, develop, and begin implementation of mandatory, comprehensive, industrywide antiterrorism and basic self-defense training for all flight attendants. Because the agency and air carriers have thus far failed to do so, despite the urging of legislation, if TSA does not take such action by December 31, 2004, Congress should consider transferring jurisdiction for this program to the Justice Department, with a statutory mandate to implement this training requirement by April 1, 2005. Furthermore, because such antiterrorist training is, inherently, a matter of national security, the federal government should assume a fair share of the cost. (**NOTE:** Representatives of the Association of Flight Attendants expressed the eagerness of their association members to receive such training. They indicated that if TSA is unwilling or unable to implement a training requirement, they would urge the transfer of the requirement to the Department of Justice.)

RECOMMENDATION 3.4.2: TSA should establish significant penalties for noncompliance with federal rules requiring that flight crews keep cockpit doors closed and locked in-flight. Federal Air Marshals should have the authority to issue citations for noncompliance with the regulation.

RECOMMENDATION 3.4.3: Federal Air Marshals should operate in a manner that maintains their anonymity and operational security to keep potential terrorists guessing. (**NOTE:** Commission staff interviewed many security experts who stressed the importance of maintaining unpredictability in security operations. We are concerned about information we received that the FAM program maintains policies including a dress code that may help potential terrorists identify air marshals and understand their procedures and tactics. In order to maximize the effectiveness of the program, DHS/TSA should take steps to ensure that FAMs are not obvious to terrorists, and that their operational procedures are not predictable or publicly well known.)

RECOMMENDATION 3.4.4: TSA should assure that federal, state, and local law enforcement officers who are passengers aboard commercial aircraft have the opportunity to receive training regarding in-flight counterterrorism procedures and tactics. This will multiply the force of personnel capable of appropriately responding to on-board contingencies.

RECOMMENDATION 3.4.5: TSA should ensure that proper procedures and safeguards are in place to confirm the identity of law enforcement officers who carry firearms into the sterile area and onto aircraft.

Cargo/Explosives

RECOMMENDATION 3.5: The use of explosives by terrorists and the potential for using cargo as a means of placing a bomb on board conveyances remains a high consequence form of attack on transportation, and TSA should continue to improve efforts to address this threat.

RECOMMENDATION 3.5.1: TSA should study and report to Congress on appropriate incentives (financial and otherwise) to encourage passenger airlines to remove cargo from passenger flights. Such study should examine the security benefits and economic costs of such incentives.

RECOMMENDATION 3.5.2: TSA should require that every passenger aircraft carrying cargo deploy at least one hardened container to carry select cargo for security purposes (including cargo chosen at random). (**NOTE:** This will provide an additional layer of security against explosives. As with the in-line screening recommendation below, a study should be conducted to determine what benefits would accrue to the air carriers from implementation of the recommendation. Cost-sharing for the containers should be based on the findings of such study.)

RECOMMENDATION 3.5.3: In-line screening of checked baggage should be implemented as expeditiously as possible as an urgent priority, beginning with the largest (category X) airports. In-line screening will result in significant improvements in both security and efficiency. Because the aviation industry will derive substantial benefits from this deployment, it should pay a fair share of the costs. To determine what that share should be, Congress should direct the National Academies of Science to conduct a study identifying the operational and security benefits and recommending the proper allocation of costs to the industry and the federal government. This report should be transmitted to Congress by no later than February 1, 2005, and Congress should fix the cost-share for in-line deployment by May 1, 2005.

RECOMMENDATION 3.5.4: Each individual identified as a selectee, by the current CAPPS I system or its successor, should have his or her person, carry-on baggage, and checked baggage subjected to explosives detection screening.

Engineering Security into Transportation Systems

RECOMMENDATION 3.6: DHS/TSA should issue standards and guidelines (in consultation with appropriate design and construction experts, owners, and operators) to ensure that new and remodeled transportation facilities, equipment, and related infrastructure are designed, constructed, operated and maintained to promote security and minimize the adverse consequences of terrorist attack. Congress should support this effort by attaching such requirements to federal infrastructure investments, starting with the pending surface transportation reauthorization legislation.

RECOMMENDATION 3.6.1: TSA should establish, by January 1, 2005, a panel for each transportation mode comprised of security experts, operational experts, design engineers, and stakeholder representatives to develop and prioritize appropriate design criteria to promote security of passengers, conveyances, and facilities.

RECOMMENDATION 3.6.2: Federal regulations governing the use of transportation grant monies should be amended to include a "best practices" guideline for the construction, design, and reconfiguration of airport and other critical transportation infrastructure, as appropriate, to promote security.

RECOMMENDATION 3.6.3: Congress should consider amending the surface transportation reauthorization bill to add the promotion of homeland security into the basic purposes of the law; requiring the states to submit (in a reasonable time frame) their plans for beginning to "build" security into their surface transportation programs; and/or authorizing certain high priority security-related proposals. (**NOTE:** We recognize that the surface transportation reauthorization bill is well along in the legislative process and that comprehensive revision as recommended would be difficult. However, given that the bill provides the largest single federal investment in transportation infrastructure, that it is multiyear and will not be due for reauthorization for five years, and that it covers transportation modes that are not the focus of current federal transportation security efforts, it represents an opportunity that we cannot afford to miss.)

RECOMMENDATION 3.6.4: Transportation security stakeholders responsible for major system operations (such as airports, air carriers, seaports, Amtrak, etc.) should maintain emergency operations centers guided by best practices and procedures necessary to provide swift, efficient, and effective emergency response. (**NOTE:** DHS, TSA, other appropriate government agencies and stakeholders should work together to establish appropriate standards and best practices for emergency operation facilities.)

Miscellaneous

RECOMMENDATION 3.7.1: TSA should set appropriate standards and practices to secure general aviation, including the designation of a General Aviation Facility Security Coordinator for selected General Aviation facilities (including those within range of high-risk, high-vulnerability targets). The Coordinator should be trained, and certified, pursuant to TSA guidelines. (**NOTE:** We believe that general aviation remains a significant transportation security vulnerability, and reasonable measures should be undertaken to make sure that general aviation aircraft are protected from unauthorized access.)

RECOMMENDATION 3.7.2: In coordination with the State Department, DHS/TSA should work, through bilateral, multilateral, and international agreements, to raise the international standards for aviation and transportation security to a level commensurate with that of the United States.

RECOMMENDATION 3.7.3: TSA should adopt an appropriate biometric standard (such as those developed by the National Institute of Standards and Technology, the National Security Agency, the International Civil Aviation Organization, or the standards planned for use in the US-VISIT program) to improve transportation security identity verification and to facilitate the ability of airports and other facilities to invest in the necessary equipment. (**NOTE:** Without such a standard, airports and others have been reluctant to invest in biometric technology. Also, we would note that it's important to realize that biometric identification can be worthless or even dangerous if the issuing agency can't confirm that a person is who they say they are when the credential is authorized. This requires appropriate policies to promote identity authentication prior to badging.)

RECOMMENDATION 3.7.4: TSA should assure that pilots and crew of foreign air carriers serving the United States undergo adequate background checks to assure that they are not a terrorist threat, and that practices and procedures necessary to protect the cockpit from intrusion are implemented and enforced.

RECOMMENDATION 3.7.5: Funding for TSA Research and Development should be increased by at least 10 percent per year above the FY2004 level of $154 million until it reaches $250 million per year. Furthermore, efforts by TSA or DHS to reprogram these funds, or by Congress to earmark them should be strongly resisted. While DHS' research and development budget has been relatively robust, TSA's has been subject to both internal reprogramming to meet operational needs and a lack of support within the budget process. For example, the FY2005 budget proposal called for a small cut in TSA R&D funding.

RECOMMENDATION 3.7.6: DHS should undertake as soon as possible its assessment of the optimal (from a security standpoint) deployment levels of Federal Air Marshals, checkpoint screeners, and checked bag screeners. This information should be reported to Congress by not later than February 1, 2005.

Principle 4: *Transportation security requires effective information sharing and coordinated teamwork among all stakeholders.*

RECOMMENDATION 4: DHS and TSA should take the lead in ensuring that all public and private organizations that are responsible for securing some part of the American transportation network are coordinated in their efforts and receive the information they need (including threat information) to carry out their security responsibilities.

RECOMMENDATION 4.1: "DHS should work with private companies to improve the two-way flow of terrorism-related information between government and industry" as recommended by the Markle Foundation.

RECOMMENDATION 4.2: Per Markle, "The DHS should help to expand the scope of all existing (industry-created) Information Sharing and Analysis Centers (ISACs) beyond cyber threats to include focus on terrorism-threat information and encourage the ISACs to share more information with the government and with other industry ISACs."[7]

RECOMMENDATION 4.3: "DHS should take the lead establishing clear procedures for providing state and local officials with better information to help guide their own homeland security decisions" as recommended by the Century Foundation.[8]

RECOMMENDATION 4.4: DHS, through TSA, should work with the various transportation stakeholders, including industry and state and local authorities, to develop a standard architecture for suspicious incident reporting that would allow such information to be shared in a timely and effective manner with federal homeland security and intelligence officials.

RECOMMENDATION 4.5: DHS/TSA should routinely develop and disseminate "tear line" intelligence reports, in which classified information is accompanied by a less classified, or unclassified, version below a tear-line (as recommended by the Markle Foundation) so that uncleared individuals have access to the security information they need to do their job properly.[9]

RECOMMENDATION 4.6: Congress, the Administration, and the courts need to provide clear guidance about what personal information may—and should—be collected for transportation security purposes, how it should be safeguarded, and how long this information should be retained (as recommended by the Century Foundation).[10]

RECOMMENDATION 4.7: An appropriate representative for each of the major transportation industries including airports, seaports, carriers, etc. should be integrated into the operation of the Terrorist Threat Integration Center (TTIC) or the National Counter Terrorism Center (NCTC) as recommended in the Commission's final report.

RECOMMENDATION 4.8: The General Aviation Facility Security Coordinator for selected General Aviation facilities suggested above should serve as the recipient of relevant security information from TSA and other federal agencies.

RECOMMENDATION 4.9: TSA should appoint a single point of contact for state and local homeland security agencies to improve the flow of communication. TSA should consider designating the senior Federal Security Director (FSD) in each state as the primary liaison and field contact.

Principle 5: Transportation security policies, practices, and procedures require vigorous oversight and enforcement to assure they remain current, relevant, and effective.

RECOMMENDATION 5: The TSA should implement measures to continuously and vigorously test and hold accountable each critical element of the U.S. transportation system in order to promote its effectiveness in preventing, responding to, and recovering from terrorist attacks.

RECOMMENDATION 5.1: TSA should provide for continuous and independent testing of civil aviation and transportation security systems, such as security checkpoints. Such testing should include the simulation of terrorist tactics in order to identify vulnerabilities and assess performance.

RECOMMENDATION 5.2: TSA, in consultation with Congress and outside experts, should establish performance goals for each element of the U.S. transportation security system.

RECOMMENDATION 5.3: The President, Congress, and TSA should develop systematic and transparent means of overseeing and holding accountable all critical elements of the U.S. transportation security system.

RECOMMENDATION 5.4: Information on the performance of transportation security systems should be shared with policy makers and stakeholders including the public, as appropriate, but in a manner that keeps the operational details of our security systems from being divulged to those who mean us harm.

RECOMMENDATION 5.5: Each House of Congress should designate one principal committee or subcommittee with expertise in transportation security policy to be kept "fully and currently" informed of the status of the transportation security system, including up-to-date information on threats, vulnerabilities, consequences, and system performance. This arrangement could follow the model established between the Congressional intelligence oversight committees and the Intelligence Community. In implementing this recommendation, in many cases this Congressional oversight should be conducted in closed sessions. Committees which maintain jurisdiction over nonsecurity aspects of transportation should be routinely updated on security issues, by the Intelligence committees and the panels with jurisdiction over transportation security to integrate vital security information and considerations into overall policy making.

RECOMMENDATION 5.6: Congress should create a Presidentially appointed and Senate-confirmed Transportation Security Oversight Board to receive and assess reports on the performance of the various components of the transportation security system, and to recommend remedial measures and initiatives.

RECOMMENDATION 5.7: TSA should consider issuing general security performance "Report Cards" measuring the relative performance of transportation security components.

RECOMMENDATION 5.8: Congress should designate either the General Accountability Office or the Department of Homeland Security Inspector General as responsible for regular monitoring and public reporting on Congressional and Administration consideration and implementation of the 9/11 Commission's transportation security recommendations.

RECOMMENDATION 5.9: TSA/DHS should establish rules and policies to assure that following any terrorist attack on transportation, comprehensive after-action reports are produced by responsible agencies to ascertain the facts and circumstances surrounding the attack, and to identify lessons learned about the prevention, response to, and recovery from the attack.

RECOMMENDATION 5.10: Congress should establish an independent board to investigate and report upon the facts and circumstances of terrorist attacks upon transportation, and issue lessons learned and remedial recommendations. Congress should consider folding this role into the National Transportation Safety Board or use the board as a model for a free-standing organization.

RECOMMENDATION 5.11: TSA and FAA should take steps to improve the survivability of flight data recorders (FDR) and cockpit voice recorders (CVR) to assure that complete and reliable information is available to investigators in the aftermath of terrorist attacks. (**NOTE:** As we saw from 9/11, maximizing the amount of evidence to re-create the events of a terrorist attack is critical to understanding precisely what happened, which in turn translates into more comprehensive "lessons learned." While the FDRs and CVRs on the 9/11 flights recorded valuable information, they did not all survive the respective crashes which deprived investigators, policy makers, and the public of valuable information.)

RECOMMENDATION 5.12: Congress should create independent "Red Teams" outside of TSA and DHS for the covert testing of all transportation modes. These teams should be placed under the jurisdiction of either a Transportation Security Oversight Board (if created), the National Research Council, and/or the Government Accountability Office.

RECOMMENDATION 5.13: As new organizations facing significant start-up issues, DHS and TSA should devote sufficient attention and resources to facilitating the oversight of their operations.

RECOMMENDATION 5.13.1: The Department of Homeland Security's Office of Inspector General (DHS IG) should be provided with adequate resources to carry out its necessary functions. (**NOTE:** With the federalization of the screener workforce, it is even more important that DHS/TSA be subject to strong independent oversight. The DHS IG should be provided with the manpower and resources commensurate with both the size of the agency and the importance of its responsibilities.)

RECOMMENDATION 5.13.2: Congress should exercise sufficient oversight to assure that the rights of whistle blowers in the transportation field are fully protected.

Appendix B: 9/11 Public Discourse Project, *Report on the Status of 9/11 Commission Recommendations: Part I: Homeland Security, Emergency Preparedness, and Response*

9/11 Public Discourse Project   September 14, 2005

Report on the Status of 9/11 Commission Recommendations

Part I: Homeland Security, Emergency Preparedness, and Response

NATIONAL STRATEGY FOR TRANSPORTATION SECURITY

"The U.S. government should identify and evaluate the transportation assets that need to be protected, set risk-based priorities for defending them, select the most practical and cost-effective ways of doing so, and then develop a plan, budget, and funding to implement the effort. The plan should assign roles and missions to the relevant authorities (federal, state, regional, and local), and to private stakeholders."(p. 391)

Grade: UNSATISFACTORY

What has happened: The Intelligence Reform and Terrorism Prevention Act of 2004 (PL 108-458) required DHS to prepare a National Strategy for Transportation Security, due April 1, 2005.

Why this is still important: With limited resources available for transportation security, resources must be allocated according to rational, risk-based priorities. Without a comprehensive assessment of the security needs of the nation's transportation system, this will be impossible.

How to fix it: DHS must produce this report as soon as possible and maintain a capability to review and modify the assessment to reflect the changing threat environment and state of transportation security.

IMPROVE AIRLINE PASSENGER PRESCREENING

"Improved use of "no-fly" and "automatic selectee" lists should not be delayed while the argument about a successor to CAPPS continues. This screening function should be performed by the TSA, and it should utilize the larger set of watch lists maintained by the federal government. Air carriers should be required to supply the information needed to test and implement this new system." (p. 393)

Grade: UNSATISFACTORY

What has happened: Contrary to the Commission recommendation, the TSA test program is combining watch list screening with the use of commercial data to verify passenger identities, which has produced controversy over privacy issues. This has delayed completion of the testing phase. TSA now hopes to begin operation of the new system in late 2005 or early 2006.

Why this is still important: With the airlines still responsible for implementing the "no fly" and "automatic selectee" lists, the names of many known or suspected terrorists are still not being included on these lists, making airline passengers less secure than they should be.

How to fix it: As recommended by the Commission and mandated by PL108-458, TSA should focus its priority attention on taking over implementation of passenger prescreening so that all names on the consolidated terrorist watch list are utilized.

IMPROVE AIRLINE SCREENING CHECKPOINTS
TO DETECT EXPLOSIVES

"The TSA and the Congress must give priority attention to improving the ability of screening checkpoints to detect explosives on passengers. As a start, each individual selected for special screening should be screened for explosives. Further, the TSA should conduct a human factors study, a method often used in the private sector, to understand problems in screener performance and set attainable objectives for individual screeners and for the checkpoints where screening takes place." (p. 393)

Grade: MINIMAL PROGRESS

What has happened: The Intelligence Reform and Terrorism Prevention Act of 2004 (PL108-458) required DHS to develop and deploy effective checkpoint explosives and WMD detection equipment, to screen all selectees and their carry-on property for explosives, and to report to Congress within 180 days on the results of any human factors study it has conducted. TSA has deployed explosives trace detection devices at all airports to examine selectees' carry-on items and installed explosives detection trace portals ("puffers") at 17 airports (with seven more airports due for installation in the near future) to scrutinize the persons of selectees. After the suicide bombing of Russian commercial aircraft in August 2004, TSA stepped up the use of "pat-down" searches for explosives, but after privacy-related protests, it took steps to reduce the "intrusiveness" of these searches. While TSA has indicated that human factors analysis is being carried out at a Research & Development facility in Atlantic City and elsewhere, it has not yet submitted to Congress the report required by statute.

Why this is still important: Following improvements in on-board defenses against suicide hijacking, explosives currently represent the major security threat to passenger aviation.

How to fix it: Congress needs to provide the funding for, and TSA needs to move as expeditiously as possible with, the installation of explosives detection trace portals at more of the nation's 441 commercial airports, while both continue to support the development of more advanced screening technology. Furthermore, until such time as the trace portals, or more effective successors, are fully deployed, TSA must utilize other means (including the canine teams and "pat-down" searches) to insure that selectees are searched for explosives, no matter what airport they fly from.

CHECKED BAG AND CARGO SCREENING
"More attention and resources should be directed to reducing or mitigating the threat posed by explosives in vessels' cargo holds. The TSA should expedite the installation of advanced (in-line) baggage screening equipment. Because the aviation industry will derive substantial benefits from this deployment, it should pay a fair share of the costs. The TSA should require that every passenger aircraft carrying cargo must deploy at least one hardened container to carry any suspect cargo. TSA also needs to intensify its efforts to identify, track, and appropriately screen potentially dangerous cargo in both the aviation and maritime sectors." (p. 393)

Grade: MINIMAL PROGRESS

What has happened: The Intelligence Reform and Terrorism Prevention Act of 2004 (PL 108-458) incorporated the Commission's recommendations for deployment of "in-line" screening equipment, converted the hardened container requirement into a pilot program, and established a detailed program for air cargo security. In response, TSA does not appear to have expedited its plans for in-line installation, with just nine operational systems and eight more under construction as of mid-2005. There has been little progress on the hardened container pilot project. The agency's air cargo security efforts have centered on a slow-moving regulatory proceeding. Efforts by the Department of Homeland Security's Customs and Border Protection (CBP) division have improved upon the pre-9/11 state of maritime cargo security, yet these programs have received relatively little funding. The Government Accountability Office, among others, has documented continuing problems in each of them.

Why this is still important: Deployment of in-line explosives detection equipment has been shown to improve security and to significantly reduce operational costs. Air and maritime cargo continue to be very vulnerable to terrorist attack.

How to fix it: The main impediment to improved checked bag and cargo security is inadequate funding. If the Congress and the administration believe these to be priorities, they must determine the costs and specify how they will pay for these improvements.

Notes

Preface

1. Available online at http://www.archives.gov/research/9-11-commission/staff-report-Sept2005.pdf. This document provides significantly more information than did the Final Report about FAA intelligence operations, though TSA "redacted" (deleted) a number of these findings on classification grounds.

2. The General Accounting Office was renamed as the Government Accountability Office, effective July 7, 2004, in order to "better reflect the modern professional services organization GAO has become." The change was made by the *GAO Human Capital Reform Act of 2004* (Public Law No. 108-271, 118 Stat. 811). To avoid confusion, this organization will generally be referred to as GAO hereafter in this book.

Chapter 1. Introduction

1. *Report of the President's Commission on Aviation Security and Terrorism* (Washington, DC, May 15, 1990), p. 57.

2. National Commission on Terrorist Attacks Upon the United States (9/11 Commission), *The 9/11 Commission Report: The Final Report of the National Commission on Terrorist Attacks Upon the United States*, Authorized Edition (New York: W.W. Norton, 2004), p. 254.

3. 9/11 Commission, *Monograph: Four Flights and Civil Aviation Security*, staff report, August 26, 2004, p. 62n478.

4. 9/11 Commission, *Testimony of Jane Garvey*, Second Public Hearing, May 22, 2003.

5. Brian Jenkins, "Aviation Security in the United States," in *Aviation Terrorism and Security*, ed. Wilkinson and Jenkins (London: Frank Cass, 1999), pp. 110–111.

6. 9/11 Commission, *Staff Statement #3*, Seventh Public Hearing, January 27, 2004.

7. 9/11 Commission, *Final Report*, pp. 339–340.

8. Public Law 107-71, 107th Cong., 1st sess. (2001).

9. Public Law 107-295, 107th Cong., 2d sess. (2002).

10. Public Law 107-296, 107th Cong., 2d sess. (2002).

11. Public Law 107-306; Title VI, 107th Cong., 2d sess. (2002).

12. White House, *December 17, 2003 Homeland Security Presidential Directive/HSPD-7* (Washington, DC, 2003).

13. Public Law 108-458, 108th Cong., 2d sess. (2004).

14. Bart Elias, Congressional Research Service, "Budget History of Aviation Security Program" (Washington, DC: March 25, 2003); Department of Homeland Security, *DHS Budget in Brief—Fiscal Year 2005* (Washington, DC: 2004), pp. 21–34; and Department of Transportation, *FY2005 Budget in Brief, Overview: Security* (Washington, DC: 2004), http://www.dot.gov/bib2005/overview.

15. The Heritage Foundation and the Center for Strategic and International Studies, *DHS 2.0: Rethinking the Department of Homeland Security* (Washington, DC, December 13, 2004), p. 7.

16. 9/11 Commission, *Final Report*, p. 391.

17. Government Accountability Office, *High Risk Series: An Update*, GAO-05-207 (Washington, DC, January 2005), p. 30.

18. Susan B. Glasser and Michael Grunwald, "Department's Mission Was Undermined from Start," *Washington Post*, December 22, 2005.

19. Paul C. Light, "Still Searching for Airport Security," *Washington Post*, April 24, 2005.

20. 9/11 Public Discourse Project, *Final Report on 9/11 Commission Recommendations* (Washington, DC, December 5, 2005).

21. Department of Homeland Security, Office of the Inspector General, *DHS Challenges in Consolidating Terrorist Watch List Information* (Washington, DC, August 2004), p. 9; and Katherine Pfleger Shrader, "Analysts Are in Great Demand," *Washington Post*, December 30, 2004.

22. Justin Rood, "Obscure Aviation Intelligence Unit Emerges From Shadows," *Congressional Quarterly*, February 24, 2005.

23. E. Marla Felcher, "Aviation Security," in *The Department of Homeland Security's First Year: A Report Card* (New York: Century Foundation, 2004), p. 51.

24. 9/11 Commission, *Final Report*, p. 392.

25. Ibid., pp. 83, 476n54; and 9/11 Commission, *Staff Statement #3*, Seventh Public Hearing, January 27, 2004.

26. Department of Homeland Security, *DHS Challenges in Consolidating Terrorist Watch List Information*, pp. 16–28.

27. 9/11 Commission, *Final Report*, pp. 392–393.

28. Ibid., pp. 84nn54–55, 392–393.

29. Government Accountability Office, *Aviation Security: Secure Flight Development and Testing Under Way, but Risks Should Be Managed as System Is Further Developed*, GAO-05-356 (Washington, DC, March 2005), p. 4.

30. Jonathan Krim, "Panel Urged to Review Passenger Screening," *Washington Post*, April 7, 2005.

31. Felcher, "Aviation Security," p. 58.

32. Department of Homeland Security, Office of the Inspector General, *Follow-up Audit of Passenger and Baggage Screening Procedures at Domestic Airports (Unclassified Summary)*, OIG-05-16 (Washington, DC, March 2005), p. 2; and Department of Homeland Security, Office of the Inspector General, *Major Management Challenges Facing the Department of Homeland Security (Excerpts from the FY2005 DHS Performance and Accountability Report)*, OIG-06-14 (Washington, DC: December 2005), p. 118.

33. Felcher, "Aviation Security," p. 46; and Government Accountability Office, *Aviation Security: Systematic Planning Needed to Optimize the Deployment of Checked Baggage Screening Systems*, GAO-05-365 (Washington, DC, March 2005), pp. 7, 45.

34. Department of Homeland Security, Office of the Inspector General, *Major Management Challenges Facing the Department of Homeland Security (Excerpts from the FY2005 DHS Performance and Accountability Report)*, OIG-06-14 (Washington, DC: December 2005), p. 118.

35. U.S. House, Committee on Transportation and Infrastructure, Subcommittee on Aviation, *Hearing on Transportation Security Administration's Perspective on Aviation Security*, Background Memo, 108th Cong., 1st sess. (Washington, DC, October 16, 2003), http://www.house.gov/transportation/aviation/10-16-03/10-16-03memo.html.

36. Felcher, "Aviation Security," p. 46.

37. Department of Homeland Security, Transportation Security Administration, *State of Aviation Security Fact Sheet*, Washington, DC, September 29, 2003.

38. *Aviation and Transportation Security Act*, Public Law 107-71, §107; and *Homeland Security Act*, Public Law 107-296, §107.

39. General Accounting Office, *Aviation Security: Federal Air Marshal Service Is Addressing Challenges of Its Mission and Workforce, but Additional Actions Needed*, GAO-04-242 (Washington, DC, November 19, 2003), p. 1.

40. Stephen McHale, interview by 9/11 Commission staff, Washington, DC, April 15, 2004.

41. Association of Flight Attendants, "TSA Fails to Provide Aviation Security Training Guidelines," news release, June 22, 2004.

42. General Accounting Office, *Aviation Security: Improvement Still Needed in Federal Aviation Security Efforts*, Highlights, pp. 13–14.

43. Felcher, "Aviation Security," p. 52; General Accounting Office, *Aviation Security: Efforts to Measure Effectiveness and Strengthen Security Programs*, GAO-04-285T (Washington, DC, November 20, 2003), p. 21; and Government Accountability Office, *General Aviation Security: Increased Federal Oversight Is Needed, but Continued Partnership With the Private Sector Is Critical to Long-Term Success*, GAO-05-144 (Washington, DC, November 2004), pp. 3–4.

44. *Associated Press*, "Report Sees Holes in U.S. Aviation Security," March 14, 2005.

45. General Accounting Office, *Aviation Security: Efforts to Measure Effectiveness and Strengthen Security Programs*, GAO-04-285T (Washington, DC, November 20, 2003), p. 20.

46. *Federal Register* 69, no. 217, November 10, 2004, pp. 65258–65291; and Associated Press, "TSA Plans More Checks on Cargo Loads," *Washington Post*, November 11, 2004.

47. U.S. Senator Ernest Hollings, "Legislative Summary: Maritime Transportation Security Act of 2002," http://hollings.senate.gov/~hollings/materials/2002B13856.html.

48. Department of Homeland Security, *Prepared Remarks of Deputy Secretary of Homeland Security James Loy, Maritime and Port Security Summit* (Washington, DC, November 16, 2004).

49. Department of Homeland Security, *DHS Budget in Brief—Fiscal Year 2006* (Washington, DC, 2005), p. 2.

50. Department of Homeland Security, *Secure Seas, Open Ports* (Washington, DC, June 21, 2004).

51. 9/11 Commission, *Testimony of Gerald Dillingham*, First Public Hearing (Washington, DC: April 1, 2003).

52. General Accounting Office, *Maritime Security: Progress Made in Implementing Maritime Transportation Security Act but Concerns Remain*, GAO-03-1155T (Washington, DC, September 9, 2003).

53. Joseph F. Bouchard, *New Strategies to Protect America: Safer Ports for a More Secure Economy* (Washington, DC: Center for American Progress, 2005), pp. 6–7.

54. Department of Homeland Security, Office of the Inspector General, *Major Management Challenges Facing the Department of Homeland Security*, OIG-05-06 (Washington, DC, December 2004), p. 18; Margaret T. Wrightson, Government Accountability Office, *Maritime Security: Enhancements Made, But Implementation and Sustainability Remain Key Challenges*, GAO-05-448T (Washington, DC, May 17, 2005), pp. 21–23; and James D. Hessman, "Port Security: A Mission Impossible for the U.S. Coast Guard?" In *The News*, March 9, 2005, http://DomesticPreparedness.com.

55. Richard Stano, General Accounting Office, *Homeland Security: Summary of Challenges Faced in Targeting Oceangoing Cargo Containers for Inspection*, GAO-04-577T (Washington, DC, March 31, 2004), p. 7.

56. Department of Homeland Security, *DHS Budget in Brief—Fiscal Year 2006*, pp. 3, 26.

57. Wrightson, *Maritime Security: Enhancements Made*, pp. 15–17.

58. Office of Management and Budget, *Budget of the U.S. Government Fiscal Year 2006* (Washington, DC, 2005), p. 38; and Government Accountability Office, *Container Security: A Flexible Staffing Model and Minimum Equipment Requirements Would Improve Overseas Targeting and Inspection Efforts*, GAO-05-557 (Washington, DC, April 2005), p. 4.

59. Government Accountability Office, *Container Security: A Flexible Staffing Model*, p. 4.

60. Antone Gonsalves, "Nation's Supply Chain Has Too Many Weak Links," November 8, 2004, http://www.securitypipeline.com/shared/article/printableArticleSrc.jhtml?articleId=52500244.

61. Institute for Security Technology Studies, *On the Road to Transportation Security* (Hanover, NH: Dartmouth College, February 2003), p. 18.

62. Department of Homeland Security, Transportation Security Administration, *Statement of David M. Stone to U.S. Senate Committee on Commerce, Science and Transportation*, February 15, 2005, pp. 7, 12.

63. U.S. Department of Transportation, *FY2006 Budget-In-Brief* (Washington, DC, 2005), pp. 9, 22–23.

64. Julie B. Hairston, "MARTA Under Pressure," *AJC Horizon*, August 15, 2005; Sewell Chan, "Funds Will Be There When Technology Is, MTA Chief Says," *New York Times*, July 13, 2005, nytimes.com; and Fred Kaplan, "Planning Gridlock," *Slate*, July 14, 2005, www.slate.com.

65. Institute for Security Technology Studies, *On the Road*, pp. 1, 20.

66. Department of Homeland Security, Office of the Inspector General, *Major Management Challenges Facing the Department of Homeland Security*, OIG-05-06 (Washington, DC, December 2004), p. 18.

67. Department of Homeland Security, Office of the Inspector General, *Major Management Challenges Facing the Department of Homeland Security (Excerpts from the FY2005 DHS Performance and Accountability Report)*, OIG-06-14 (Washington, DC: December 2005), p. 119.

68. Clark Kent Ervin, "A To-Do List for Chertoff," *Washington Post*, February 7, 2005.

69. 9/11 Commission, *Final Report*, p. 83; and 9/11 Commission, *Testimony of James Loy*, Seventh Public Hearing, January 27, 2004.

70. Office of Management and Budget, *Budget of the U.S. Government Fiscal Year 2006*, pp. 38, 40.

71. Department of Homeland Security, Transportation Security Administration, *Statement of David M. Stone to U.S. Senate Committee on Commerce, Science and Transportation* (Washington, DC, February 15, 2005), p. 6.

72. Congressional Research Service, *Homeland Security Department: FY2006 Appropriations* (Washington, DC, June 13, 2005), pp. 18, 32–33; and U.S. Senate, Committee on Appropriations, *DHS Appropriations Bill, 2006*, 109th Cong., 1st sess. (Washington, DC, July 16, 2005), S. Report 109-83, p. 43.

73. 9/11 Commission, *Final Report*, p. 391.

74. The November 2004 proposed rule making for air cargo, the November 2002 *Maritime Transportation Security Act*, and the May 2004 Rail Security Directives, respectively.

Chapter 2. The Pre-9/11 Aviation Security System

1. 9/11 Commission, *Monograph: Four Flights and Civil Aviation Security*, staff report, August 26, 2004, p. 62n478.

2. 9/11 Commission, *Staff Statement #3*, Seventh Public Hearing, January 27, 2004; and 9/11 Commission, *Monograph: Four Flights and Civil Aviation Security*, pp. 54–55n108.

3. Alexander T. Wells, *Commercial Aviation Safety*, 3rd ed. (New York: McGraw-Hill, 2001), p. 303.

4. Ibid., p. 303.

5. *Report of the President's Commission on Aviation Security and Terrorism* (Washington, DC, May 15, 1990), pp. 1–2.

6. Laura Parker, "U.S. Agency Orders Measures to Improve Airline Security," *Washington Post*, April 4, 1989.

7. *Report of the President's Commission on Aviation Security and Terrorism*, p. i.

8. Public Law 104-604, 104th Cong., 2d sess. (1990); and *Report of the President's Commission on Aviation Security and Terrorism*, pp. 40–61.

9. Federal Aviation Administration, *Criminal Acts Against Civil Aviation 1996* (Washington, DC, 1997), pp. 50–52, 56–57.

10. Daniel Benjamin and Steven Simon, *The Age of Sacred Terror* (New York: Random House, 2002), pp. 20–26.

11. While some reports indicated that "bojinka" was derived from the Serbo-Croatian word for "big bang," plotter Khalid Shaikh Mohammed told U.S. investigators that it was a "nonsense word he adopted after hearing it on the front lines in Afghanistan." 9/11 Commission, *Final Report*, p. 147n7.

12. 9/11 Commission, *Testimony of Jane Garvey*, Second Public Hearing, May 22, 2003.

13. Andrew R. Thomas, *Aviation Insecurity: The New Challenges of Air Travel* (Amherst, NY: Prometheus Books, 2003), p. 248n10.

14. 9/11 Commission, *Testimony of Jane Garvey*.

15. Aviation Security Advisory Committee (ASAC) Security Baseline Working Group, *Summary and Recommendations of the Final Report of the Baseline Working Group* (Washington, DC, December 12, 1996), available online at http://www.securitymanagement.com/library/asac.html.

16. Ibid., *Summary*.

17. Ibid.

18. Ibid.

19. U.S. Department of Transportation, Federal Aviation Administration, *Study and Report to Congress on Civil Aviation Security Responsibilities and Funding* (Washington, DC: 1998), p. 47.

20. Executive Order no. 13015, *Federal Register* 61, no. 167 (August 27, 1996), p. 43937.

21. *Final Report of the White House Commission on Aviation Safety and Security* (Washington, DC, 1997), available online at http://www.fas.org/irp/threat/212fin~1.html.

22. Ibid.

23. *White House Commission on Aviation Safety and Security DOT Status Report* (Washington, DC, February 1998); *White House Commission on Aviation Safety and Security DOT Status Report* (Washington, DC, February 1999); and *White House Commission on Aviation Safety and Security Status of Implementation of Recommendations: Public Version* (Washington, DC, October 2000).

24. White House, *Final Report of the White House Commission on Aviation Safety and Security* (Washington, DC: 1997); White House, *White House Commission on Aviation Safety and Security DOT Status Report* (Washington, DC: February 1998); White House, *White House Commission on Aviation Safety and Security DOT Status Report* (Washington, DC: February 1999); and White House, *White House Commission on Aviation Safety and Security Status of Implementation of Recommendations: Public Version* (Washington, DC: October 2000).

25. "Appendix A, Commissioner Cummock Dissent Letter," in *Final Report of the White House Commission on Aviation Safety and Security* (Washington, DC, 1997), available online at http://www.fas.org/irp/threat/212fin~1.html.

26. 9/11 Commission, *Testimony of Cathal "Irish" Flynn*, Seventh Public Hearing, January 27, 2004.

27. *Federal Aviation Reauthorization Act of 1996*; Public Law 104-264; 104th Cong., 2d sess., 110 Stat. 3213.

28. *Airport Security Improvement Act of 2000*; Public Law 106-528; 106th Cong., 2d sess., 114 Stat. 2521.

Chapter 3. Attributes of the Security System

1. 49 USC 449 Subtitle VII, Part A; Alexander T. Wells, *Commercial Aviation Safety*, 3rd ed. (New York: McGraw-Hill, 2001), p. 307; and Legal Information Institute, *US Code Collection*, http://www4.law.cornell.edu/uscode/49/40101.html.

2. 14 CFR 108, 1-01-01 ed.

3. 9/11 Commission, Testimony of Kenneth Mead, Second Public Hearing, May 22, 2003; and Andrew R. Thomas, *Aviation Insecurity: The New Challenge of Air Travel* (Amherst, NY: Prometheus Books, 2003), p. 44.

4. 14 CFR 107.

5. Steven Brill, *After: How America Confronted the September 12 Era* (New York: Simon & Schuster, 2003), p. 31.

6. *Final Report of the White House Commission on Aviation Safety and Security* (Washington, DC, 1997), available online at http://www.fas.org/irp/threat/212fin~1.html.

7. U.S. House, *Conference Report to accompany HR 3539, Federal Aviation Reauthorization Act of 1996*, 104th Cong., 2d sess. (Washington, DC, 1996), H. Report 104-848, p. 92.

8. Wells, *Commercial Aviation Safety*, p. 307.

9. *Report of the President's Commission on Aviation Security and Terrorism* (Washington, DC, May 15, 1990), p. 53.

10. *Report of the Special Advisory Task Force on Massport* (Boston, MA: December 4, 2001), p. 5.

11. The Commission attributed the FAA's "reliance" on reaction to a lack of visibility of its security function, a lack of a sufficient information base for decision making, insufficient staffing for security, and the division of security responsibilities with no single entity accountable. *Report of the President's Commission on Aviation Security and Terrorism*, pp. i, 53.

12. Thomas, *Aviation Insecurity*, p. 115.

13. Wells, *Commercial Aviation Safety*, p. 308.

14. Richard J. Kent, Jr., *Safe, Separated and Soaring: A History of Federal Civil Aviation Policy: 1961–1972* (Washington, DC: U.S. Department of Transportation, Federal Aviation Administration, 1980), p. 338; Federal Aviation Administration, *FAA Historical Chronology, 1926–1996*, www.faa.gov; U.S. Senate, Committee on Governmental Affairs, *Testimony of Paul Busick at Hearing on "Weak Links: How Should the Federal Government Manage Airline Passenger and Baggage Screening?"* 107th Cong., 1st sess. (Washington, DC, September 25, 2001), S. Hrg. 107-208, p. 110; and *1974 CQ Almanac* (Washington, DC: Congressional Quarterly, 1975), pp. 275–276.

15. Kent, *Safe, Separated and Soaring*, p. 338; and U.S. Department of Transportation, Federal Aviation Administration, *Study and Report to Congress on Civil Aviation Security Responsibilities and Funding* (Washington, DC, 1998), p. 20.

16. *Report of the President's Commission on Aviation Security and Terrorism* (Washington, DC, 1990), p. i; and *The Aviation Security Improvement Act of 1990*, Public Law 104-604, 104th Cong., 2d sess.

17. Office of the President, *Executive Order 13015 Federal Register* Document 96-21996 (Washington, DC, August 22, 1996); *Final Report of the White House Commission on Aviation Safety and Security* (Washington, DC, 1997); *White House Commission on Aviation Safety and Security DOT Status Report* (Washington, DC, February 1998); *White House Commission on Aviation Safety and Security* (Washington, DC, February 1999); *White House Commission on Aviation Safety and Security Status of Implementation of Recommendations: Public Version* (Washington, DC, October 2000); *Federal Aviation Reauthorization Act of 1996*; Public Law 104-264; 104th Cong., 2d sess., 110 Stat. 3213; and *Airport Security Improvement Act of 2000*; Public Law 106-528, 106th Cong., 2d sess., 114 Stat. 2521.

18. Wells, *Commercial Aviation Safety*, pp. 220–221.

19. 9/11 Commission, *Testimony of Cathal "Irish" Flynn*, Seventh Public Hearing, January 27, 2004.

20. Peter St. John, "The Politics of Aviation Terrorism," in Wilkinson and Jenkins, eds., *Aviation Terrorism and Security* (London: Frank Cass, 1999), p. 28.

21. 9/11 Commission, *Testimony of Cathal "Irish" Flynn*.

22. As of 9/11, the entire regulatory process could take up to 217 steps, though some of these could be dispensed with under certain circumstances. Wells, *Commercial Aviation Safety*, pp. 220–221.

23. Cost–benefit analysis was required of federal rules by Executive Order 12866, the *Regulatory Flexibility Act of 1980* and the OMB impact statement on foreign trade.

24. 9/11 Commission, *Staff Statement #3*, Seventh Public Hearing, January 27, 2004.

25. Wells, *Commercial Aviation Safety*, pp. 220–221.

26. Brill, *After*, p. 63.

27. 9/11 Commission, *Testimony of Kenneth Mead*.

28. *Federal Register*, July 17, 2001, pp. 37335–37336.

29. Ibid., p. 37339.

30. Ibid., pp. 37340–37341.

31. 9/11 Commission, *Testimony of James C. May*, Second Public Hearing, May 22, 2003.

32. 9/11 Commission, *Testimony of Cathal "Irish" Flynn*.

33. National Commission on Terrorist Attacks Upon the United States (9/11 Commission), *The 9/11 Commission Report: The Final Report of the National Commission on Terrorist Attacks Upon the United States*, authorized ed. (New York: W.W. Norton, 2004), p. 83nn52–53.

34. The Office of Civil Aviation Security Intelligence (ACI) exclusively handled threat assessments for the FAA, whereas vulnerability assessments were primarily conducted by the Office of Civil Aviation Security Operations (ACO), with the Office of Civil Aviation Security Policy and Planning (ACP) also having a role.

35. Including, among others, *Aviation Security: Additional Actions Needed to Meet Domestic and International Challenges* (GAO/RCED-94-38, January 27, 1994); *Aviation Security: Urgent Issues Need to Be Addressed* (GAO/T-RCED/NSIAD-96-251, September 11, 1996); *Aviation Security: Slow Progress in Addressing Long-Standing*

Screener Performance Problems (GAO/T-RCED-00-125, March 16, 2000); and *Aviation Security: Long-Standing Problems Impair Airport Screeners' Performance* (GAO/RCED-00-75, June 28, 2000).

36. Including *Audit Report on Deployment of Explosives Detection Systems*, October 5, 1998 (AV-1999-001); *Statement on Aviation Security by Alexis Stefani*, Deputy Assistant Inspector General for Aviation, before House Subcommittee on Aviation, May 14, 1998 (AV-1998-134); *Statement on Aviation Security by Alexis Stefani*, Deputy Assistant Inspector General for Aviation, before House Subcommittee on Aviation, March 10, 1999 (AV-1999-068); and *Statement on Aviation Security* by Alexis Stefani, Deputy Assistant Inspector General for Aviation, before Senate Aviation Subcommittee, April 6, 2000 (AV-2000-076).

37. 9/11 Commission, *Final Report*, p. 83nn52–53.

38. 9/11 Commission, *Staff Statement #3*.

39. *Federal Register*, July 17, 2001, pp. 37335–37352.

40. U.S. Centennial of Flight Commission, *The Federal Aviation Administration and Its Predecessor Agencies*, http://www.centennialofflight.gov/essay/Government_Role/FAA_History/POL8.htm).

41. Thomas, *Aviation Insecurity*, p. 42.

42. *Federal Aviation Act of 1958*; Public Law 85-726, 85th Cong., 2d sess.; 72 Stat. 737; 49 U.S.C. App. 1301 *et. seq.*

43. Mary Schiavo, *Flying Blind, Flying Safe* (New York: Avon Books, 1997), p. 51.

44. Federal Aviation Administration, *FAA Historical Chronology, 1926–1998*, www.faa.gov.

45. *Congressional Record,* 104th Cong., 2d sess., July 16, 1996, p. S7897.

46. U.S. House, *Conference Report to accompany HR 3539, Federal Aviation Reauthorization Act of 1996*, 104th Cong., 2d sess. (Washington, DC, 1996), H. Report 104-848, p. 92.

47. Legal Information Institute, *US Code Collection*, http://www4.law.cornell.edu/uscode/49/40101.html.

48. Wells, *Commercial Aviation Safety*, pp. 302–303.

49. National Research Council, *Making the Nation Safer: The Role of Science and Technology in Countering Terrorism* (Washington, DC: The National Academies Press, 2002), p. 219.

50. *U.S. Centennial of Flight Commission*, *The Federal Aviation Administration and Its Predecessor Agencies*, http://www.centennialofflight.gov/essay/Government_Role/FAA_History/POL8.htm.

51. Jenkins, "Aviation Security in the United States," p. 102.

52. Air Transport Association, *Remarks of Carol B. Hallett, President to the ALPA Safety Forum* (Washington, DC, August 16, 2001).

53. 9/11 Commission, *Testimony of Cathal "Irish" Flynn*.

54. 9/11 Commission, *Testimony of Jane Garvey*, Second Public Hearing, May 22, 2003.

55. Jenkins, "Aviation Security in the United States," p. 104.

56. Ibid., p. 103.

57. 9/11 Commission, *Testimony of Gerald Dillingham*, First Public Hearing, May 1, 2003.

58. Ibid.

59. U.S. Senate, Committee on Governmental Affairs, *Testimony of Kenneth Mead*, 107th Cong., 1st sess. (Washington, DC, November 14, 2001), S. Hrg. 107-263, pp. 79–81.

60. 9/11 Commission, *Testimony of Bogdan Dzakovic*, Second Public Hearing, May 22, 2003.

61. U.S. Senate, Commerce, Science and Transportation Committee, Subcommittee on Aviation, *Testimony of Gerald Dillingham at hearing on" Vulnerabilities in the Aviation Security System*," 106th Cong., 2d sess. (Washington, DC, April 6, 2000).

Chapter 4. The 9/11 Hijackings

1. National Commission on Terrorist Attacks Upon the United States (9/11 Commission), *The 9/11 Commission Report: The Final Report of the National Commission on Terrorist Attacks Upon the United States*, authorized ed. (New York: W.W. Norton, 2004), p. 85n63; and 9/11 Commission, *Testimony of Jane Garvey*, Second Public Hearing, May 22, 2003.

2. 9/11 Commission, *Final Report*, pp. 85–86; and *Testimony of Jane Garvey.*

3. ABC News Poll by TNS Intersearch, November 1999, N=1,024, MoE ± 3%: "Which do you feel is safer: flying in a commercial airplane or driving in a car?" Flying 58%, Driving 39%, No Opinion 8%; and Fox News/Opinion Dynamics Poll, Nov. 3–4, 1999, N=900, MoE ± 3%: "Which do you think is the greater threat to airline safety: terrorist attacks or poor maintenance?" Poor Maintenance 78%, Terrorist Attacks 15%, Not Sure 7%.

4. Brian Jenkins, "Aviation Security in the United States," in *Aviation Terrorism and Security*, ed. Wilkinson and Jenkins (London: Frank Cass, 1999), p. 104.

5. Prior to 9/11, the aviation industry was forecasting 2001 net losses of $3.5 billion. Air Transport Association, *Airlines in Crisis: The Perfect Economic Storm* (Washington, DC, May 2003), p. 9.

6. 9/11 Commission, *Testimony of Kenneth Mead*, Second Public Hearing, May 22, 2003.

7. 9/11 Commission, *Final Report*, p. 84n55.

8. 9/11 Commission, *Staff Statement #3*, Seventh Public Hearing, January 27, 2004; and 9/11 Commission, *Final Report*, p. 84n57.

9. 9/11 Commission, *Final Report*, p. 84n58.

10. Ibid., p. 85n60.

11. Ibid., pp. 83–84n54.

12. Ibid., pp. 1–4nn2, 5, 9, 10, 12, 18.

13. Ibid., pp. 1n1, 3nn14–16.

14. Ibid., p. 19nn109–110.

15. Ibid., pp. 11–12n79.

16. Ibid., p. 9n55.

17. Ibid., p. 10n67.

18. Ibid., pp. 32–33.

19. Ibid., p. 19n111.

20. 9/11 Commission, *Monograph: Four Flights and Civil Aviation Security*, staff report (Washington, DC, August 26, 2004), pp. 21–22n171.

21. 9/11 Commission, *Final Report*, p. 22nn127–128.

22. Ibid., p. 10n67.

23. Ibid., p. 11n69.

24. Ibid., p. 11n70.

25. Ibid., p. 11n69.

26. Ibid., p. 1n1.

27. Ibid., p. 84n56.

28. Ibid., p. 84n57.

29. 9/11 Commission, *Staff Statement #4*, Seventh Public Hearing, January 27, 2004.

30. Air Transport Association, *Airlines in Crisis*, p. 9; and United Airlines, "UAL Corporation Reports Low for Second Quarter," news release, July 18, 2001.

31. 9/11 Commission, *Testimony of Kenneth Mead*, and General Accounting Office, *Aviation Security: Long-Standing Problems Impair Airport Screeners' Performance*, GAO/RCED-00-75 (Washington, DC, June 28, 2000).

32. 9/11 Commission, *Final Report*, p. 83n52.

33. Ibid., pp. 10–11nn65–69.

Chapter 5. Response to 9/11

1. National Research Council, *Making the Nation Safer: The Role of Science and Technology in Countering Terrorism* (Washington, DC: The National Academies Press, 2002), p. 220.

2. E. Marla Felcher, "Aviation Security," in *The Department of Homeland Security's First Year: A Report Card* (New York: Century Foundation, 2004), p. 39.

3. Democratic Members of the House Select Committee on Homeland Security, "America at Risk: Closing the Security Gap" (Washington, DC, February 2004).

4. General Accounting Office, *Airport Security: Challenges to Airport Passenger and Baggage Screening*, GAO-04-440T (Washington, DC, February 12, 2004), pp. 3, 16.

5. Department of Homeland Security, *DHS Budget in Brief—Fiscal Year 2005* (Washington, DC, 2004), p. 30.

6. Sec. 4023 of the Intelligence Reform and Terrorism Prevention Act of 2004, the implementing legislation for the 9/11 Commission recommendations, called for TSA to submit to Congress a report on the "standards for determining the aviation security staffing for all airports at which screening is required," in order to "(1) provide necessary levels of aviation security; and (2) ensure that the average aviation security-related delay experienced by airline passengers is minimized." Apparently, however, such determinations are not to include the size of the screener workforce because, under the same section, DHS is to study the feasibility of combining the operations of "aviation security-related functions" with "Federal employees involved in screening," thereby indicating that the latter is regarded as a separate function from aviation security, per se. Public Law 108-458; §4023.

7. National Commission on Terrorist Attacks Upon the United States (9/11 Commission), *The 9/11 Commission Report: The Final Report of the National Commission on Terrorist Attacks Upon the United States*, authorized ed. (New York: W.W. Norton, 2004), p. 39.

8. *Report of the President's Commission on Aviation Security and Terrorism* (Washington, DC, 1990), p. 47.

9. Public Law 107-71, §101, 107th Cong., 1st sess.

10. Public Law 107-295, 107th Cong., 2d sess.

11. Public Law 107-296, 107th Cong., 2d sess.

12. White House, *December 17, 2003 Homeland Security Presidential Directive/HSPD-7* (Washington, DC, 2003).

13. U.S. House, Select Committee on Homeland Security, Subcommittee on Infrastructure and Border Security, *Testimony of Stephen J. McHale*, 108th Cong., 2d sess. (Washington, DC, May 12, 2004).

14. U.S. Senate, Committee on Commerce, Science and Transportation, *Testimony of Asa Hutchinson*, 108th Cong., 2d sess. (Washington, DC, August 16, 2004).

15. Public Law 107-306; §602, 107th Cong., 2d sess.

16. 9/11 Commission, *Final Report*, p. xv.

17. Ibid., p. 391.

18. Ibid., pp. 392–393.

19. The Senate adopted its version of the legislation by a vote of 96 to 2 on October 6, 2004. The two votes in opposition to the measure were from Democratic Senators Byrd (WV) and Hollings (SC), who objected to the haste in which the Senate was considering such major changes in governmental structure. *Congressional Record*, 108th Cong., 2d sess., October 6, 2004, pp. S10512–10513. On October 8, 2004, the House of Representatives, by a vote of 282 to 134, passed HR 10. The House vote was much more along party lines, with Republicans supporting it by a margin of 213 to 8, and Democrats opposing by a vote of 69 to 125. Prior to the final vote, House Democrats had sought to replace HR 10 with the language from the Senate-passed bill because they felt the Senate version was closer to the 9/11 Commission recommendations, but the effort failed, 193 to 223. On that vote, Republicans opposed, 2 to 219, whereas Democrats supported, 190 to 4. Independent Bernard Sanders of Vermont sided with a majority of Democrats on both votes. *Congressional Record*, 108th Cong., 2d sess., October 8, 2004, pp. H8975–8976. The House adopted the conference report on December 7, 2004, by a vote of 336 to 75, with sixty-seven Republicans and eight Democrats voting against it. Charles Babington, "House Approves Intelligence Bill," *Washington Post*, December 8, 2004. On the next day, the Senate approved the legislation by a margin of 89 to 2, with Democrat Robert Byrd (WV) and Republican James Inhofe (OK) dissenting. Walter Pincus, "Intelligence Bill Clears Congress," *Washington Post*, December 9, 2004.

20. Consisting of John Raidt, former director of the Senate Commerce Committee for Senator John McCain (R-AZ), Dr. Gerald Dillingham, on loan to the Commission from his position at the GAO, and myself, former senior policy advisor for Sen. Max Cleland (D-GA).

21. Although the staff recommendations were fully consistent with the 9/11 Commission report findings and recommendations, the Commission did not formally endorse them.

22. 9/11 Public Discourse Project, *Report on the Status of 9/11 Commission Recommendations, Part I: Homeland Security, Emergency Preparedness and Response* (Washington, DC, September 14, 2005).

23. 9/11 Public Discourse Project, *Final Report on 9/11 Commission Recommendations* (Washington, DC, December 5, 2005).

Chapter 6. The New Organization of Transportation Security

1. Federal Aviation Administration, *Administrator's Fact Book* (Washington, DC, October 2001), p. 16; and Federal Aviation Administration, *Civil Aviation Security Handbook* (Washington, DC, May 1999), pp. 117–118.

2. Air Transport Association, *Airlines In Crisis: The Perfect Economic Storm* (Washington, DC, May 2003), p. 9.

3. 9/11 Commission, *Testimony of Gerald L. Dillingham*, First Public Hearing, April 1, 2003.

4. National Research Council, *Making the Nation Safer*, p. 212.

5. Most of this amount, 1.7 million miles, is in the form of natural gas distribution pipelines, which transport natural gas from transmission pipelines to residential, commercial, and industrial customers. General Accounting Office, *Pipeline Safety: The Office of Pipeline Safety Is Changing How It Oversees the Pipeline Industry*, GAO/RCED-00-128 (Washington, DC, May 15, 2000), p. 6.

6. U.S. Coast Guard, *Maritime Strategy for Homeland Security* (Washington, DC, 2004), p. 30.

7. Office of Management and Budget, *Budget of the United States Government Fiscal Year 2005* (Washington, DC: 2004), p. 166.

8. 9/11 Commission, *Testimony of Gerald L. Dillingham*.

9. National Research Council, *Making the Nation Safer*, p. 213.

10. Markle Foundation, *Creating a Trusted Network for Homeland Security* (New York: Markle Foundation, 2003), p. 3.

11. Department of Homeland Security, Office of the Inspector General, *Major Management Challenges Facing the Department of Homeland Security*, OIG-05-06 (Washington, DC, December 2004), p. 19.

12. Ibid., p. 1; and Department of Homeland Security, Office of the Inspector General, *Major Management Challenges Facing the Department of Homeland Security (Excerpts from the FY2005 DHS Performance and Accountability Report)*, OIG-06-14, December 2005, pp. 110–111.

13. The Heritage Foundation and the Center for Strategic and International Studies, *DHS 2.0: Rethinking the Department of Homeland Security* (Washington, DC, December 13, 2004), p. 7.

14. John Mintz, "Infighting Cited at Homeland Security," *Washington Post*, February 2, 2005.

15. Susan B. Glasser and Michael Grunwald, "Department's Mission Was Undermined From Start," *Washington Post*, December 22, 2005.

16. Paul C. Light, "Still Searching for Airport Security," *Washington Post*, April 24, 2005.

17. Partnership for Public Service, *Best Places to Work in the Federal Government*, September 14, 2005, www.bestplacestowork.org.

18. National Commission on Terrorist Attacks Upon the United States (9/11 Commission), *The 9/11 Commission Report: The Final Report of the National Commission on Terrorist Attacks Upon the United States*, Authorized Edition (New York: W.W. Norton, 2004) p. 391.

19. Department of Homeland Security, *Interim National Infrastructure Protection Plan* (Washington, DC, February 2005), p. 2.

20. Department of Homeland Security, "National Infrastructure Protection Plan Status Update," PowerPoint presentation provided to House Committee on Homeland Security staff, Washington, DC, November 1, 2005, cited in U.S. House, Committee on Homeland Security, Democratic staff, *Leaving the Nation at Risk: 33 Unfulfilled Promises from the Department of Homeland Security,* 109th Cong, 1st sess. (Washington, DC, December 27, 2005), p. 4.

21. 9/11 Public Discourse Project, *Final Report on 9/11 Commission Recommendations* (Washington, DC: December 5, 2005).

22. Clark Kent Ervin, "A To-Do List for Chertoff," *Washington Post*, February 7, 2005.

23. U.S. Senate, Committee on Homeland Security and Governmental Affairs, *Statement of Kip Hawley at hearing on "Transit Security,"* 109th Cong., 1st sess. (Washington, DC, September 21, 2005).

24. Department of Homeland Security and Department of Transportation, *National Strategy for Transportation Security: Overview* (Washington, DC, 2005).

25. 9/11 Public Discourse Project, *Final Report on 9/11 Commission Recommendations* (Washington, DC: December 5, 2005).

26. 9/11 Commission, *Testimony of Gerald Dillingham.*

27. 9/11 Commission, *Final Report*, p. 391.

28. Asa Hutchinson, interview by 9/11 Commission staff, Washington, DC, December 22, 2003.

29. James Loy, interview by 9/11 Commission staff, Washington, DC, December 15, 2003.

30. Charles Mitchell and Chris Decker, "Applying Risk-Based Decision-Making Methods and Tools to U.S. Navy Antiterrorism Capabilities," February 2004, http://www.homelandsecurity.org/journal/Articles/Mitchell_Decker.html.

31. Department of Homeland Security, *Securing Our Homeland: U.S. Department of Homeland Security Strategic Plan* (Washington, DC, 2004), p. 54.

32. Ibid., p. 10.

33. Ibid., p. 11.

34. Gregory F. Treverton, "Intelligence Gathering, Analysis, and Sharing," in *The Department of Homeland Security's First Year: A Report Card* (New York: Century Foundation, 2004), p. 73.

35. 9/11 Commission, Testimony of James M. Loy, 7th Public Hearing, January 27, 2004; and U.S. House, Committee on Homeland Security, Subcommittee on Infrastructure and Border Security, *Testimony of Stephen J. McHale*, 108th Cong., 2d sess. (Washington, DC, May 12, 2004).

36. Treverton, "Intelligence Gathering," p. 72.

37. Clark Kent Ervin, "A To-Do List for Chertoff."

38. Government Accountability Office, *Passenger Rail Security: Enhanced Federal Leadership Needed to Prioritize and Guide Security Efforts*, GAO-05-851 (Washington, DC, September 2005), pp. 20–25.

39. Government Accountability Office, *Passenger Rail Security: Enhanced Federal Leadership Needed to Prioritize and Guide Security Efforts*, GAO-05-851 (Washington, DC, September 2005), Highlights.

40. Transportation Security Administration, *Fact Sheet: CAPPS II At a Glance* (Washington, DC, February 12, 2004).

41. Department of Homeland Security, *FY 2005 Budget Presentation* (Washington, DC, 2004), p. 30.

42. Transportation Security Administration, *Fiscal Year 2004 Budget Briefing* (Washington, DC, February 3, 2003).

43. Office of Management and Budget, *Budget of the United States Government Fiscal Year 2005* (Washington, DC: 2004), p. 166.

44. 9/11 Commission, Site Visit to National Targeting Center, Herndon, VA, July 25, 2003.

45. Government Accountability Office, *High Risk Series: An Update*, GAO-05-207 (Washington, DC, January 2005), p. 30.

46. John Mintz, "Infighting Cited at Homeland Security."

47. The Heritage Foundation and the Center for Strategic and International Studies, *DHS 2.0*, p. 11.

48. Department of Homeland Security, *Transcript of Press Conference with Acting Secretary of Homeland Security Admiral James Loy on the FY2006 Budget* (Washington, DC, February 7, 2005).

49. U.S. House, Committee on Appropriations, *Conference Report to accompany HR 2360, Making Appropriations for the Department of Homeland Security for the Fiscal Year ending September 20, 2006*, 109th Cong., 1st sess. (Washington, DC, September 2005), H. Report 109-241, p. 31.

50. Department of Homeland Security, *DHS Budget in Brief—Fiscal Year 2006* (Washington, DC, 2005), p. 37.

51. Steven Brill, *After: How America Confronted the September 12 Era* (New York: Simon & Schuster, 2003), p. 408.

52. Department of Homeland Security, *DHS Budget in Brief*, p. 40; and Transportation Security Administration, *Statement of David M. Stone, before U.S. Senate Committee on Commerce, Science & Transportation* (Washington, DC, February 15, 2005), pp. 5–6.

53. 50,696 out of 52,504 "full time equivalent" positions (FTEs). Transportation Security Administration, *FY2006 TSA Budget Request* (Washington, DC, February 2005), p. 15.

54. The FY2006 DHS appropriations bill transferred the WMD detection equipment funding from CBP to a new Domestic Nuclear Detection Office (DNDO) within the Science and Technology directorate, and focused the program on the "testing, development, and deployment of radiation portal monitors at the Nation's ports-of-entry." U.S. House, Committee on Appropriations, *Conference Report to accompany HR 2360, Making Appropriations for the Department of Homeland Security for the Fiscal Year ending September 20, 2006*, 109th Cong., 1st sess. (Washington, DC, September 2005), H. Report 109-241, p. 79.

55. Office of Management and Budget, *Budget of the U.S. Government Fiscal Year 2006* (Washington, DC, 2005), pp. 35–38, 151–156; and Department of Homeland Security, *Department of Homeland Security FY2006 Budget Request Includes Seven Percent Increase*, fact sheet (Washington, DC, February 8, 2005).

56. Department of Homeland Security, *DHS Budget in Brief*, pp. 19–22.

57. FY2005 funding for port, rail, truck, intercity bus, and nongovernmental organization security grants totaled $340 million. Margaret T. Wrightson, Government Accountability Office, *Maritime Security: Enhancements Made, But*

Implementation and Sustainability Remain Key Challenges, GAO-05-448T (Washington, DC, May 17, 2005), p. 22.

58. Office of Management and Budget, *Budget of the U.S. Government Fiscal Year 2006* (Washington, DC, 2005), p. 156.

59. Ibid., p. 154.

60. Congressional Research Service, *Homeland Security Department FY2006 Appropriations*, 109th Cong., 1st sess. (Washington, DC, June 13, 2005), p. 33; U.S. Senate, Committee on Appropriations, *Department of Homeland Security Appropriations Bill, 2006*, 109th Cong., 1st sess. (Washington, DC, 2005), S. Report 109-83, p. 49; and U.S. House, Committee on Appropriations, *Conference Report to accompany HR 2360, Making Appropriations for the Department of Homeland Security for the Fiscal Year ending September 20, 2006*, 109th Cong., 1st sess. (Washington, DC, September 2005), H. Report 109-241, p. 35.

61. Congressional Research Service, *Homeland Security Department FY2006 Appropriations*, 109th Cong., 1st sess. (Washington, DC, June 13, 2005), pp. 43–44; U.S. House, Committee on Appropriations, *Department of Homeland Security Appropriations Bill, 2006*, 109th Cong., 1st sess. (Washington, DC, 2005); U.S. Senate, Committee on Appropriations, *Department of Homeland Security Appropriations Bill, 2006*, p. 67; and U.S. House, Committee on Appropriations, *Conference Report to accompany HR 2360, Making Appropriations for the Department of Homeland Security for the Fiscal Year ending September 20, 2006*, 109th Cong., 1st sess. (Washington, DC, September 2005), H. Report 109-241, p. 64.

62. U.S. Department of Transportation, *FY2006 Budget in Brief* (Washington, DC, 2005), pp. 9, 22–23; and Office of Management and Budget, *Budget of the United States Government Fiscal Year 2006, "Appendix: Homeland Security Mission Funding by Agency and Budget Account."*

63. U.S. Department of Energy, *FY2006 Congressional Budget Request: National Nuclear Security Administration*, Volume 1 (Washington, DC, February 2005), p. 490.

Chapter 7. The Current State of Transportation Security

1. Public Law 107-296, § 424, 107th Cong., 2d sess.

2. For example, see Sara Kehaulani Goo, "Proposed Budget Would Strip TSA of Its Biggest Programs," *Washington Post*, February 9, 2005.

3. Proposed in Administration's FY2006 budget request for DHS. Department of Homeland Security, *U.S. Department of Homeland Security FY2006 Budget Request Includes Seven Percent Increase*, fact sheet (Washington, DC, February 8, 2005).

4. Although such a lead role for the Coast Guard was also envisioned by MTSA, that law left the ultimate "assignment of duties and responsibilities" for maritime security to its mandated National Maritime Transportation Security Plan (Public Law 107-295, §70103).

5. John Mintz, "Infighting Cited at Homeland Security," *Washington Post*, February 2, 2005.

6. The transfer took place on November 2, 2003, and was justified by Secretary Ridge as allowing for the centralized cross-training of air marshals, immigration

agents, and customs agents within ICE in order to create a "surge capacity" to respond to a variety of security threats. General Accounting Office, *Aviation Security: Federal Air Marshal Service Is Addressing Challenges of Its Expanded Mission and Workforce, But Additional Actions Needed*, GAO-04-242 (Washington, DC, November 19, 2003), p. 1.

7. Department of Homeland Security, "Homeland Security Secretary Michael Chertoff Announces Six-Point Agenda for Department of Homeland Security," news release, July 13, 2005, p. 3.

8. Department of Homeland Security, *DHS Budget in Brief—Fiscal Year 2005* (Washington, DC, 2004), p. 29.

9. Goo, "Proposed Budget."

10. Department of Homeland Security, *DHS Budget in Brief—Fiscal Year 2006* (Washington, DC, 2005), p. 19.

11. Ibid., pp. 19–21.

12. National Commission on Terrorist Attacks Upon the United States (9/11 Commission), *The 9/11 Commission Report: The Final Report of the National Commission on Terrorist Attacks Upon the United States*, Authorized Edition (New York: W.W. Norton, 2004), p. 387.

13. Goo, "Proposed Budget."

14. U.S. House, Committee on Appropriations, *Conference Report to accompany HR 2360, Making Appropriations for the Department of Homeland Security for the Fiscal Year ending September 20, 2006*, 109th Cong., 1st sess. (Washington, DC, September 2005), H. Report 109-241, p. 35.

15. Sara Kehaulani Goo, "Air Security Agency Faces Reduced Role," *Washington Post*, April 8, 2005; and Sara Kehaulani Goo, "High Turnover at Agency Raises Concern for Air Safety," *Washington Post*, April 9, 2005.

16. Department of Homeland Security, *DHS Budget in Brief—Fiscal Year 2005*, p. 45.

17. Department of Homeland Security, Office of the Inspector General, *DHS Challenges In Consolidating Terrorist Watch List Information* (Washington, DC, August 2004), pp. 5–7.

18. Ibid., p. 7.

19. Ibid., pp. 7, 9.

20. Markle Foundation, *Creating a Trusted Network for Homeland Security* (New York: Markle Foundation, 2003), pp. 7–8.

21. 9/11 Commission, *Testimony of Russell Travers*, Seventh Public Hearing, January 26, 2004, transcript, pp. 102–103.

22. Department of Homeland Security, *DHS Challenges In Consolidating Terrorist Watch List Information*, pp. 7–10.

23. Ibid., p. 6.

24. 9/11 Commission, *Final Report*, pp. 392–393.

25. 9/11 Public Discourse Project, *Final Report on 9/11 Commission Recommendations* (Washington, DC, December 5, 2005).

26. Eric Lichtblau, "Government Report on U.S. Aviation Warns of Security Holes," *New York Times*, March 14, 2005.

27. 9/11 Commission, *Final Report*, p. 83n51.

28. *Report of the President's Commission on Aviation Security and Terrorism* (Washington, DC, May 15, 1990), p. 40.

29. Department of Homeland Security, *DHS Challenges In Consolidating Terrorist Watch List Information*, p. 9; and Katherine Pfleger Shrader, "Analysts Are in Great Demand," *Washington Post*, December 30, 2004.

30. Justin Rood, "Obscure Aviation Intelligence Unit Emerges From Shadows," *Congressional Quarterly*, February 24, 2005.

31. Former head of both FAA Intelligence and TSIS Claudio Manno testified to the 9/11 Commission about the training of FAA intelligence analysts in aviation security operations and in tactics used in previous attacks specifically against civil aviation, which he felt made them "uniquely qualified to evaluate threats to civil aviation." 9/11 Commission, *Testimony of Claudio Manno*, Seventh Public Hearing, January 27, 2004. It has been reported that "most" intelligence specialties require an analyst to spend seven to ten years in mastering the subject matter. Katherine Pfleger Shrader, "Analysts Are in Great Demand," *Washington Post*, December 30, 2004.

32. 9/11 Commission, *Final Report*, p. 1n1; and 9/11 Commission, *Staff Statement #3*, Seventh Public Hearing, January 27, 2004.

33. E. Marla Felcher, "Aviation Security," in *The Department of Homeland Security's First Year: A Report Card* (New York: Century Foundation, 2004), pp. 50–51.

34. TSA originally projected that it would test a TWIC prototype in 2003 and issue the first identification cards by August 2004. However, the program has been significantly delayed, in part because of TSA's shift to DHS and inadequate communication and coordination between the two entities. Furthermore, GAO received reports from a number of seaport stakeholders that TSA had not been sufficiently responsive to their input, for example in determining precisely which felony convictions should disqualify a worker from receiving the credential. Margaret T. Wrightson, Government Accountability Office, *Maritime Security: Enhancements Made, But Implementation and Sustainability Remain Key Challenges*, GAO-05-448T (Washington, DC, May 17, 2005), pp. 3, 21.

35. Department of Homeland Security, *DHS Budget In Brief—Fiscal Year 2005*, p. 30.

36. Department of Homeland Security, *DHS Budget In Brief—Fiscal Year 2006*, p. 19.

37. Felcher, "Aviation Security," p. 51.

38. 9/11 Commission, *Final Report*, p. 392.

39. *"Report of the Secure Flight Working Group,"* presented to the Transportation Security Administration (Washington, DC, September 19, 2005), p. 17, http://www.epic.org/privacy/airtravel/secureflight.html.

40. 9/11 Commission, *Final Report*, p. 83n54; and 9/11 Commission, *Staff Statement #3*.

41. Department of Homeland Security, *DHS Challenges In Consolidating Terrorist Watch List Information*, pp. 16–28.

42. 9/11 Commission, *Final Report*, pp. 392–393. There were 270,000 entries on the consolidated terrorist watch list as of Spring 2005, though a number of these were aliases of the same individual. *"Report of the Secure Flight Working Group,"* p. 17, http://www.epic.org/privacy/airtravel/secureflight.html; and Sara Kehaulani Goo, "Panel Criticizes Screening Plan," *Washington Post*, September 24, 2005.

43. This was reported in a June 2005 statement by the Department of Justice Inspector General and was based on that office's audit of the TSC conducted between April and November 2004. Mark Sherman, "Review of Terrorism Database Finds Flaws," *Associated Press*, June 14, 2005.

44. 9/11 Commission, *Final Report*, pp. 84nn54–55, 392–393.

45. In March 2004, GAO reported to Congress "TSA . . . has not completely addressed seven of the eight issues identified by the Congress as key areas of interest related to the development, operation, and public acceptance of CAPPS II." The only issue to have been fully resolved at the time of the report was the creation of an internal CAPPS II advisory board. The unresolved issues, which had not been addressed "due in part to the early stage of the system's development," included the accuracy of data, "stress testing" of the proposed system, abuse prevention, unauthorized access prevention, operation and use policies, specific privacy concerns, and the redress process. General Accounting Office, *Challenges Delay Implementation of Computer-Assisted Passenger Prescreening System*, GAO-04-504T (Washington, DC, March 12, 2004).

46. 9/11 Commission, *Testimony of James Loy*, Seventh Public Hearing, January 27, 2004.

47. "Transportation Security Administration, Docket No. TSA-2004-19160, Privacy Impact Assessment: Secure Flight Test Phase," *Federal Register* 69, no. 185 (September 24, 2004), pp. 57352–57355.

48. Section 522 of Public Law 108-334, 108th Cong., 2d sess. (2004).

49. Government Accountability Office, *Aviation Security: Secure Flight Development and Testing Under Way, but Risks Should Be Managed as System Is Further Developed*, GAO-05-356 (Washington, DC: March 2005), p. 4.

50. Ibid.

51. Sara Kehaulani Goo, "Air Passenger Screening Program Behind Schedule," *Washington Post*, March 25, 2005.

52. 9/11 Public Discourse Project, *Report on the Status of 9/11 Commission Recommendations, Part I: Homeland Security, Emergency Preparedness and Response* (Washington, DC, September 14, 2005); and "Secure Flight Test Records: Privacy Impact Assessment," Docket No. TSA-2004-19160, *Federal Register* 70, no. 119 (June 23, 2005), p. 36321.

53. Government Accountability Office, *Aviation Security: Transportation Security Administration Did Not Fully Disclose Uses of Personal Information During Secure Flight Testing in Initial Privacy Notes, But Has Recently Taken Steps to More Fully Inform the Public*, GAO-05-864R (Washington, DC, July 22, 2005), p. 2.

54. Jonathan Krim, "Panel Urged to Review Passenger Screening," *Washington Post*, April 7, 2005.

55. *"Report of the Secure Flight Working Group,"* p. 17. and Goo, "Panel Criticizes Screening Plan."

56. U.S. House, Committee on Appropriations, *Conference Report to accompany HR 2360, Making Appropriations for the Department of Homeland Security for the Fiscal Year ending September 20, 2006*, 109th Cong., 1st sess. (Washington, DC, September 2005), H. Report 109-241, pp. 22, 54.

57. 9/11 Public Discourse Project, *Final Report on 9/11 Commission Recommendations* (Washington, DC, December 5, 2005).

58. Sara Kehaulani Goo, "No-Fly Gaps Irk Airlines, DHS," *Washington Post*, May 25, 2005.

59. Sara Kehaulani Goo, "U.S. Modifies Air Passenger List Proposal," *Washington Post*, June 1, 2005.

60. Sara Kehaulani Goo, "Program for Registered Fliers Slow to Expand," *Washington Post*, February 5, 2005.

61. Sara Kehaulani Goo, "Airports Look to Expand Registered Traveler Plan," *Washington Post*, July 15, 2005.

62. Sara Kehaulani Goo, "Registered Traveler Test Is Ending Inconclusively," *Washington Post*, September 27, 2005.

63. Transportation Security Administration, "TSA Announces Key Elements of Registered Traveler Program," news release, January 20, 2006.

64. Leslie Miller, "TSA Toughens Registered Traveler Rules," *Washington Post*, January 21, 2006.

65. While requiring that checkpoint screening be taken over by federal employees by November 2002, ATSA also authorized up to five airports to participate in a pilot program using private contractors under TSA supervision. (The five airports ultimately selected for the program were in San Francisco, CA; Tupelo, MS; Kansas City, MO; Rochester, NY; and Jackson, WY.) ATSA further provided that, starting on November 19, 2004, all airports could petition TSA to leave the federalized screening system and return to a privatized screener workforce. Robert S. Kirk, Congressional Research Service, *Selected Aviation Security Legislation in the Aftermath of the September 11 Attack*, RL31150 (Washington, DC, December 14, 2001), p. 6. The pilot program at the five airports concluded on November 18, 2004. A preliminary assessment was delivered at an April 2004 hearing before the House Transportation and Infrastructure Committee's Aviation Subcommittee. The DHS Inspector General and the GAO both testified that the performance of the federal and private screeners was comparable, but poor, and needed further improvement. U.S. House of Representatives, Committee on Transportation and Infrastructure, "Decentralized Airport Security Screening System With Strong Federal Oversight Recommended at Congressional Hearing," press release, April 22, 2004; and Department of Homeland Security, *Statement of Clark Kent Ervin, before House Transportation and Infrastructure Committee Subcommittee on Aviation* (Washington, DC, April 22, 2004). TSA has begun to develop guidelines and procedures for the opt-out program, but specific measures have not yet been finalized. However, the agency has indicated that the ability of screeners to detect test threat objects, including both knives and handguns, will be a key performance requirement. Government Accountability Office, *Aviation Security: Preliminary Observations on TSA's Progress to Allow Airports to Use Private Passenger and Baggage Screeners*, GAO-05-126 (Washington, DC, November 2004).

66. Felcher, "Aviation Security," p. 38.

67. Ibid., pp. 39–45.

68. Ibid., p. 58.

69. General Accounting Office, *Aviation Security: Improvement Still Needed in Federal Aviation Security Efforts*, GAO-04-592T (Washington, DC, March 30, 2004), p. 11.

70. Department of Homeland Security, *Statement of Clark Kent Ervin.*

71. Sara Kehaulani Goo, "Airport Security Screeners Overworked, Report Says," *Washington Post*, October 13, 2004.

72. Department of Homeland Security, Office of the Inspector General, *Follow-up Audit of Passenger and Baggage Screening Procedures at Domestic Airports (Unclassified Summary)*, OIG-05-16 (Washington, DC, March 2005), p. 2.

73. Felcher, "Aviation Security," p. 46; and Government Accountability Office, *Aviation Security: Systematic Planning Needed to Optimize the Deployment of Checked Baggage Screening Systems*, GAO-05-365 (Washington, DC, March 2005), pp. 7, 45.

74. General Accounting Office, *Aviation Security: Improvement Still Needed in Federal Aviation Security Efforts*, GAO-04-592T (Washington, DC, March 30, 2004), p. 12.

75. Department of Homeland Security, Office of the Inspector General, *Major Management Challenges Facing the Department of Homeland Security, (Excerpts from the FY2005 DHS Performance and Accountability Report)*, OIG-06-14 (Washington, DC, December 2005), p. 118.

76. Public Law 108-458 §4013.

77. Transportation Security Administration, "TSA Expands Its Passenger Explosives Detection Capability," news release, July 29, 2005.

78. Transportation Security Administration, *Pat-down, Other Screening Enhancements Must Be Carried Out Appropriately*, fact sheet (Washington, DC, December 2004).

79. U.S. House, Committee on Transportation and Infrastructure, Subcommittee on Aviation, *Hearing on Transportation Security Administration's Perspective on Aviation Security*, Background memo, 108th Cong., 1st sess. (Washington, DC, October 16, 2003), http://www.house.gov/transportation/aviation/10-16-03/10-16-03.memo.html.

80. Felcher, "Aviation Security," p. 46.

81. TSA has estimated that a typical lobby-based screening unit can screen an average of 376 bags per hour and employ 19 screeners, whereas an in-line unit can screen 425 bags per hour utilizing just 4.25 screeners. Furthermore, the agency's cost–benefit analysis at the nine airports where TSA was helping to fund in-line installation found that deployment of these systems could produce significant cost savings for the federal government, with the initial federal investment being recoverable in a little more than a year via lower operating costs. Government Accountability Office, *Aviation Security: Systematic Planning Needed to Optimize the Deployment of Checked Baggage Screening Systems*, pp. 4, 23, 41–42.

82. Public Law 108-176, 108th Cong., 2d sess.

83. Bert Elias, Congressional Research Service, "Aviation Security-Related Findings and Recommendations of the 9/11 Commission," RL32541 (Washington, DC, October 13, 2004), p. 2.

84. U.S. House, Committee on Appropriations, *Conference Report to accompany HR 2360, Making Appropriations for the Department of Homeland Security for the Fiscal Year ending September 20, 2006*, 109th Cong., 1st sess. (Washington, DC, September 2005), H. Report 109-241, p. 51.

85. *Consolidated Appropriations Resolution, 2003*, Public Law 108-7, 108th Cong., 1st sess.

86. Elias, "Aviation Security-Related Findings, p. 7; U.S. House, Committee on Transportation and Infrastructure, Subcommittee on Aviation, *Hearing on In-Line Explosive Detection Systems: Financing and Deployment, staff memo*, 108th Cong., 2d sess. (Washington, DC, July 14, 2004); and Transportation Security Administration, *Statement of David M. Stone to U.S. Senate Committee on Commerce, Science and Transportation* (Washington, DC, February 15, 2005), p. 5.

87. Atlanta, Boston, Dallas–Ft. Worth, Denver, Las Vegas, Los Angeles and Ontario, CA, Phoenix, and Seattle.

88. Government Accountability Office, *Aviation Security: Systematic Planning*, pp. 28, 32–35; and U.S. House, Committee on Appropriations, *Conference Report to accompany HR 2360, Making Appropriations for the Department of Homeland Security for the Fiscal Year ending September 20, 2006*, 109th Cong., 1st sess. (Washington, DC, September 2005), H. Report 109-241, p. 51.

89. The FY2006 budget request provided an additional $144 million in federal funds for a total of $394 million, to purchase and install EDS, including Next Generation EDS and Explosives Trace Detection devices. Transportation Security Administration, *Statement of David M. Stone*, p. 10.

90. Elias, *Aviation Security-Related Findings*, p. 7; Transportation Security Administration, *Statement of David M. Stone*, p. 5; and U.S. House, Committee on Appropriations, *Conference Report to accompany HR 2360, Making Appropriations for the Department of Homeland Security for the Fiscal Year ending September 20, 2006*, 109th Cong., 1st sess. (Washington, DC, September 2005), H. Report 109-241, p. 51.

91. 9/11 Commission, *Final Report*, p. 393.

92. 9/11 Public Discourse Project, *Final Report on 9/11 Commission Recommendations* (Washington, DC, December 5, 2005).

93. Rep. John Mica, Chairman of House Transportation and Infrastructure Committee Subcommittee on Aviation, "Problems In Equipping Commercial Airports With Effective & Efficient Screening Systems By 2006," news release, July 14, 2004.

94. Department of Homeland Security, Office of the Inspector General, *Major Management Challenges Facing the Department of Homeland Security*, OIG-05-06 (Washington, DC, December 2004), p. 16.

95. General Accounting Office, *Aviation Security: Improvement Still Needed in Federal Aviation Security Efforts*, pp. 12–13.

96. Department of Homeland Security, *DHS Budget In Brief—FY2006*, pp. 40, 77.

97. U.S. House, Committee on Appropriations, *Conference Report to accompany HR 2360, Making Appropriations for the Department of Homeland Security for the Fiscal Year ending September 20, 2006*, 109th Cong., 1st sess. (Washington, DC, September 2005), H. Report 109-241, p. 82.

98. Department of Homeland Security, Office of the Inspector General, *Major Management Challenges Facing the Department of Homeland Security (Excerpts from the FY2005 DHS Performance and Accountability Report)*, OIG-06-14 (Washington, DC: December 2005), p. 118.

99. Department of Homeland Security, *State of Aviation Security Fact Sheet* (Washington, DC, September 29, 2003).

100. ATSA, Public Law 107-71, §107; and *Homeland Security Act*, Public Law 107-296, §107.

101. General Accounting Office, *Aviation Security: Federal Air Marshal Service Is Addressing Challenges of Its Mission and Workforce, But Additional Actions Needed*, GAO-04-242 (Washington, DC: November 19, 2003), p. 1.

102. Stephen McHale, interview by 9/11 Commission staff, Washington, DC, April 15, 2004.

103. Former FAA Administrator Jane Garvey told the 9/11 Commission that, with respect to the "Common Strategy": "No one had to order that policy changed. The men and women on the fourth airplane that crashed in Pennsylvania changed that policy. It will never be our country's policy again." 9/11 Commission, *Testimony of Jane Garvey*, Second Public Hearing, May 22, 2003.

104. Association of Flight Attendants, "TSA Fails to Provide Aviation Security Training Guidelines," news release, June 22, 2004.

105. Letter from Joann Matley, APFA National Safety Coordinator, to Senators McCain and Hollings, and Representatives Young and Oberstar, October 30, 2003.

106. Association of Flight Attendants, "AFA Lauds Training Recommendation by September 11 Commission, Statement by International President Patricia Friend," news release, 2004.

107. Government Accountability Office, *Aviation Security: Flight and Cabin Crew Member Security Training Strengthened, But Better Planning and Internal Controls Needed*, GAO-05-781 (Washington, DC, September 2005), pp. 3, 7.

108. 9/11 Commission, *Final Report*, p. 85n62.

109. General Accounting Office, *Improvement Still Needed in Federal Aviation Security Efforts*, Highlights, pp. 13–14.

110. Audrey Hudson, "Air Marshals' Secrecy Ruined by Dress Code," *Washington Times*, July 9, 2004; and Brian Wingfield, "Dress Code May Hinder Their Work, Air Marshals Say," *New York Times*, July 17, 2004.

111. Stephen Barr, "Association Representing Air Marshals Applauds Dress Code Modifications," *Washington Post*, August 12, 2005.

112. General Accounting Office, *Aviation Security: Federal Air Marshal Service Is Addressing Challenges*, pp. 25–26.

113. Department of Homeland Security, "Homeland Security Secretary Michael Chertoff Announces Six-Point Agenda," p. 3.

114. Audrey Hudson, "Air Marshals Cover Only a Few Flights," *Washington Times*, August 16, 2004. In recognition of some of these problems, Section 4016 of the *Intelligence Reform and Terrorism Prevention Act of 2004*, which was enacted in December 2004 to implement the recommendations of the 9/11 Commission, required that the Director of the Federal Air Marshal program "continue operational initiatives to protect the anonymity of Federal Air Marshals," and authorized an additional $83 million for FY2005–2007 to increase the size of the air marshal force. Public Law 108-458, §4016.

115. General aviation accounts for three-fourths of all takeoffs and landings in the United States, utilizing 19,000 general aviation airports. Its major categories include recreational flying, medical services, aerial advertising, aerial mapping and photography, and aerial application of seeds or chemicals. Government Accountability Office, *General Aviation Security: Increased Federal Oversight Is Needed, But Continued Partnership With the Private Sector Is Critical to Long-Term Success*, GAO-05-144 (Washington, DC, November 2004).

116. Felcher, "Aviation Security," pp. 52–56.

117. Public Law 107-71, §132.

118. Transportation Security Administration, *Report of the General Aviation Airport Security Working Group* (Washington, DC, 2003); and Transportation Security Administration, "TSA Outlines Security Recommendations for General Aviation," news release, December 1, 2003.

119. Transportation Security Administration, *Statement of David M. Stone*, p. 3.

120. U.S. House, Committee on Appropriations, *Conference Report to accompany HR 2360, Making Appropriations for the Department of Homeland Security for the Fiscal Year ending September 20, 2006*, 109th Cong., 1st sess. (Washington, DC, September 2005), H. Report 109-241, p. 53.

121. Felcher, "Aviation Security," p. 52; General Accounting Office, *Aviation Security: Efforts to Measure Effectiveness and Strengthen Security Programs*, GAO-04-285T (Washington, DC, November 20, 2003), p. 21; and Government Accountability Office, *General Aviation Security: Increased Federal Oversight Is Needed*, pp. 3–4.

122. *Associated Press*, "Report Sees Holes in U.S. Aviation Security," March 14, 2005.

123. General Accounting Office, *Aviation Security: Vulnerabilities and Potential Improvements for the Air Cargo System*, GAO-03-344 (Washington, DC, December 20, 2002), p. 9; and Congressional Research Service, *Air Cargo Security*, RL32022 (Washington, DC, September 11, 2003). The "limited amount" of cargo being screened is attributed to the "large volume of air cargo and the fact that its delivery is generally considered time-critical." General Accounting Office, *Aviation Security: Vulnerabilities*, p. 20.

124. General Accounting Office, *Aviation Security: Efforts to Measure Effectiveness and Strengthen Security Programs*, GAO-04-285T (Washington, DC,: November 20, 2003), p. 20.

125. *Federal Register* 69, no. 217 (November 10, 2004), pp. 65258–65291.

126. *Associated Press*, "TSA Plans More Checks on Cargo Loads," November 11, 2004.

127. John F. Fritelli, Congressional Research Service, *Maritime Security: Overview of Issues*, RS21079 (Washington, DC, December 5, 2003), p. 1.

128. Institute for Security Technology Studies, *On the Road to Transportation Security* (Hanover, NH: Dartmouth College, February 2003), p. 15.

129. Wrightson, *Maritime Security: Enhancements Made*, p. 5.

130. General Accounting Office, *Maritime Security: Progress Made in Implementing Maritime Transportation Security Act But Concerns Remain*, GAO-03-1155T (Washington, DC, September 9, 2003), pp. 5–7. The law implementing the 9/11 Commission recommendations imposes deadlines for a number of MTSA provisions, including the National Maritime Transportation Security Plan, vessel and facility vulnerability assessments, and Transportation Security Card regulations. Public Law 108-458 §4072.

131. Government Accountability Office, *Better Planning Needed to Help Ensure an Effective Port Security Assessment Program*, GAO-04-1062 (Washington, DC, September 2004), pp. 2–4. The Coast Guard reported that the facility inspections were all completed by the end of 2004, and the vessel inspections are to be finished by July 1, 2005. Wrightson, *Maritime Security: Enhancements Made*, p. 8.

132. U.S. Senator Ernest Hollings, "Legislative Summary: Maritime Transportation Security Act of 2002," http://hollings.senate.gov/~hollings/materials/2002B13856.html.

133. Department of Homeland Security, *Prepared Remarks of Deputy Secretary of Homeland Security James Loy, Maritime and Port Security Summit* (Washington, DC, November 16, 2004).

134. Department of Homeland Security, *DHS Budget in Brief—Fiscal Year 2006*, p. 2.

135. Department of Homeland Security, *Prepared Remarks of Deputy Secretary of Homeland Security James Loy*; and Department of Homeland Security, *DHS Budget in Brief—Fiscal Year 2006*, p. 2.

136. Department of Homeland Security, *The National Strategy for Maritime Security* (Washington, DC, September 2005); and Department of Homeland Security, "National Strategy for Maritime Security Supporting Plans Announced," news release, October 26, 2005.

137. Department of Homeland Security, *Maritime Commerce Security Plan* (Washington, DC, October 26, 2005).

138. Department of Homeland Security, *Secure Seas, Open Ports* (Washington, DC, June 21, 2004).

139. Joseph F. Bouchard, *New Strategies to Protect America: Safer Ports for a More Secure Economy* (Washington, DC: Center for American Progress, 2005), pp. 6–7.

140. John F. Fritelli, Congressional Research Service, *Maritime Security: Overview of Issues*, RS21079 (Washington, DC, December 5, 2003), p. 5.

141. Department of Homeland Security, Office of the Inspector General, *Statement of Richard L. Skinner before U.S. Senate Committee on Commerce, Science, and Transportation* (Washington, DC, May 17, 2005), p. 4.

142. Bouchard, *New Strategies to Protect America*, p. 11.

143. Department of Homeland Security, *Major Management Challenges*, p. 18.

144. James D. Hessman, "Port Security: A Mission Impossible for the U.S. Coast Guard?" In *The News*, March 9, 2005, DomesticPreparedness. com.

145. The oversight agency's own analysis of the first four rounds of port security grants during FY2002–2004 indicated that, although $489 million was awarded, the total amount requested was more than $3.3 billion. Wrightson, *Maritime Security: Enhancements Made*, pp. 21–23.

146. Department of Homeland Security, *Statement of Richard L. Skinner*, pp. 3–4.

147. Department of Homeland Security, Office of the Inspector General, *Review of the Port Security Grant Program*, OIG-05-10 (Washington, DC, January 28, 2005), p. 4; and Department of Homeland Security, *Statement of Richard L. Skinner*, pp. 4–5.

148. Operation Safe Commerce was transferred from CBP to DHS' Office for Domestic Preparedness (ODP) in FY2005.

149. Richard Stano, General Accounting Office, *Homeland Security: Summary of Challenges Faced in Targeting Oceangoing Cargo Containers for Inspection*, GAO-04-577T (Washington, DC, March 31, 2004), p. 7.

150. Department of Homeland Security, *DHS Budget in Brief—Fiscal Year 2006*, pp. 3, 26.

151. Stephen Flynn, *America the Vulnerable: How Our Government Is Failing to Protect Us From Terrorism* (New York: Harper Collins, 2004), p. 107.

152. Wrightson, *Maritime Security: Enhancements Made*, pp. 15–17.

153. Richard M. Stana, Government Accountability Office, *Homeland Security: Key Cargo Security Programs Can Be Improved*, GAO-05-466T (Washington, DC, May 26, 2005), pp. 3–4.

154. Department of Homeland Security, Office of the Inspector General, *Audit of Targeting Oceangoing Cargo Containers (Unclassified Summary)*, OIG-05-26 (Washington, DC, July 2005), p. 2.

155. Flynn, *America the Vulnerable*, pp. 107–108. The Bush Administration had initially attempted to redirect $28 million of the FY2003 appropriation for Operation Safe Commerce to other homeland security programs, but relented under pressure from Congress. The entire $58 million was subsequently allocated to the ports of Los Angeles/Long Beach, New York/New Jersey, and Seattle/Tacoma for what the Administration regarded as a time-limited pilot project. Charles Pope, "Entire $58 Million Going to Security at Three Ports," *Seattle Post-Intelligencer*, June 12, 2003. The Administration requested no funding for Operation Safe Commerce in its budgets for Fiscal Years 2004, 2005, and 2006, but Congress added $17 million in the FY2004 DHS appropriation bill, which was again awarded to the same three ports. Office of U.S. Senator Patty Murray, "Senator Murray Announces Over $17 Million in Grants for Operation Safe Commerce," news release, April 11, 2005.

156. CBP "screens" such cargo by using its risk assessment programs, but only the very small number identified by these programs as risky are actually examined. Office of Management and Budget, *Budget of the U.S. Government Fiscal Year 2006* (Washington, DC, 2005), p. 38. Moreover, a GAO analysis found that only 43 percent of all container shipments to the United States are actually being subjected to risk assessment prescreening. Government Accountability Office, *Container Security: A Flexible Staffing Model and Minimum Equipment Requirements Would Improve Overseas Targeting and Inspection Efforts*, GAO-05-557 (Washington, DC, April 2005), p. 4.

157. Department of Homeland Security, Customs and Border Protection, *Statement of Robert C. Bonner before U.S. House Appropriations Subcommittee on Homeland Security* (Washington, DC, March 15, 2005).

158. Department of Homeland Security, *FY06 Budget in Brief* (Washington, DC, 2005), p. 26.

159. Department of Homeland Security, Briefing to staff of House Committee on Homeland Security, Washington, DC, February 10, 2005, cited in U.S. House, Committee on Homeland Security, Democratic staff, *Leaving the Nation at Risk: 33 Unfulfilled Promises from the Department of Homeland Security*, 109th Cong., 1st sess. (Washington, DC, December 27, 2005).

160. Department of Homeland Security, "Nation's Busiest Seaports to Have Complete Radiation Detection Coverage by End of 2005," news release, June 3, 2005.

161. DOE anticipates completing installation at three additional ports by the end of FY2005, with another five to be finished during FY2006. U.S. Department of Energy, *FY2006 Congressional Budget Request: National Nuclear Security Administration, Volume 1* (Washington, DC, February 2005), p. 485.

162. Government Accountability Office, *Preventing Nuclear Smuggling: DOE Has Made Limited Progress In Installing Radiation Detection Equipment*, GAO-05-375 (Washington, DC: March 2005), pp. 3–6.

163. Department of Homeland Security, *Statement of Richard L. Skinner*, pp. 2–3.

164. Scott Higham and Robert O'Harrow, Jr., "Contracting Rush For Security Led To Waste, Abuse," *Washington Post*, May 22, 2005.

165. Stana, *Homeland Security: Key Cargo Security*, p. 4.

166. Office of U.S. Rep. Ed Markey, "Markey, Thompson Release Scientific Assessment of Nuke Detection Equipment Used at U.S. Ports," news release, June 21, 2005.

167. Sen. Patty Murray (D-WA), "Operation Safe Commerce—An Early Picture of Success," news release, September 2, 2004.

168. Antone Gonsalves, "Nation's Supply Chain Has Too Many Weak Links," November 8, 2004, http://www.securitypipeline.com/shared/article/printableArticleSrc.jhtml?articleId=52500244.

169. Wrightson, *Maritime Security: Enhancements Made*, p. 11.

170. There are currently only three Interagency Operational Centers: Charleston, SC; Norfolk, VA; and San Diego, CA. Wrightson, *Maritime Security: Enhancements Made*, p. 13.

171. Government Accountability Office, *Maritime Security: New Structures Have Improved Information Sharing, But Security Clearance Processing Requires Further Attention*, GAO-05-394 (Washington, DC, April 15, 2005), p. 29; and. Wrightson, *Maritime Security: Enhancements Made*, p. 19.

172. Wrightson, *Maritime Security: Enhancements Made*, p. 20; and Government Accountability Office, *Homeland Security: Process for Reporting Lessons Learned From Seaport Exercises Needs Further Attention*, GAO-05-170 (Washington, DC, January 2005), pp. 5–6.

173. Fritelli, *Maritime Security: Overview of Issues*, p. 5.

174. Flynn, *America the Vulnerable*, p. 58.

175. Wrightson, *Maritime Security: Enhancements Made*, pp. 23–24.

176. Institute for Security Technology Studies, *On the Road*, p. 13.

177. 9/11 Commission, *Testimony of Gerald Dillingham*.

178. Wrightson, *Maritime Security: Enhancements Made*, Highlights.

179. Institute for Security Technology Studies, *On the Road*, p. 18.

180. U.S. House, Committee on Transportation, Subcommittee on Highways, Transit & Pipelines, *Public Transportation Terrorism Prevention and Response Act of 2004, HR 5082*, 108th Cong., 2d sess. (Washington, DC, October 6, 2004), H. Report 108-746, p. 7.

181. RAND Corporation, *Statement of Jack Riley, Director of RAND Public Safety and Justice, before the U.S. Senate Committee on Commerce, Science and Transportation* (Washington, DC, March 23, 2004).

182. The Blue Ribbon Panel on Bridge and Tunnel Security that was formed at the request of AASHTO and FHWA, and which was comprised of engineering experts.

183. Federal Highway Administration, The Blue Ribbon Panel on Bridge and Tunnel Security, *Recommendations for Bridge and Tunnel Security* (Washington, DC, September 2003), p. 1n2.

184. Department of Homeland Security, *Testimony of James Loy Before the U.S. Senate Select Committee on Intelligence* (Washington, DC: February 16, 2005).

185. Department of Homeland Security, *DHS Budget in Brief—Fiscal Year 2006*, p. 38.

186. Transportation Security Administration, *Statement of David M. Stone to U.S. Senate Committee on Commerce, Science and Transportation* (Washington, DC: February 15, 2005), p. 7.

187. Transportation Security Administration, *Statement of David M. Stone*, p. 12.

188. Department of Homeland Security, *Fact Sheet: Rail and Transit Security Initiatives* (Washington, DC: 2004), http://dhs.gov/dhspublic/display?theme=43&content=3377&print=true.

189. In the early morning of March 11, 2004, ten bombs exploded on four crowded commuter trains in Madrid, Spain, killing 191 and injuring more than 1,800. Three unexploded bombs were discovered nearby and another unexploded bomb, of the same type used in the March 11 attacks, was found in the same area three weeks later. Though the Spanish government initially identified the Basque separatist group Eta as the main suspect, evidence soon uncovered pointed to Islamic terrorists as the responsible parties. *BBC News*, "Timeline: Madrid Investigation," April 28, 2004, http://news.bbc.co.uk/go/pr/fr/-/1/hi/world/europe/3597885.stm and Al Goodman, "Aznar to Testify at Madrid Probe," CNN, September 15, 2004, http://www.cnn.com/2004/WORLD/europe/09/15/madrid.aznar/index.html.

190. During the morning rush hour on July 7, 2005, four small bombs (each estimated as containing less than ten pounds of explosives) were detonated in London, England, three on underground trains and the fourth on a doubledecker bus. Glenn Frankel, "Bombers Strike London At Rush Hour," *Washington Post*, July 8, 2005. Fifty-two were killed and more than 700 wounded. Paul Duggan and Lyndsey Layton, "Transit Security Seen and Unseen," *Washington Post*, July 14, 2005.

191. Department of Homeland Security, *Fact Sheet: Rail and Transit Security Initiatives.*

192. Transportation Security Administration, *Statement of David M. Stone*, p. 3.

193. Department of Homeland Security, *Fact Sheet: Rail and Transit Security Initiatives.*

194. Transportation Security Administration, *Testimony of Chet Lunner before the U.S. House Committee on Transportation and Infrastructure Subcommittee on Highways, Transit & Pipelines* (Washington, DC, June 22, 2004), p. 4.

195. Congressional Research Service, *Homeland Security Department: FY2006 Appropriations*, 109th Cong., 1st sess., RL32863 (Washington, DC, June 13, 2005), p. 43.

196. Department of Homeland Security, *FY2005 Transit Security Grant Program Allocations* (Washington, DC, April 12, 2005).

197. Department of Homeland Security, "U.S. Department of Homeland Security Announces Over $9.5 Million in Grants to Secure Intercity Bus Programs," news release, April 22, 2005.

198. U.S. House, Committee on Appropriations, *Conference Report to accompany HR 2360, Making Appropriations for the Department of Homeland Security for the Fiscal Year ending September 20, 2006*, 109th Cong., 1st sess. (Washington, DC, September 2005), H. Report 109-241, p. 64.

199. U.S. Department of Transportation, *FY2006 Budget In Brief* (Washington, DC, 2005), p. 23.

200. American Public Transportation Association, *Survey of United States Transit System Security Needs and Funding Priorities, Summary of Findings* (Washington, DC, April 2004), pp. 4–5.

201. General Accounting Office, *Mass Transit: Challenges in Securing Transit Systems*, GAO-02-1075T (Washington, DC, September 18, 2002), pp. 15–19.

202. As of July 2005, annexes for mass transit, rail, and research and development were being developed. Government Accountability Office, *Passenger Rail Security: Enhanced Federal Leadership Needed to Prioritize and Guide Security Efforts*, GAO-05-851 (Washington, DC, September 2005), pp. 42–43.

203. U.S. House, Committee on Transportation and Infrastructure, *Public Transportation Terrorism Prevention and Response Act of 2004*, 108th Cong., 2d sess. (Washington, DC, October 6, 2004), House Committee Report 108-746, p. 9.

204. Julie B. Hairston, "MARTA Under Pressure," *AJC Horizon*, August 15, 2005.

205. Sewell Chan, "Funds Will Be There When Technology Is, MTA Chief Says," *New York Times*, July 13, 2005, nytimes.com; and Fred Kaplan, "Planning Gridlock," *Slate*, July 14, 2005, www.slate.com.

206. John P. Hamilton and Henry Goldman, "Lockheed Awarded New York Security Contract," *Bloomberg News*, August 24, 2005.

207. Transportation Security Administration, *Statement of David M. Stone*, p. 3.

208. Transportation Security Administration, *Testimony of Chet Lunner*.

209. U.S. House, Committee on Transportation and Infrastructure, Subcommittee on Highways, Transit and Pipelines, *Testimony of William W. Millar, President of the American Public Transportation Association*, 108th Cong., 2d sess. (Washington, DC, June 22, 2004).

210. Government Accountability Office, *Passenger Rail Security: Enhanced Federal Leadership Needed to Prioritize and Guide Security Efforts*, GAO-05-851 (Washington, DC, September 2005), pp. 36–37.

211. Transportation Security Administration, "TSA Expanding National Explosives Detection Teams to Mass Transit and Commuter Rail Systems," news release, September 28, 2005; and Michael Alison Chandler, "Bomb-Dog Noses Pressed Into Transit Duty," *Washington Post*, September 29, 2005.

212. American Public Transportation Association, *Public Transportation Fact Book*, 5th ed. (Washington, DC, 2005), pp. 94–99.

213. U.S. House, Committee on Appropriations, *Conference Report to accompany HR 2360, Making Appropriations for the Department of Homeland Security for the Fiscal Year ending September 20, 2006*, 109th Cong., 1st sess. (Washington, DC, September 2005), H. Report 109-241, p. 53.

214. RAND Corporation, *Statement of Jack Riley*.

215. Steve Johnson, "U.S. Rail Network Still Vulnerable to Terror," *MSNBC*, July 7, 2005.

216. Fred Millar, *New Strategies To Protect America: Putting Rail Security on the Right Track* (Washington, DC: Center for American Progress, 2005), pp. 1–2.

217. *CSX Transportation, Inc. v. Anthony A. Williams, et al.*, United States District Court for the District of Columbia, Civ. Action No-05-338 (EGS), April 18, 2005, at 3–5, 72.

218. U.S. Department of Transportation, *Overview, U.S. DOT FY 2005 Budget in Brief* (Washington, DC, 2004), http://www.dot.gov/bib2005/ overview.html and

U.S. Department of Transportation, *Overview, U.S. DOT FY 2006 Budget in Brief* (Washington, DC, 2005), p. 22.

219. Federal Highway Administration, *Recommendations for Bridge and Tunnel Security*, pp. 1–4.

220. Julia Malone, "Security Department Faces Challenges," *Atlanta Journal-Constitution*, December 26, 2004.

221. Paul W. Parfomak, Congressional Research Service, *Pipeline Security: An Overview of Federal Activities and Current Policy Issues*, 108th Cong., 2d sess. (Washington, DC, February 5, 2004), Summary.

222. See, for example, Brian D. Taylor, *Security Planning for Transit* (Los Angeles: UCLA Institute of Transportation Studies, 2005), which reported that more policing, improved technology, and better system design were perceived by transit system operators as the most effective security measures. (See"Table 16: Perceived Effectiveness of Strategies in Security Planning.")

223. Institute for Security Technology Studies, *On the Road to Transportation Security*, pp. 1, 20.

224. Department of Homeland Security, *Major Management Challenges*, p. 18.

225. Department of Homeland Security, Office of the Inspector General, *Major Management Challenges Facing the Department of Homeland Security (Excerpts from the FY2005 DHS Performance and Accountability Report)*, OIG-06-14 (Washington, DC: December 2005), p. 119.

226. Clark Kent Ervin, "A To-Do List for Chertoff."

Chapter 8. "Looking Back to Look Forward": The Post-9/11 Policy Failure of Transportation Security

1. For example, as of September 2003, seaport, waterway, and coastal security activities accounted for only 34 percent of Coast Guard "resource hours" utilization of its ships, boats, or aircraft. Margaret T. Wrightson, Government Accountability Office, *Maritime Security: Enhancements Made, But Implementation and Sustainability Remain Key Challenges*, GAO-05-448T (Washington, DC, May 17, 2005), p. 12.

2. Government Accountability Office, *Aviation Security: Flight and Cabin Crew Member Security Training Strengthened, But Better Planning and Internal Controls Needed*, GAO-05-781 (Washington, DC, September 2005), Highlights.

3. National Commission on Terrorist Attacks Upon the United States (9/11 Commission), *The 9/11 Commission Report: The Final Report of the National Commission on Terrorist Attacks Upon the United States*, Authorized Edition (New York: W.W. Norton, 2004), p. 83; and 9/11 Commission, *Testimony of James Loy*, Seventh Public Hearing, January 27, 2004.

4. National Research Council, *Making the Nation Safer: The Role of Science and Technology in Countering Terrorism* (Washington, DC: The National Academies Press, 2002), pp. 13–14.

5. Ibid.

6. Jonathan Weisman and Jim VandeHei, "Road Bill Reflects the Power of Pork," *Washington Post*, August 11, 2005.

7. U.S. Department of Transportation, *Overview, U.S. DOT FY 2006 Budget in Brief* (Washington, DC, 2005), p. 40.

8. *Final Report of the White House Commission on Aviation Safety and Security* (Washington, DC, February 12, 1997), pp. 20–21.

9. Office of Management and Budget, *Budget of the U.S. Government Fiscal Year 2006* (Washington, DC, 2005), p. 40.

10. Ibid., p. 38.

11. Transportation Security Administration, *Statement of David M. Stone to U.S. Senate Committee on Commerce, Science and Transportation* (Washington, DC, February 15, 2005), p. 6. Both houses of Congress rejected the fee increase during their consideration of the FY2006 DHS Appropriations bill. Congressional Research Service, *Homeland Security Department: FY2006 Appropriations* (Washington, DC, June 13, 2005), p. 18, 32–33; and U.S. Senate, Committee on Appropriations, *DHS Appropriations Bill, 2006*, 109th Cong., 1st sess. (Washington, DC, July 16, 2005), S. Report 109-83, p. 43.

Chapter 9. Key Questions, Hard Choices

1. Dana Priest and Josh White, "War Helps Recruit Terrorists, Hill Told," *Washington Post*, February 17, 2005.

2. Department of Homeland Security, *Testimony of James Loy before the Senate Select Committee on Intelligence* (Washington, DC, February 16, 2005).

3. The mailing of anthrax spores to news media representatives and members of Congress resulted in twenty-two confirmed cases of anthrax and five deaths between September and November of 2001. The United States Senate's Hart Office Building was closed for more than three months and mail processing centers in the District of Columbia, Maryland, and New Jersey were shut down for even longer periods. To date, the perpetrator or perpetrators have not been identified but speculation has centered on the possibility of a lone attacker. Congressional Research Service, *The U.S. Postal Service Response to the Threat of Bioterrorism Through the Mail*, 107th Cong,, 2d sess., RL31280 (Washington, DC, February 11, 2002), p. 1; Congressional Research Service, *Small Scale Terrorist Attacks Using Chemical and Biological Agents: An Assessment Framework and Preliminary Comparisons*, 108th Cong,, 2d sess., RL32391 (Washington, DC, June 23, 2004), p. 1; and Allan Lengel, "Little Progress in FBI Probe of Anthrax Attacks," *Washington Post*, September 16, 2005.

4. Stephen Flynn, *America the Vulnerable: How Our Government Is Failing to Protect Us From Terrorism* (New York: Harper Collins, 2004), p. 60.

5. *Imperial Hubris* (Washington, DC: Bressey's, 2004), pp. 100–101.

6. Margaret T. Wrightson, Government Accountability Office, *Maritime Security: Enhancements Made, But Implementation and Sustainability Remain Key Challenges*, GAO-05-448T (Washington, DC, May 17, 2005), p. 3.

7. Department of Homeland Security, *Interim National Infrastructure Protection Plan* (Washington, DC, February 2005), p. 29.

8. 9/11 Commission, *Testimony of James Loy*, Seventh Public Hearing, January 27, 2004.

9. Congressional Budget Office, *Homeland Security and the Private Sector* (Washington, DC, December 2004), pp. 1–3.

10. Clark Kent Ervin, "A To-Do List for Chertoff," *Washington Post*, February 7, 2005.

11. National Commission on Terrorist Attacks Upon the United States (9/11 Commission), *The 9/11 Commission Report: The Final Report of the National Commission on Terrorist Attacks Upon the United States*, Authorized Edition (New York: W.W. Norton, 2004), p. 391.

12. Public Law 108-458,§ 4001.

13. Ariel Merari, "Attacks on Civil Aviation: Trends and Lessons," in Wilkinson and Jenkins, eds., *Aviation Terrorism and Security* (London: Frank, 1999), p. 26.

14. Congressional Budget Office, *The Budget and Economic Outlook: Fiscal Years 2006 to 2015*, 109th Cong., 1st sess. (Washington, DC, January 2005), pp. xiii–xv.

15. "CBO Says Bush Budget Would Deepen Deficit," *Washington Post*, March 3, 2005.

16. Congressional Budget Office, *Budget and Economic Outlook: An Update*, 109th Cong., 1st sess. (Washington, DC, August 2005), p. ix.

17. Jim VandeHei and Peter Baker, "Bush Pledges Historic Effort to Help Gulf Coast Recover," *Washington Post*, September 16, 2005.

18. Bill Brubaker, "Low-Fare and Hoping," *Washington Post*, January 9, 2005.

19. Keith L. Alexander,"Airlines Hope to Begin Ascent in '06," *Washington Post*, January 6, 2006.

20. Wrightson, *Maritime Security: Enhancements Made,* pp. 23–24.

21. The strategic plan called for by the 9/11 Commission and contained in the Senate-passed version of the implementing legislation provided that it include a "budget and funding to implement" the necessary security measures. 9/11 Commission, *Final Report*, p. 391.

22. The November 2004 proposed rule making for air cargo, the November 2002 Maritime Transportation Security Act, and the May 2004 Rail Security Directives, respectively.

23. Even in passenger aviation security, the area that has received by far the most federal funding post-9/11, efforts are being made to limit the federal financial burden by shifting the cost onto users in the form of higher passenger fees. Both the original passenger security fee (in Section 118 of ATSA) and the FY2006 Administration budget request to more than double the original fee are designed "to pay the costs of providing civil aviation security services." These fees covered 41 percent of TSA's aviation security costs in FY2004 and would offset almost 80 percent of such costs in FY2006 if the fee increase is approved. Transportation Security Administration, *Statement of David M. Stone to U.S. Senate Committee on Commerce, Science and Transportation* (Washington, DC, February 15, 2005), p. 6.

Chapter 10. Principles for Action

1. The DHS and other departmental requests in this paragraph exclude fee-funded activities, which in the case of DHS total $4.8 billion in the FY2006 request. Office of Management and Budget, *Budget of the United States Government Fiscal Year 2006* (Washington, DC, 2005), p. 166.

2. These amounts are all based on the President's FY2006 budget request. Office of Management and Budget, *Budget of the United States Government Fiscal Year 2006*,

Table S-3. Growth in Discretionary Budget Authority by Major Agency (Washington, DC, 2005), p. 345.

3. 9/11 Commission, *Testimony of Gerald L. Dillingham*, First Public Hearing, April 1, 2003.

4. Ibid.

5. General Accounting Office, *Testimony of Raymond J. Decker to House Committee on Government Reform Subcommittee on National Security, Veterans Affairs and International Relations Hearing on Homeland Security*, GAO-02-150T (Washington, DC, October 12, 2001), p. 5.

6. Department of Homeland Security, "National Infrastructure Protection Plan Status Update," PowerPoint presentation provided to House Committee on Homeland Security staff, Washington, DC, November 1, 2005, cited in U.S. House, Committee on Homeland Security, Democratic staff, *Leaving the Nation at Risk: 33 Unfulfilled Promises from the Department of Homeland Security,* 109th Cong., 1st sess. (Washington, DC, December 27, 2005), p. 4.

7. Michael Crowley, "Playing Defense: Bush's Disastrous Homeland Security Department," *The New Republic*, March 15, 2004, http://www.tnr.com/doc.mhtml?i=20040315&s=crowley031504.

8. Council on Foreign Relations, *America—Still Unprepared, Still in Danger* (Washington, DC, 2002), p. 3.

9. The Heritage Foundation and the Center for Strategic and International Studies, *DHS 2.0: Rethinking the Department of Homeland Security* (Washington, DC, December 13, 2004), p. 24.

10. Transportation Security Administration, *Remarks of Kip Hawley on "Aviation Security Enhancements" to National Press Club* (Washington, DC, December 2, 2005).

11. Sara Kehaulani Goo, "TSA Would Allow Sharp Objects on Airliners," *Washington Post*, November 30, 2005; and Hope Yen, "TSA Defends Move to Allow Sharp Tools," *Washington Post*, December 12, 2005.

12. Sara Kehaulani Goo, "Marshals to Patrol Land, Sea Transport," *Washington Post*, December 14, 2005.

13. Sara Kehaulani Goo, "New TSA Surveillance Tactic Curtailed," *Washington Post*, December 15, 2005.

14. Council on Foreign Relations, *America—Still Unprepared, Still in Danger*, p. 19.

15. Transportation Research Board, National Academies of Science, *Deterrence, Protection and Preparation,* Special Report 270 (Washington, DC: National Academies Press, 2002), pp. 6–7.

16. Aviation Security Advisory Committee (ASAC) Security Baseline Working Group, *Summary and Recommendations of the Final Report of the Baseline Working Group* (Washington, DC, December 12, 1996), http://www.securitymanagement.com/library/asac.html.

17. Michele Dyson, "Security and Safety: Metro's Systematic Shortfalls," *Washington Post*, August 21, 2005.

18. International Civil Aviation Organization (ICAO), "Appendix 5—A Risk Assessment Model," in *Security Manual for Safeguarding Civil Aviation Against Acts of Unlawful Interference*, 6th ed. (Montreal, Quebec, Canada: ICAO, 2002).

19. E. Marla Felcher, "Aviation Security," in *The Department of Homeland Security's First Year: A Report Card* (New York: Century Foundation, 2004), p. 60.

20. 9/11 Commission, *Testimony of James Loy*, Seventh Public Hearing, January 27, 2004.

21. National Research Council, *Making the Nation Safer: The Role of Science and Technology in Countering Terrorism* (Washington, DC: The National Academies Press, 2002), p. 4.

22. Ibid., p. 15.

23. Brian D. Taylor, *Security Planning For Transit* (Los Angeles: UCLA Institute of Transportation Studies, 2005).

24. One TSA official told 9/11 Commission staff that, although he felt that the agency was headed in the right direction, more resources were needed for inspection. "In the big budget debates, it's a fairly small item like inspection that tends to get squeezed." Stephen McHale, interview by 9/11 Commission staff, Washington, DC, April 15, 2004.

25. Transportation Security Administration, *FY2005 TSA Budget Request* (Washington, DC, February 2004), p. 5.

26. Congressional Research Service, *Homeland Security Department: FY2006 Appropriations*, 109th Cong., 1st sess. (Washington, DC, June 13, 2005), p. 31; U.S. Senate, Committee on Appropriations, *Department of Homeland Security Appropriations Bill, 2006*, 109th Cong., 1st sess. (Washington, DC, 2005), S. Report 109-83, p. 46; and U.S. House, Committee on Appropriations, *Conference Report to accompany HR 2360, Making Appropriations for the Department of Homeland Security for the Fiscal Year ending September 20, 2006*, 109th Cong., 1st sess. (Washington, DC, September 2005), H. Report 109-241, p. 52.

27. Public Law 107-71, §101, which authorizes TSA to "issue the regulation or security directive without providing notice or an opportunity for comment," if it is determined that such action must be taken "immediately in order to protect transportation security."

28. Department of Homeland Security, *DHS Budget in Brief—Fiscal Year 2005* (Washington, DC, 2004), p. 29.

29. Markle Foundation, *Creating a Trusted Network for Homeland Security* (New York: Markle Foundation: 2003), pp. 1–5, 11.

30. Century Foundation, *The Department of Homeland Security's First Year: A Report Card* (New York: Century Foundation, 2004), pp. 19–21.

31. "This area has received increased attention but the federal government still faces formidable challenges sharing information among stakeholders in an appropriate and timely manner." Government Accountability Office, *High Risk Series—An Update*, GAO-05-207 (Washington, DC, January 2005), Highlights, pp. 15–16.

32. Department of Homeland Security, Office of the Inspector General, *Major Management Challenges Facing the Department of Homeland Security (Excerpts from the FY2005 DHS Performance and Accountability Report)*, OIG-06-14 (Washington, DC, December 2005), p. 115.

33. 9/11 Commission, *Final Report*, p. 83nn52–53.

34. Government Accountability Office, *High Risk Series*, pp. 19–20.

35. 9/11 Commission, *Final Report*, p. 419.

36. Markle Foundation, *Creating a Trusted Network*, p. 21.

37. Century Foundation, *The Department of Homeland Security's First Year: A Report Card*, p. 21.

38. Ibid., p. 21.

39. Markle Foundation, *Creating a Trusted Network,* p. 23n40.

40. 9/11 Commission, *Testimony of James May*, Second Public Hearing, May 22, 2003.

41. 9/11 Commission, *Testimony of Claudio Manno*, Seventh Public Hearing, January 27, 2004.

42. Department of Homeland Security, Office of Inspector General, *DHS' Efforts to Develop the Homeland Secure Data Network*, OIG-05-19 (Washington, DC, April 2005), p. 3.

43. Lara Jakes Jordan, "Homeland Security Information Network Criticized," *Washington Post*, May 10, 2005.

44. Department of Homeland Security, *DHS' Efforts to Develop the Homeland Secure Data Network*, pp. 7–8.

45. U.S. House, Committee on Appropriations, *Conference Report to accompany HR 2360, Making Appropriations for the Department of Homeland Security for the Fiscal Year ending September 20, 2006*, 109th Cong., 1st sess. (Washington, DC, September 2005), H. Report 109-241, p. 37.

46. 9/11 Commission, *Final Report*, pp. 242n133, 245n149.

47. Gabriel Weissmann, "www.terror.net: How Modern Terrorism Uses the Internet," Special Report 116 (Washington, DC: United States Institute of Peace, 2004); and Heritage Foundation and CSIS, *DHS 2.0: Rethinking the Department of Homeland Security*, p. 20.

48. Heritage Foundation and CSIS, *DHS 2.0: Rethinking the Department of Homeland Security*, p. 20.

49. Canada Standards Association, *Risk Management: Guidelines for Decision-Makers* (Etobicoke, Ontario, Canada: Canada Standards Association, October 1997), pp. 19–27.

50. Quoted in Joel Achenbach, "Threat Level Gray: When The Danger Is Relative, Assessing Risk Can Be Well, Risky," *Washington Post*, February 8, 2004.

51. Lerner, Gonzalez, Small, and Fischhoff, "Effects of Fear and Anger on Perceived Risks of Terrorism: A National Field Experiment," *Psychological Science* 14, no. 2 (March 2003), pp. 144–150; and *Washington Post*, "Science Notebook," March 31, 2003.

52. Brian Michael Jenkins and Frances Edwards-Winslow, *Saving City Lifelines: Lessons Learned in the 9-11 Terrorist Attacks*, MTI Report 02-06 (San Jose, CA: Mineta Transportation Institute, September 2003), p. 37.

53. "Security Warnings Need Review, Ridge Says," *Washington Post*, December 15, 2004.

54. Dan Eggen and Sari Horwitz, "As Jan. 20 Nears, Terror Warnings Drop," *Washington Post*, January 18, 2005.

55. John Mintz, "Skepticism of Terrorism Alerts Cited," *Washington Post*, May 4, 2005.

56. According to a May 2005 report in the *Washington Post*, DHS officials presented incoming DHS Secretary Michael Chertoff with a number of alternatives to the current warning system, including utilizing the DHS Web site instead of news conferences to issue the alerts, employing numbers or letters instead of colors, and

shifting the focus to a long-term public education campaign to improve general awareness of possible terrorist attacks. John Mintz, "DHS Considers Alternatives to Color-Coded Warnings," *Washington Post*, May 10, 2005.

57. The Heritage Foundation and CSIS, *DHS 2.0: Rethinking the Department of Homeland Security*, p. 14.

58. National Research Council, *Making the Nation Safer*, p. 17.

59. Department of Homeland Security, "Department of Homeland Security Secretary Tom Ridge Approves National Incident Management System (NIMS)," news release, March 1, 2004.

60. Department of Homeland Security, *Fact Sheet: Ready Campaign* (Washington, DC, November 22, 2004).

61. Department of Homeland Security, *Remarks by Secretary Tom Ridge at the "News and Terrorism: Communicating in a Crisis," Roundtable* (Washington, DC, August 11, 2004).

62. The Heritage Foundation and CSIS, *DHS 2.0: Rethinking the Department of Homeland Security*, p. 14.

63. Stephen Flynn, *America the Vulnerable: How Our Government Is Failing to Protect Us From Terrorism* (New York: Harper Collins, 2004), p. 9.

64. Ibid., p. 131.

65. White House, *Homeland Security Presidential Directive 13 (HSPD-13), Maritime Security Policy* (Washington, DC, December 21, 2004), pp. 3, 7–8.

66. Department of Homeland Security, "Maritime Infrastructure Recovery Plan" (Washington, DC, October 2005), http://www.dhs.gov/dhspublic/display?theme=67&content=4914&print=true.

67. Joseph F. Bouchard, *New Strategies to Protect America: Safer Ports for a More Secure Economy* (Washington, DC: Center for American Progress, 2005), p. 17.

68. Office of Management and Budget, *Budget of the U.S. Government Fiscal Year 2006* (Washington, DC, 2005), p. 153.

69. Department of Homeland Security, *DHS Budget in Brief—Fiscal Year 2005*, p. 60.

70. Chet Lunner, interview by 9/11 Commission staff, Washington, DC, June 10, 2004.

71. The FY2006 budget request would increase funding for the National Pre-Disaster Mitigation (PDM) Fund by $50 million, restoring it to the FY2004 level. Department of Homeland Security, *DHS Budget in Brief—Fiscal Year 2006* (Washington, DC, 2005), p. 61. FEMA's operations budget had been cut by 14.5 percent over the three preceding years. Spencer S. Hsu, "Brown Defends FEMA's Efforts," *Washington Post*, September 28, 2005.

72. Jon Elliston, "Disaster in the Making," September 22, 2004, http://indyweek.com/durham/2004-09-22/cover.html.

73. Partnership For Public Service, *Best Places to Work in the Federal Government 2005* (Washington, DC,2005), www.bestplacestowork.org and Spencer S. Hsu, "Inside FEMA: Leaders Lacking Disaster Experience," *Washington Post*, September 9, 2005.

74. Susan B. Glasser and Michael Grunwald, "The Steady Build-up to a City's Chaos," *Washington Post*, September 11, 2005.

75. Spencer S. Hsu, "Inside FEMA."

76. Ibid.

77. Transportation Security Administration, *TSA's Mission, Vision and Values,* available online at http://www.tsa.gov.

78. This number was reduced to 79 by organizational changes made at the start of the 108th Congress in early 2005. CSIS and Business Executives for National Security, *Untangling the Web: Congressional Oversight and the Department of Homeland Security* (Washington, DC, December 10, 2004), p. 2.

79. 9/11 Commission, *Final Report*, p. 421.

80. CSIS and Business Executives for National Security, *Untangling the Web*, p. 1.

81. George Washington University Homeland Security Policy Institute, "Top Officials Call for Homeland Security Jurisdiction to Track Armed Services Committee Model," news release, December 30, 2004.

82. Julia Malone, "Security Department Faces Challenges," *Atlanta Journal-Constitution*, December 26, 2004.

83. 9/11 Commission, *Final Report*, p. 396.

Chapter 11. Reassessment and a Test

1. Department of Homeland Security, "Homeland Security Secretary Michael Chertoff Announces Six-Point Agenda for Department of Homeland Security," news release, July 13, 2005.

2. Department of Homeland Security, *Secretary Michael Chertoff, U.S. Department of Homeland Security Second Stage Review Remarks* (Washington, DC, July 13, 2005).

3. Spencer S. Hsu and Sara Kehaulani Goo, "30-Minute Airport Rule To Be Lifted," *Washington Post*, July 14, 2005; and Editorial, "Mr. Chertoff's Challenge," *Washington Post*, July 14, 2005.

4. Department of Homeland Security, *Securing Our Homeland: U.S. Department of Homeland Security Strategic Plan* (Washington, DC, 2004), p. 54.

5. Government Accountability Office, *High Risk Series: An Update*, GAO-05-207 (Washington, DC, January 2005), p. 30.

6. The Heritage Foundation and the Center for Strategic and International Studies, *DHS 2.0: Rethinking the Department of Homeland Security* (Washington, DC, December 13, 2004), p. 11.

7. National Commission on Terrorist Attacks Upon the United States (9/11 Commission), *The 9/11 Commission Report: The Final Report of the National Commission on Terrorist Attacks Upon the United States*, Authorized Edition (New York: W.W. Norton, 2004), p. 391.

8. 9/11 Public Discourse Project, *Final Report on 9/11 Commission Recommendations* (Washington, DC, December 5, 2005).

9. Hsu and Goo, "30-Minute Airport Rule To Be Lifted"; and Editorial, "Mr. Chertoff's Challenge."

10. Editorial, "Mr. Chertoff's Challenge."

11. Department of Homeland Security, *Secretary Michael Chertoff, U.S. Department of Homeland Security Second Stage Review Remarks*; and Department of Homeland Security, "Homeland Security Secretary Michael Chertoff Announces Six-Point Agenda."

12. U.S. House, Committee on Appropriations, *Conference Report to accompany HR 2360, Making Appropriations for the Department of Homeland Security for the Fiscal Year ending September 20, 2006*, 109th Cong., 1st sess. (Washington, DC, September 2005), H. Report 109-241, p. 30.

13. Intelligence Reform and Terrorism Prevention Act of 2004, Public Law 108-458, §4001(b)(2).

14. Steven Pearlstein, "Crisis Planning: Waiting for Mr. Big," *Washington Post*, September 16, 2005.

15. Michael Grunwald and Susan B. Glasser, "Brown's Turf Wars Sapped FEMA's Strength," *Washington Post*, December 23, 2005.

16. Eric Holdeman, "Destroying FEMA," *Washington Post*, August 30, 2005.

17. Hsu and Goo, "30-Minute Airport Rule To Be Lifted"; and Editorial, "Mr. Chertoff's Challenge."

18. Department of Homeland Security, "Homeland Security Secretary Michael Chertoff Announces Six-Point Agenda."

19. Department of Homeland Security, *Secretary Michael Chertoff, U.S. Department of Homeland Security Second Stage Review Remarks*.

20. Ibid.

21. Department of Homeland Security, "Homeland Security Secretary Michael Chertoff Announces Six-Point Agenda."

22. Department of Homeland Security, *Secretary Michael Chertoff, U.S. Department of Homeland Security Second Stage Review Remarks*.

23. Ibid.

24. Congressional Research Service, *Homeland Security Department: FY2006 Appropriations*, 109th Cong., 1st sess. (Washington, DC, June 13, 2005), p. 18, 32–33; and U.S. Senate, Committee on Appropriations, *Department of Homeland Security Appropriations Bill, 2006*, 109th Cong., 1st sess., July 16, 2005, S. Report 109-83, p. 43.

25. "Katrina Chronology," *Washington Post,* September 4, 2005.

26. "Katrina Chronology," *Washington Post,* September 21, 2005.

27. Susan B. Glasser and Josh White, "Storm Exposed Disarray at the Top," *Washington Post*, September 4, 2005.

28. Peter Baker, "An Embattled Bush Says 'Results Are Not Acceptable,'" *Washington Post*, September 3, 2005.

29. Manuel Raig-Franzia and Spencer Hsu, "Many Evacuated, but Thousands Still Waiting," *Washington Post*, September 4, 2005.

30. Department of Homeland Security, *National Response Plan* (Washington, DC, December 2004), p. 43.

31. Mark Fischetti, "Drowning New Orleans," *Scientific American*, Vol. 285, No. 4, October 1, 2001, pp. 76–85.

32. Department of Homeland Security, *National Response Plan* (Washington, DC, December 2004), pp. 43–44.

33. Glasser and White, "Storm Exposed Disarray at the Top."

34. Susan B. Glasser and Michael Grunwald, "The Steady Buildup to a City's Chaos," *Washington Post*, September 11, 2005.

35. Shailagh Murray and Jim VandeHei, "Katrina's Cost May Test GOP Harmony," *Washington Post*, September 21, 2005.

Appendix A. Transmittal Letter and Recommendations of 9/11 Commission Aviation and Transportation Security Staff

1. Throughout the recommendations, the reader will see that we have offered specific deadlines. The dates chosen reflect our best estimate about the time necessary to complete the relevant task. We recognize that more in-depth analysis and discussion with the agency might be required to establish the most appropriate possible deadlines. However, the point that we wish to make is that the establishment of firm deadlines is vital in order to ensure implementation and accountability. We urge Congress to set and provide oversight of responsible and specific deadlines.

2. Setting risk-based priorities includes (1) gathering and analyzing intelligence information to identify terrorist threats at home and abroad; (2) conducting vulnerability assessments to identify weaknesses in national, state, and local transportation systems; and (3) determining the consequences—in lives lost, injuries sustained, and property damaged—that might result from successful attacks.

3. Selecting the most practicable, cost-effective methods of protection involves identifying the required personnel, actions, or technologies; determining their capability, availability, and cost in the near and long term; and choosing the methods that will provide the greatest protection at the least cost now and in the future.

4. See *The White House Commission on Aviation Safety and Security: Final Report* (Washington, DC, February 12, 1997); General Accounting Office, *Homeland Security: A Risk Management Approach Can Guide Preparedness Efforts*, GAO-02-208T (Washington, DC, Oct. 31, 2001); 9/11 Commission, *Testimony of Gerald Dillingham*, First Public Hearing, May 1, 2003; General Accounting Office, *Transportation Security: Post-September 11 Initiatives and Long-Term Challenges*, GAO-03-616T (Washington, DC, Apr. 1, 2003); and Robert W. Poole, Jr., with George Passantino, *A Risk-Based Airport Security Policy* (Los Angeles: Reason Foundation, May 2003).

5. National Research Council, *Making the Nation Safer: The Role of Science and Technology in Countering Terrorism* (Washington, DC: The National Academies Press, 2002), p. 17.

6. ASAC Security Baseline Working Group, "Summary and Recommendations," December 12, 1996.

7. *Creating a Trusted Network for Homeland Security* (New York: Markle Foundation: 2003), p. 21.

8. *The Department of Homeland Security's First Year: A Report Card* (New York: Century Foundation, 2004), p. 21.

9. *Creating a Trusted Network for Homeland Security*, p. 23n40.

10. *The Department of Homeland Security's First Year: A Report Card*, p. 21.

Index

About the Author

R. WILLIAM JOHNSTONE served on the transportation security staff of the National Commission on Terrorist Attacks Upon the United States (9/11 Commission) after working for over twenty years as a Congressional staff member. He is currently a consultant on homeland and national security matters.